Innovation Ecosystems in Africa

Innovation Ecosystems in Africa

Solving the problems that we have

**Edited by
Olugbenga Adesida,
Geci Karuri-Sebina,
João Resende-Santos
& Mammo Muchie**

Published by Amalion 2023
In collaboration with the Africa Innovation Summit (AIS)

Amalion
BP 5637 Dakar-Fann
Dakar CP 10700
Senegal
http://www.amalion.net

ISBN 978-2-35926-115-8 (Paperback)
ISBN 978-2-35926-116-5 (ebook)

Cover designed by Lindiwe Gugushe
Pagelayout by Amalion

Contents

Tables

Figures

Contributors

Olugbenga Adesida is a Development Policy and Scenarios Planning specialist and co-founder of the Africa Innovation Summit and the technology enterprise Bonako based in Cabo Verde. He is Associate Editor of the *African Journal of Science, Technology, Innovation and Development,* Director of the Africa Leadership Institute, and a board member of the Pedro Pires Leadership Institute. He holds a doctorate from the London School of Economics, UK, with a thesis on the role of intermediary institutions in the diffusion of complex technological innovations.

Yap Boum II is General Director of Institute Pasteur of Bangui in the Central African Republic and the former Regional Representative for Epicentre in Africa, the research arm of Médecins sans Frontières (MSF). He has conducted several studies on tuberculosis, malaria, Ebola, and COVID-19 in Cameroon, DR Congo, Guinea and Uganda among others. Prof Boum teaches Public Health and Microbiology at Mbarara University of Sciences and Technology (Uganda) and at the Universities of Virginia (USA) and University of Yaoundé I (Cameroon). He has held an array of leadership and advisory positions at the national and international level. Currently, Boum serves on the International Editorial Board of *The Lancet Global Health,* and is also co-founder of Kmerpad, a nonprofit that developed washable sanitary pads to empower women, and iDocta, a digital platform that takes healthcare services to the community.

In his capacity as a full-time faculty of the Gordon Institute of Business Science, Dr **Jeff Chen** serves as the Lead Faculty for the MBA Consulting Stream and various other corporate education programmes. Much of his academic interests, coaching and consulting focus on improving the innovation performance of individuals, teams and organisations.

Liza Rose Cirolia is a senior researcher at the African Centre for Cities. Her work is largely focused on the social, political, technical and institutional dimensions of urban infrastructure, decentralization, and human settlements in African cities. Cirolia has led several projects including, the Post-networked City: Sanitation, Water and Energy – GCRF (2020–2023). She received both her PhD and a Masters in City and Regional Planning from the University of Cape Town, South Africa; and her undergraduate degree in Development Studies from the University of California, Berkeley, USA.

Jeremy de Beer is a Full Professor at the University of Ottawa's Faculty of Law, where he creates and shapes ideas about technology innovation, intellectual property, and global trade and development. He is also a Faculty Member of the Centre for Law, Technology and Society, a Senior Fellow at the Centre for International Governance Innovation, and a Senior Research Associate at the University of Cape Town's IP Unit. As co-founder and co-director of the Open African Innovation Research network, Open AIR, his current work helps solve practical challenges related to innovation in the digital economy, life science industries, and clean technology sector.

Pauline Anna Marie Delay is currently an Operations Analyst at the International Finance Corporation (IFC), where she works to develop new and innovative investments in the private sector, with a focus on leveraging new technology and non-bank platforms to increase access to finance in the region. Delay was previously a Financial Sector Analyst and Communications Specialist for the World Bank Group's Finance, Competitive, and Innovations Global Practice in Africa, where she led financial education programs in multiple countries to increase awareness, uptake, and responsible use of new financial products and services, including credit bureaus, collateral registries, insurance, and finance leasing. She has a BA in Foreign Affairs from the University of Virginia (USA) and an MSc in International Business from the University of London's School of Oriental and African Studies (UK).

Aidan Eyakuze, an economist, is Executive Director of Twaweza East Africa. Twaweza works to enable children to learn, citizens to exercise agency, and governments to be more open and responsive in Tanzania, Kenya and Uganda. In May 2016, Aidan was appointed to the global Steering Committee of the Open Government Partnership (OGP). In June 2017, he was appointed to the Board of the Global Partnership for Sustainable Development Data (GPSDD). Before joining Twaweza, Eyakuze was Associate Regional Director of the Society for International Development (SID) based in Tanzania.

Kareem Ibrahim is an Egyptian architect and urban researcher who graduated from Cairo University's Faculty of Architectural Engineering.

He has worked on a number of urban rehabilitation projects in Egypt, including a UNDP rehabilitation plan for Historic Cairo and The Aga Khan Trust for Culture's al-Darb al-Ahmar's Revitalisation project. He co-founded Takween Integrated Community Development in 2009 in response to a foreseen growing demand for innovative urban solutions in Egypt. In 2018, Ibrahim received the Egyptian State Award for architecture for Takween's work designing and building for local communities in informal areas. In 2019, he was selected to be a member of jury for the prestigious Aga Khan Award for Architecture.

Daniel Irurah currently serves as Associate Professor of Sustainable Architecture & Cities in the School of Architecture & Planning at the University of the Witwatersrand (Johannesburg, South Africa), where he conducts research and supervises masters and doctoral studies in related fields and topics. He holds a BArch with Hons (University of Nairobi, Kenya), MArch and MUP (University of Oregon, USA) and PhD (University of Pretoria, South Africa). His PhD study focused on application of input–output model in analyses of embodied energy of construction materials and buildings in South Africa. His MArch studies focused on climatic response, energy conservation and renewable energy for buildings within inter-tropical regions. His MUP studies focused on energy and environmental policy-analyses/planning for cities. He is a registered Architect in Kenya and South Africa. He currently serves as a board member of Sustainable Energy Africa (SEA), focusing on municipal support in policy and responses in energy and climate change for cities, and previously served as a board member of the Green Building Council of South Africa (GBCSA). In 2017, he was elected as a Fellow of the Mind & Life Institute, USA.

Heinrich Kammeyer (PhD) started his practicing and academic ventures in Architecture in 1972 after qualifying at University of Cape Town (UCT), South Africa. He also holds a Masters and PhD in Architecture from the University of Pretoria. Heinrich has served in teaching and research in architecture at University of Pretoria and University of the Witwatersrand in South Africa. His passion for practice and teaching has guided his research interests, especially within the field of vernacular architecture with phenomenology as his core philosophical foundation, including a PhD thesis on reciprocity in the process of Basotho woman making and the expression of care for her family and community. Prior research work at the Council for Scientific and Industrial Research (CSIR) allowed for his engaged practice in the planning, design and development of schools and academic institutions over an extended period of his career. Even in his retirement age, Heinrich is well acknowledged and appreciated by diverse cohorts of academic and practicing architects as an empathetic mentor and teacher who has contributed immensely to their career paths in the profession and life in general.

Geci Karuri-Sebina is an Associate Professor with the University of Witwatersrand's School of Governance, Adjunct Professor at University of Cape Town (African Centre for Cities), Associate of the South African Cities Network, and a founding Director of the Southern African Node of the Millennium Project. She is active across a number of sectors including as board member and Vice President of AfricaLics, organizer of the Civic Tech Innovation Network, and Africa Regional Editor for the journal *foresight*.

Deena Khalil is currently the Research and Advocacy Unit Manager at Takween Integrated Community Development, an urban development consultancy focusing on urban issues and underserved communities in Egypt. She is also a PhD candidate at the University College London (UCL) where she is studying the politics of access to potable water and infrastructure in Cairo's informal settlements. Prior to this, she obtained her MA in the Economics of International Development at the American University in Cairo, and worked as a project coordinator and researcher on studies related to HIV-AIDS, water and sanitation, and monitoring and evaluation in Egypt, Sudan, and the MENA region more broadly.

Erika Kraemer-Mbula is a Professor of Economics and is currently the Chair holder of the DSI/NRF/Newton Fund Trilateral Chair in Transformative Innovation, the Fourth Industrial Revolution and Sustainable Development, based at the College of Business and Economics University of Johannesburg, South Africa. She specialises in the analysis of innovation systems in connection to equitable development and inclusive development, and has done pioneering work on innovation in the African informal sector.

Taibat Lawanson is Associate Professor of Urban Planning at the University of Lagos, Nigeria, where she leads the Pro-Poor Development Research Cluster and serves as Co-Director at the Centre for Housing and Sustainable Development. She holds a PhD in Urban and Regional Planning from the Federal University of Technology, Akure, Nigeria. Her research focuses on the interface of social complexities, urban realities and the quest for environmental justice. She is particularly interested in how formal and informal urban systems synthesize in emerging African contexts. She is a member of the board of directors of Lagos Studies Association and a member of the International Advisory Committee of the UNHABITAT flagship 'State of the World's Cities Report'.

Sechaba Maape is an architect and senior lecturer at the Wits School of Architecture and Planning, South Africa. He holds a PhD in Architecture with a thesis that explored people/place relationships, ritual and climate change adaptation among prehistoric indigenous communities in Kuruman in the Northern Cape Province, engaging archaeological and paleontological material in-depth. In his research Maape investigates the manner in which people survive change and variability, especially environmental change. His main finding, that rituals play a significant role in fostering psychological, social and thus ecological adaptation, allows for deepening our understanding of the role of ritual practices and places in modern South African society.

Samuel Munzele Maimbo is the Chief of Staff in the Office of the President of the World Bank Group. Prior to his current role, he was Director of the International Development Association (IDA) Resource Mobilization and the International Bank for Reconstruction and Development (IBRD) Corporate Finance department, and Senior Advisor in the Office of the Managing Director and Chief Financial Officer at the World Bank. He has also worked on a diverse range of operations and countries and held various positions in the Finance Markets and Innovations Global Practice, including Financial Sector Specialist (South Asia Region, Africa Region, and Europe and Central Asia Region); Practice Manager for Strategy and Operations; and Practice Manager for Long-Term Finance & Risk Management. Before joining the World Bank, Maimbo held the position of Bank Inspector at the Bank of Zambia and Auditor at PricewaterhouseCoopers (PWC). Maimbo holds a PhD in Public Administration (Banking) from the University of Manchester, an MBA in Finance from the University of Nottingham, a BSc in Accounting from Copperbelt University, Zambia, and is a Fellow Chartered Certified Accountant (FCCA, UK).

Shadreck Mapfumo is a Senior Financial Specialist and Insurance Advisory Services Practice Group Lead for Africa at the International Finance Cooperation, World Bank Group, with responsibility for providing agricultural and index-based insurance advisory services to insurance companies and intermediaries in Africa, the Caribbean, and Asia as part of the Global Index Insurance Facility. He is a lead author of a World Bank Publication "Risk Modeling for Appraising Named Peril Index Insurance Products – A Guide for Practitioners, April 2017". Prior to joining IFC, he worked for the African Risk Capacity as Head of Risk Management, MicroEnsure as Vice President for Agriculture Insurance, Zimbabwe Reinsurance Company and Mercantile and General Reinsurance Company as Treaties Reinsurance Manager. Mapfumo holds a Master's degree in Actuarial Studies from the Australian National

University, Canberra; and a BCom (Hons) in Insurance and Risk Management from the National University of Science and Technology in Zimbabwe. He is an Associate in Reinsurance, and Associate of the Chartered Insurance Institute (UK).

Ntombini Marrengane is the Senior Manager at the Bertha Centre for Social Innovation and Entrepreneurship at the Graduate School of Business at the University of Cape Town, South Africa. She is an international development practitioner by training with a specialisation in governance and public health in African cities. Her current research interests centre on how social innovation can be used to enhance governance systems and service delivery in under-resourced local authorities in the Global South.

Martin Mbaya is a Doctoral Fellow at Strathmore University Business School in Nairobi, Kenya. He teaches, researches and consults in the areas of public policy, digital learning, entrepreneurship, innovation, trade and sustainability. Mbaya holds an S.B. degree in Mechanical Engineering from MIT and an MPP from Harvard Kennedy School of Government, USA. He is currently a doctoral candidate at the University of Pretoria's Graduate School of Technology Management. Martin serves in governance roles at the African Centre for Technology Studies (ACTS), the African Population and Health Research Center (APHRC) and the Alliance High School Endowment Funds. He is a co-founder and Investor in Nairobi Capital Inc. He is also a 2015 Archibishop Desmond Tutu Fellow.

Mammo Muchie is a South Africa National Research Foundation Research (SARChI) Chair-holder and Professor of Innovation Studies at Tshwane University of Technology, and currently Adjunct Professor at Bahir Dar University and the University of Gondar both in Ethiopia and the Africa Centre of Excellence in Data Science in Rwanda. He is a scientific board member of Globelics and the Globelics Academy; founder and Chief Editor of the *African Journal on Science, Technology, Innovation and Development;* and co-editor along with Bengt-Åke Lundvall and Peter Gammeltoft of the seminal book *Putting Africa First: The Making of African Innovation Systems* (Aalborg University Press, 2003), and author of numerous articles and academic papers. He holds a DPhil in Science, Technology, and Innovation for Development (STI4D) from the University of Sussex, UK.

Professor **Robert Mudida** is currently the Director of the Research Department of the Central Bank of Kenya and former Professor of Political Economy at Strathmore University, Nairobi, Kenya. He is the author of four books and numerous articles in top peer reviewed international journals. His most recent book *An Emerging Africa in the Age of Globalization* is published by Routledge (2022). He has also carried out consulting assignments with the World Bank and the United Nations Economic Commission for Africa.

Omar Nagati is a practising architect and urban planner, and the co-founder of the Cairo Lab for Urban Studies, Training and Environmental Research (CLUSTER), an urban design and research platform down-town Cairo. Having graduated from Cairo University, he studied and taught at UBC, Vancouver, Canada and UC Berkeley, USA. Nagati adopts an interdisciplinary approach to urban history and design, and engages in empirical research and critical mapping of urban informality. He teaches part-time Urban Design Studio at the MSA University in Giza and most recently a visiting professor at the University of Sheffield, UK.

Caroline Ncube is a Professor and the DST/NRF SARChI Research Chair in Intellectual Property, Innovation and Development in the Department of Commercial Law at the University of Cape Town (UCT), South Africa. She is the co-lead of the Open African Innovation Research (Open AIR) network's Cape Town hub and a member of the African Policy, Research & Advisory Group on STI, a member of the Advisory Board of the African Network of International Economic Law (AfIELN) and of the Academy of Science of South Africa (ASSAf). She also serves on the AU Scientific Technical Research Commission ASRIC Taskforce on IP Protection in Joint Research and Collaboration During Outbreaks.

Chidi Oguamanam holds the Research Chair in Bio-Innovation, Indigenous Knowledge Systems and Global Knowledge Governance, University of Ottawa, affiliated with the Centre for Law, Technology and Society, the Centre for Environmental Law and Global Sustainability, and the International Law Group. He is the director of Access and Benefit Sharing Canada (ABS-Canada) and co-founder of the Open African Innovation (Open AIR) Partnership and holds senior research fellowships with the Centre for International Governance Innovation (CIGI), the University of Cape Town Intellectual property Unit and the Centre for International Sustainable Development Law.

Brian Omwenga, a practising software and systems engineer, is currently a doctoral candidate in Computer Science at the University of Nairobi, Kenya, where he has also been a part-time lecturer in the Design and Analysis of Algorithms as well as Innovation Studies. He holds an MSc in Technology and Policy from MIT and a BSc in IT from Strathmore University. He is a holder of several filed and granted software patents and a lead enterprise architect of various large scale national

ICT projects. He is currently the team lead at the Tech Innovators Network Ltd (THiNK), a community-driven initiative for the discovery and delivery of local grassroot innovations and digital solutions. He also founded the Tech Innovators Sacco for the collaborative support of tech innovators.

João Resende-Santos is Associate Professor of Global Studies at Bentley University in Massachusetts, USA. He is author of *Neorealism, States, and the Modern Mass Army* (Cambridge University Press, 2007), and is active as a policy practitioner and international consultant in the areas of economic development policy, entrepreneurship, and trade policy. He has been a consultant for a number of international organizations and for the Government of Cabo Verde.

Davlin Richardson is currently an Associate Director at a global consulting firm, aligned to the Technology Strategy and Operations practice serving clients across the energy and utilities sector. Before moving to Atlanta, USA in 2018, Davlin was based in Johannesburg, South Africa where he served as the Technology and Infrastructure Executive for an international mining and engineering firm headquartered in Canada. With over 23 years experience in Information Technology, Davlin is a technology professional, passionate about innovation, continuous improvement and collaborative business processes. Davlin has built extensive experience in large-scale ERP cloud deployments, Agile Project Management, IT Operations and Infrastructure Management, Technology strategy and execution. He has developed deep international project experience, working with organizations across Africa, Australia, Canada, Europe and North America. He holds a BSc. in Computer Science from the University of South Africa, a Master of Business Administration (MBA) from GIBS Business School (Gordon Institute of Business Science) and various project management certifications.

Nagla Rizk is Professor of Economics and Founding Director of the Access to Knowledge for Development Center (A2K4D) at the American University in Cairo's School of Business. Her research area is the economics of knowledge, technology and development, with focus on the platform economy, digitally mediated work, knowledge and data governance, artificial intelligence, innovation, gender and inclusive growth in the Middle East and North Africa. She leads the North African Hub of the Open African Innovation Research Partnership and has affiliations and teaching experience at several global universities including Harvard, Yale, Columbia, the University of Ottawa and the University of Toronto. She also has affiliations with several international organizations and national policy bodies.

Margot Rubin is the South African Research Chair in Spatial Analysis and City Planning at the University of the Witwatersrand in Johannesburg. Since 2002, she has worked as a researcher, and policy and development consultant focusing on housing and urban development issues, and has contributed to a number of research reports on behalf of the National Department of Housing, the Johannesburg Development Agency, SRK Engineering, World Bank, Ekurhuleni Metropolitan Municipality and Urban LandMark. Her PhD in Urban Planning and Politics interrogates the role of the legal system in urban governance and its effect on the distribution of scarce resources and larger questions around democracy. Of late, Rubin has been writing about inner-city regeneration, housing policy and is currently engaged in work around mega housing projects and issues of gender and the city.

Vipua Inata Rukambe is a Namibian doctoral candidate in Architecture at the University of the Witwatersrand, South Africa. Her PhD research seeks to tackle one of the critical gaps in sustainable city transitioning towards capacitating African cities to re-envision their futures, with a specific anchoring on the temporal dimension. Through the application of multiple theoretical and methodological lenses, her research is focused on defining pathways towards desirable futures for African cities. Based on architect's future-crafting skills in exploring desirable futures, her current research interests are influenced by Afrofuturistic future crafting through African cultural frames with uBuntu as a primary reference. With a passion for co-creating, collaborating and cultivating new networks. Using her skills outside the production of buildings, she has joined Kollective Kaboom and is currently exploring decolonial re/membering in Berlin, working with the temporal dimension of colonialism and the decolonialization of memory and place.

Isaac Rutenberg is an Associate Professor and founder of the Center for Intellectual Property and Information Technology Law (CIPIT) at Strathmore Law School in Nairobi, Kenya. Dr. Rutenberg teaches numerous courses on IP and IT law. His research covers data protection and privacy, artificial intelligence, digital identity, contextualized innovation, and the interface between IT law and intellectual property law. He is registered to practice law in California, and is registered to practice before the United States Patent and Trademark Office and the Kenya Industrial Property Institute. He holds a JD (law degree) and a PhD in chemistry.

Youdi Schipper is a research economist at Twaweza East Africa and a senior fellow at the Amsterdam Institute for International Development. Youdi's work focuses on education reform, results based finance, impact evaluation and mobile data collection. He manages the KiuFunza teacher performance pay trials and scale-up in Tanzania. He is a principal investigator in the RISE Tanzania country research team. Previously he led the team that designed and initiated Sauti za Wananchi Tanzania, the first nationwide mobile phone panel survey in Africa.

Tobias Schonwetter (PhD) is Director of the Intellectual Property Unit (IP Unit), Faculty of Law, University of Cape Town (UCT), and the Founding Director of the iNtaka Centre for Law & Technology at UCT and its LawTechLab. He is a Steering Committee member of the Open African Innovation Research (Open AIR) and co-lead of the Open AIR Cape Town hub. As an Associate Professor at UCT, Schonwetter teaches IP and IT law. He has decades of experience exploring IP issues and regularly advises various government and non-governmental entities on issues relating to IP and, in particular, copyright and open access.

1.

INTRODUCTION

Innovation Ecosystems to Create African Solutions to African Problems

Olugbenga Adesida, Geci Karuri-Sebina,
João Resende-Santos & Mammo Muchie

The global pandemic that swept across the globe during 2020 was a stark reminder of the many different kinds of challenges and diversity of sources that threaten economic growth and social wellbeing in all countries, rich and poor alike. Such disease outbreaks and pandemics destabilize economies in multiple ways. As the 2020 pandemic revealed, even the most technologically sophisticated, advanced industrial countries that dominate the world economy succumbed in rapid, spectacular fashion to a virus that neither their advanced technologies nor sophisticated economies were prepared to deal with.

The African continent, unhappily, has had a long and distressing experience with pandemics and intractable diseases that have ravaged African societies and undermined economic progress. Such diseases – many of which are preventable – not only stress already brittle and inadequate healthcare systems but they damage short- and long-term economic growth through the impact on the health of the labour force, business interruptions and shutdowns, trade and supply chains disruptions, social fear and malaise causing drastic changes in economic and social behaviour, and the confidence of domestic as well as international investors. What the advanced industrial countries experienced in 2020 is what most countries in post-colonial Africa have been experiencing for decades as they aspire to grow and transform their economies.

However, the 2020 crisis also revealed something else – a strength and promise for Africa that reinforces the urgency of fostering innovation of all kinds. It revealed the critical importance of what this project on the African Innovation Summit (AIS) has been insisting all along: the value and centrality of everyday, bottom-end innovations and simple, low-cost, low-technology solutions to the continent's many challenges and opportunities. Among the world's most desperately poor and ill-equipped countries, the countries of West Africa managed to control their latest outbreak of Ebola in 2014 not through high-end medical or technological breakthroughs, but through low-cost, low-technology solutions and practices that focused on building social trust, collective action, improved management and decision, improving access to and community trust of health facilities, grassroots involvement, and even co-opting traditional leaders.

International donor support was critical to their efforts, and there were many errors, gaps and failures. Yet these poorest of the poor countries embraced low-end innovations in organizational practices, approaches to public services delivery, and social policies to foster community engagement and inclusion so critical to finding and isolating cases, door-to-door contact tracing, and changing social behaviour. High-end medical and technological breakthroughs and infrastructure play a critical role, of course, in controlling pandemics. An equally critical part of stopping a pandemic is early identification and isolation of cases as well as contact tracing, simple, everyday innovations and solutions involving improved delivery, building social trust, and community inclusion.

As we have insisted since the launch of the AIS project, Africa needs both kinds of innovation, what we have referred to as high-end and low-end innovation, and across all aspects of social, economic, and institutional life. Innovation must be at the centre of development. And we have insisted, there are vast opportunities and widespread existing initiatives in Africa in low-end, everyday innovations to solve social and economic problems retarding growth and transformation. The rich, technologically advanced countries in 2020 confronted major difficulties in contact tracing, despite the promises of high-end technological solutions, fiscal resources, and vast infrastructure. West African countries, where street addresses and signs are practically non-existent in many cases, managed to effectively deploy a grassroots door-to-door contact tracing that became a vital component of stopping the 2014 Ebola outbreak.

As much as the 2014 Ebola outbreak in West Africa demonstrated the promise and opportunities of low-end innovation in Africa, it also exposed the many impediments and gaping holes in the ecosystem of innovation so vital to growth, transformation and social progress. From inadequate infrastructure, high-cost and adverse business and investment climate, poor governance and frail public administration, inadequate investment in human capital, to the many market failures and distortions characterizing post-colonial African economies. Put differently, the challenges to growth and transformation are many as they are profound and persistent. Innovation is not a panacea for poverty and underdevelopment. Indeed, African countries are confronted with an array of enormous challenges, not just the onerous task of building a national innovation ecosystem. They face simultaneous gargantuan tasks – such as transforming their economies into globally competitive, growth-sustaining economies and building up the strength and credibility of state institutions, to solving basic, post-colonial challenges such as nation-building, governance stability, and social peace in many cases. The thesis in this book, however, is that these challenges can only be addressed through innovation, given the emerging context and realities.

Enabling and mainstreaming both high-end and low-end innovation are necessary parts of the broader strategy for transforming African economies, spurring robust growth and competitiveness, in addition to poverty alleviation and redressing common everyday challenges such as disease mitigation, improving access to clean water and energy, raising farm productivity, and generally building up resilience of communities through low-cost, low-tech solutions. Moreover, growth and transformation of African economies takes place in a highly competitive world economy whose functioning and rules have proven onerous for poorer countries to catch up, compete, or escape the middle-income trap. Yet high- and low-end innovation will play a critical part in Africa's growth and transformation going forward – perhaps all the more so because of the challenges presented by the world's economy.

Innovation, along with entrepreneurship and good management of the state, will be a key driver for growth and human development in Africa. This volume, *Innovation Ecosystems in Africa: Solving the Problems We Have*, offers a fresh and critical survey of the advances, trends, challenges and gaps in innovation on the African continent. This is the second in a series of scholarly works that examines innovation in Africa. It is a follow-up work to the novel and well-received volume, *Innovation Africa: Emerging Hubs of Excellence* (2016). These works are scholarly outputs of the much broader initiative, organized under the umbrella Africa Innovation Summit (AIS), to raise public awareness, foster research interest, promote innovators and entrepreneurs, and draw policy attention to the opportunities and challenges facing innovation and its enabling ecosystem on the African continent.

As in the first volume, *Innovation Ecosystems in Africa* brings together scholars, experts and practitioners who offer in-depth case studies across the continent that examine innovation activities. By examining closely country-cases of innovation initiatives in all regions of the continent, the works in tandem provide the empirical basis for demonstrating that rich innovation is happening in Africa, examining how it is happening, and synthesizing key lessons and recommendations for African innovation systems in policy and practice. As one of the authors observes, Africa is a region today with extensive innovation activities, but the many initiatives by entrepreneurs, firms, non-profits, social enterprises, and the public sector remain overlooked and obscure, misconstrued, isolated, and unsupported.

This second volume builds upon this same basic approach, this time examining how innovation systems in Africa are serving to address the most basic conditions of human, socio-economic and institutional development required on the continent. Linked to the second Africa Innovation Summit (6–8 June 2018, Kigali, Rwanda), the book continues to build upon the position that African countries must innovate and build robust national and local systems that promote and nourish innovation to ensure structural transformation. This is crucial if they are to advance and significantly benefit from some of the vibrant cultures of innovation that are emerging within various communities on the continent.

Countries in Africa need to recognize that innovation is taking place everywhere to address daily challenges and opportunities, and that policymakers must systematically see how to sense or tap into what is happening, promote and build on them as an efficient way to build effective innovation-driven societies on the continent. To do this, it is crucial, in turn, that countries address policy and institutional deficits and reforms, decisively tackling endemic challenges such as access to finance, education and training, research, entrepreneurship, partnerships/collaboration, and intellectual property regimes.

FOSTERING AN INNOVATION ECOSYSTEM

Inside and outside Africa the misperception persists of a continent that is bereft of innovation and entrepreneurial activities. These scholarly works of the AIS intentionally contest these misperceptions and stereotypes, while simultaneously drawing attention to the many challenges facing innovation activities and, importantly, the wider national innovation ecosystem that affects them. In similar fashion, these works adopt a much broader perspective and conceptualization of innovation, which is too narrowly associated with capital- and technology-intensive activities often driven by new scientific discoveries.

For us, Africa needs all kinds of innovation, and in all spheres of social, economic and political life – what we have referred to as high-end and low-end innovation. Given the continent's many needs and deficits, especially the sum total of the human development challenges and other social deficits, innovation in the African context can neither be an abstraction nor narrowly associated with technology parks and digital-age discoveries. That is, while African economies urgently need to build up their internal capacity for science- and technology-based innovation (that is, high end, capital and technology-intensive innovation), it is equally critical to recognize the role of low-end innovation in economic growth and human development, given the continent's socioeconomic deficits as well as its vast natural endowments.

Low-end innovation includes diffusely developed low-cost and low-technology solutions that capitalize on locally available and sustainable inputs to solve everyday problems from energy, housing, education, health, agricultural production, and clean water resources. So that while Africa might arguably need to foster the emergence of its own Silicon Valleys, it must also promote the invention and adoption of more efficient wood-fuelled stoves that burn less wood and thus limit deforestation and combat climate change. As some of the chapters in this book show, rethinking and redesigning our organizational models for public services delivery, such as learning and teaching or healthcare, are important types of much-needed low-end innovations.

In some cases, high-end and low-end innovation overlaps, as in the vast potential to tap into Africa's vast natural endowments to generate sustainable green energy solutions. High-end and low-end innovation are not separate but linked and mutually reinforcing. An ecosystem that enables both creates growth opportunities, economic gains and entrepreneurial spaces. Using low-tech, low-cost drones to deliver medicines or the widespread use of mobile payments may be considered low-end innovations but they also involve at the back-end more intensive innovations involving software design, programming, and engineering that may open up opportunities for local firms and entrepreneurs.

The book is, thus, very much grounded in the realities facing African countries, on the initiatives and trends at all levels and sectors, and on the practical policy interventions necessary to foster these and improve their enabling ecosystem. As such, the subtitle of the volume, *Solving the Problems We Have*, is deliberate in its effort to draw multi-stakeholder attention to what is happening, to what is missing, and to what is needed to drive forward the African development agenda. A third characteristic feature of these volumes is our insistence that as much as the individual innovation initiatives are important, much more critical is the larger ecosystem. Our view is that without a robust ecosystem, it is highly unlikely for an innovation culture to take root and to ensure an innovation-driven society.

This volume, embedded in the larger AIS project, adopts a systems approach to innovation – viewing the entire country as an ecosystem encompassing the many actors, individuals, organizations, networks, clusters and communities, interactions, and flows of knowledge and learning that enable (or hinder) innovation activities. To be sure, given a globalized, integrated world economy as well as efforts at regional integration, innovation process and interactions do not happen only at the national level; nor is economic development merely a national process or outcome. Identifying and supporting the micro-level firms, individual entrepreneurs, hubs and clusters are important, but these are embedded in a larger context that requires national-level policies, institutions, infrastructure, and so on.

An innovation ecosystem is a fancy way to describe a society characterized by institutions, practices, policies, infrastructure, linkages, and interactions that foster and support knowledge creation and sharing, individual and organizational learning, entrepreneurial activity and risk taking, problem-solving attitudes and practices, and low barriers to product and knowledge dissemination. Given the historical origins of the concept, and its close connotation with Silicon Valley and the high-technology industry, the 'ecosystem' has become closely associated with science- and technology-promoting industries, government policy, and research institutions.

Moreover, the concept has become closely associated with the private sector and commercially-oriented production, and the manufacturing and digital technology industries in particular. Too often, the innovation ecosystem is viewed by policymakers and lay people as limited to high-end science and technology policy, infrastructure and actors; or as just an isolated clustering of tech start-ups and app developers occupying abandoned warehouses or in some 'science parks'. Still others narrowly view the ecosystem as government-funded university–industry collaboration. Supporting the creativity, knowledge production, learning, networking, collaboration, and successful commercialization of new knowledge and ideas by the firms and individuals in these clusters and elsewhere is crucial, as is supporting and enabling social enterprises, communities, and individuals in producing, devising and applying solutions to the problems they face every day. However, the innovation ecosystem is much more comprehensive, and involves many other facets, linkages and interactions, institutions, and components. We adopt a view of the concept as a national-level ecosystem. Our conception is consistent with those of Freeman (2008) and Lundvall (2007) and many other works that emphasize the national innovation system approach. It encompasses micro-level behaviour and interactions as well as macro-level institutions and interactions.

The ecosystem of innovation has four distinctive dimensions. The first is on non-linearity of the knowledge to generate innovative products and solutions. The second is how different products and practices are produced from the interaction with production networks that collaborate, be they firms, social or political organizations, or social and non-profit enterprises. The third is the importance of promoting innovation through ecosystem-based design. The fourth feature is policy learning to facilitate institutional, social and economic transformation. In other words, critical components of the ecosystems include governance institutions, private sector entrepreneurship, and institutions of learning and research.

As ecosystem, the concept puts a critical focus on the interactions, relations, and collaboration of the many components and actors in the system. Yet these are themselves embedded in larger, deeper layers. As Lundvall (2007) and others remind us, the ecosystem is a national context that fosters, supports and facilitates knowledge and learning, and the wide dissemination or commercialization of the products, practices, and applications generated. In Africa, despite the frailty of the private sector or research institutions, there is no shortage of good ideas, entrepreneurial drive, high-end and low-end innovative product ideas and solutions. As the following chapters will show, the larger political and market environment often stifles or undermines their dissemination, adoption and commercialization.

Innovation ecosystems are not the result of some carefully designed blueprint or master plan that is implemented in some mechanistic, sequential fashion in some short period of time. They are organic, historical and non-linear. However, an ecosystem of innovation is not a randomized, chance or accidental outcome. An enabling ecosystem is not a fluke nor a spontaneous outcome. Whether we look to Silicon Valley's development or the successful cases of innovation ecosystems in both rich and developing countries, governance institutions and policies deliberately designed to foster its development have been crucial, especially to support learning institutions and capacities, reduce market failures and distortions, and support entrepreneurship. In building, deepening and enlarging its innovation ecosystem, Africa does not have to reinvent the wheel. While easier said than done, some essential steps, practices, components and policies to build and foster an innovation ecosystem are both universal and successfully tried widely. While taking stock of their needs and specificities, African countries can take best practices and success factors from each other as well as internationally.

Nevertheless, the task of creating and fostering a national innovation ecosystem is as daunting as it is long term. Yet, it is important to emphasize, it is *not* a separate endeavour from the task of social and economic transformation that African countries *must* engage in if they wish to prosper and avoid falling further by the wayside in the global system. They are one and the same, in many ways. Strengthening and diversifying the productive capacities of the economy, building human capital, reducing or removing structural constraints and market failures, strengthening institutions and the regulatory framework, and all the other critical measures necessary to enable transformation is to enable an innovation ecosystem.

As we have emphasized in the AIS and as highlighted in the chapters below, a critical aspect is governing institutions and policies. This is not a claim the state must take the lead, nor that all that is needed is better policies, institutions and good governance. This is not a call for state-led growth or *dirigisme* of old. It is, however, acknowledgment of the important, necessary and universal, role the state plays in creating an enabling environment in which private actors and organizations can thrive, create, produce, innovate, and prosper through their own efforts and creative energies.

It is also an acknowledgement of the vital importance that policy and institutions have played everywhere in supporting the innovation activities of private firms and individuals, promoting learning institutions and capabilities, fostering networks and collaboration such as university–industry collaboration, removing or mitigating market failures, seeding basic research and development, incentivizing social entrepreneurship, investment in economic and social infrastructure, improving the regulatory and business climate, and otherwise creatively using fiscal, social, macroeconomic and even trade policies (Block and Keller 2016). It is difficult to conceive of economic transformation, and the urgent necessity of development that Africa must engage in, without a robust and well-managed state to build the enabling environment (UNECA 2011).

African countries must become more entrepreneurial and agile, not only because of the enormous challenges to solve at home but also because of an inhospitable external environment. The highly integrated and intensely competitive global economy makes entry harder and opportunities fewer, especially given the domination by China and other large emerging markets at the lower end of industrial production and global value chains that African economies would need as part of their transformation. In addition, global governance does not help. The rich and advanced countries of today were able to play an active and direct role building up, intervening and managing their economic transformation through their industrial policies and other mechanisms. Of course, many still do so today, in hidden as well as overt ways. World trade rules have drastically reduced the scope and manner in which states can engage in economic management and promotion. The weakness and vulnerability of African states further reduces their scope of action.

As noted above, fostering an enabling environment that nourishes and broadens all types of innovation, while not a panacea, is necessarily a key component of the larger and difficult task of economic transformation. The diversity of African societies and economies means this transformation will follow different pathways. Each country will have to devise growth models and strategies based on its peculiar conditions, endowments, and circumstances internally and externally. Regardless of the individual pathways, and specificities of each transformation strategy, enabling innovation at the top end and the bottom will be vital. Building globally competitive firms and industries require it. So too is building up the resilience and capabilities of individual citizens and communities – especially in the sense of giving them the capacities and enabling environment to solve their own everyday problems.

RATIONALE AND OBJECTIVES OF THE BOOK

The first AIS scholarly output, the *Innovation Africa* volume (published by Emerald in 2016), presented itself as a novel, grounded, voyage of exploration towards a systematic approach to studying and supporting innovation-driven development for Africa. Tackling the question of how innovation is concentrating or clustering to drive industry-scale economic development, it used a variety of country-based case studies to provide an empirical basis for demonstrating that rich innovation is happening in Africa, examining how it is happening, and synthesizing key lessons and recommendations for policy and practice.

This second book builds upon the same basic approach, but this time examining how innovation systems in Africa are serving to address the most basic conditions of socio-economic and institutional development required on the continent. Linked to the second Africa Innovation Summit (Rwanda, June 2018), the book develops learning case studies to examine various sectoral exemplars and transversal dimensions which could help inform insights about how policymakers and practitioners might develop more effective and impactful innovation-driven strategies, ecosystems and enterprises.

As in the first volume, this edited collection uses multi-country, cross-sectoral case studies to advance an empirically grounded, analytically rigorous, appreciative investigation of how innovation is being used to address fundamental development challenges on the continent, and how the African innovation ecosystems could be made more enabling into the future. Exploring these dynamics based on empirical work is the purpose of this book, as well as working towards robust policy guidance on how to solve Africa's most urgent challenges.

The edited volume has simultaneous academic, policy and practice objectives. The general purpose of the book is to broaden the visibility and deepen interrogation of African innovation systems in practice by offering relatively unique, serious academic analysis of the emergence, growth and future prospects of endogenous innovation practices and

The AIS

The Africa Innovation Summit (AIS) was launched by interested innovators and scholars based on the simple idea that innovation must be at the centre of Africa's agenda if the continent is to ensure socioeconomic development and structural transformation. Since its launch in 2012, the AIS has emerged as 'innovation system in action' and it is emerging as a hybrid 'marketplace' aimed at deepening and scaling up innovation in Africa. The AIS has become a platform bringing all stakeholders – from heads of state, policymakers, investors, activists, entrepreneurs, academics, researchers to innovators – together to share ideas and learn, as well as facilitate the necessary collaboration and collective actions to overcome the challenges of getting innovations to market and scaling up innovations to truly impact upon Africa's development.

In June 2018, we the group of editors were involved in convening the 2nd Africa Innovation Summit (AIS), which was held in Kigali under the patronage of His Excellencies President Paul Kagame of Rwanda and Former President Pedro Pires of Cabo Verde. Here, 50 young innovators from 44 African countries and about two thousand delegates – scholars, policymakers, financiers and commercialists – from over 70 countries converged to engage with each other about where innovation is required in Africa's development trajectory, and to diagnose what ecosystem factors are hampering the viability and efficacy of innovations and innovators.

lessons across the continent. Beyond disseminating knowledge about these cases of innovation in Africa and sparking public interest, the book is also intended as a policy-oriented work to help inform policymakers and practitioners throughout Africa on how to develop more enabling innovation ecosystems. The individual case studies aim to isolate the key factors driving the developmentally-oriented innovations, and to distil the main policy- and practice-useful lessons that can inspire and inform governments and business leaders in their efforts to recognize and nurture these efforts in their respective local and national innovation systems. As a policy-relevant exercise, the book aims to provide policymakers, business leaders and opinion leaders both inspiration and useful policy 'take-aways' that can inform strategies and concrete measures to foster and speed up the pace of developmentally impactful innovation on the continent.

The premise of the book is that there are critically useful lessons to be learned from under-recognized emergent praxis in various places and at different societal levels. These efforts demonstrate important potential to find relevant response to some of Africa's most fundamental or critical development challenges. However, there has not been enough of a focus on studying cases which may not have been easily understood or reconciled in conventional policy terms. This may be partly due to overly formalized, bureaucratized or exogenous approaches with narrow economic considerations to studying innovation. The book thus supports a self-reflection and learning approach grounded in unearthing and learning from a range of both conventional and unconventional case studies.

As with its predecessor, the volume adopts the 'structured case study' method. The case chapters are structured and written as an analytical narrative style that offers readers a clear and succinct analysis of the origins, characteristics, growth and critical issues surrounding each innovation and its ecosystem in relation to the challenge issue. The goal is for the cases to present an in-depth but succinct picture of the subject matter that isolates and discusses the most critical aspects and factors behind the context and performance of the innovation case, combining theory with empirical evidence.

BOOK STRUCTURE

The volume is presented as a series of eight diverse case studies exploring grounded instances of developmental innovation in Africa, seeking out policy and practice lessons for how its innovation ecosystem could be more enabling. The series of cases begin with the very pragmatic fields of health, education and housing, then progress to considering economic and governance issues. The latter studies on cognitive leadership qualities and paradigmatic shifts begin to explore the prospects for building new capabilities to drive systemic change.

Boum's chapter 'Reinventing African Healthcare Systems' [Chapter 2] is located in the Democratic Republic of Congo (DRC), discussing innovation in the context of some of Africa's biggest health challenges. In fact, the 2018 Ebola outbreak was a pandemic threat of global scale that had its epicentre in some of Africa's poorest communities in the DRC provinces of Equateur and North Kivu. The question of how healthcare solutions already implemented in many countries might innovatively combine with 'homegrown' systems and solutions within an African health innovation ecosystem can result not only in improved global health security but also in universal healthcare coverage across the continent. The paper argues that the high burden of diseases, coupled with the lack of infrastructure and trained healthcare workers in Africa, presents the demand and opportunity to use both new technologies and traditional health systems, where traditional healers and community healthcare workers play an established role in patient management and disease surveillance. This would result in a new African healthcare ecosystem that could significantly improve the management of pandemics.

What is required, it is proposed, is for the private sector, philanthropists and African diasporas to support initiatives that creatively combine modern and homegrown solutions to the health challenges that Africa faces.

Eyakuze and Schipper then explore the innovative idea of 'Paying Teachers for Performance' [Chapter 3] in Tanzania, where schooling is expensive and government's expenditure on education has been steadily growing. As in most other countries, teacher pay there does not differentiate between the quality of teaching and learning that takes place, despite research showing substantial differences in teacher quality within schools. Having a good or a bad teacher affects the learning and lifetime incomes of students, but teacher quality differences are difficult to observe. In addition, a teacher's salary is based in large part on experience, but research shows that more experience does not correlate well with teaching effort and quality (apart from during the first years of a teacher's career). This chapter provides an account of the KiuFunza teacher incentive programme in Tanzania implemented by the NGO Twaweza. This implementation of incentive pay over the last four years shows that introducing a modest salary component related to measured performance can inspire teachers to improve learning. After discussing how a global and domestic innovation ecosystem produced ideas that affected the history of Tanzania's education sector, the KiuFunza innovation based on teacher performance pay is described. The development of the practical design of the experimental programme is detailed, followed by a discussion of the programme's impact on student learning, and considerations for how the programme might be scaled through partnering approaches and additional experiments.

Maimbo, Mapfumo and Delay tackle the idea of 'Insurance as an Effective Development Instrument' [Chapter 4]. Insurance, they argue, can both help a country's economy grow and contribute to reducing poverty, including through helping households manage risk, and improving resilience mitigating the effects of climate change. However, although many insurance products are aligned with public policy priorities in Africa, several barriers need to be overcome to develop insurance markets and increase penetration in the region. One particular innovative insurance product is weather-based index insurance, which is insurance linked to an index such as rainfall or temperature. Such a product can be an effective tool for increasing insurance penetration on the continent, provided insurance companies and regulators understand how to design and implement such a complex and labour-intensive product. This paper uses case studies from Nigeria and Zambia to demonstrate how capacity-building can have a positive impact on the creation of sustainable insurance markets in Africa. Long-term sustainability will require insurance companies and other stakeholders in the ecosystem to develop local product-design capacity, making them more cost efficient. They will also be able to use their local knowledge and insights to develop and offer innovative products that are specifically suited to African markets

Marrengane et al. write on 'Innovative Approaches to Sustainable Housing' [Chapter 5], which uses a recent comparative study of the four largest African city-regions, where they examine the institutional, political, and material realities influencing different city-region approaches to informality and affordable housing delivery. The background is a body of research that examines contemporary African cities and the varied dimensions of unmet service delivery needs that has grown consistently in the last decade. Scholars across disciplines have documented the absence of effective planning regimes, the lack of infrastructure, and the shortages of decent and affordable shelter. These seemingly intractable features of African cities are amplified as the region experiences unprecedented urban growth. This research on Cairo, Egypt; Addis Ababa, Ethiopia; Lagos, Nigeria; and Gauteng, South Africa illuminates both the starkly different urban realities and the common need for sustainable solutions. The research also reveals that while it is useful to distil 'best practices' where they exist, it is vital to face the complexity, constraints, and contradictions encountered in each context. Attention to local conditions and the need for governance practices which embed principles of sustainability in line with the New Urban Agenda and the post Habitat III policy environment, provide an opportunity to assess institutional capacities and practices against an innovation systems framework. These case studies offer insight into the spectrum of governance environments on the continent and opportunities for innovations and adaptive approaches to urban management.

Mbaya, Mudida and Omwenga write about 'Innovative Governance Systems' [Chapter 6], examining two national cases (Kenya and Rwanda) and the implementation of Africa's Agenda 2063 through the African Continental Free Trade Area (AfCFTA), a newly ratified regional free market initiative enabling the free movement of people, goods and services across traditional borders, supported by logistics, payments and dispute resolution. This advances the goals of Africa's ambitious Agenda 2063 which requires a continental, multi-sectoral innovation ecosystem. AfCFTA is envisioned as a digital, free trade area that is effectively anchored upon an ICT innovation ecosystem. This requires an innovative governance system with optimized linkages across other innovation system pillars. This chapter examines case studies of innovative governance systems at national and sub-national level with strong linkages to the rest of the ICT innovation ecosystems: Kenya's devolution through the revenue-sharing formula and improved service delivery through the Huduma Centres, and Rwanda's experience with Umushyikirano (National Dialogue). Both countries have in place ICT policies that are based on clearly defined problems and supported by strong implementation efforts through well-evaluated projects and programmes. Their experience illustrates good practice in implementing projects and explains their willingness to extend their successes to AfCFTA. The authors argue that the success stories of Kenya and Rwanda in the ICT sector and their experience with innovative governance systems can offer models for the rest of the African continent. These governance systems are structured to maximize the provision of public goods underpinned by a social contract and embracing the SDGs, and tend to be innovative, inclusive, integrated and supportive of the Fourth Industrial Revolution.

Kraemer-Mbula et al. extend the economic conversation into 'Collaborative Innovation and Networked Entrepreneurship in Africa' [Chapter 7], acknowledging that in spite of needing to focus on formal arrangements, the reality is that the majority of African innovators still operate in the informal economy and remain at the margins of the broader innovation ecosystem. Research done by the Open African Innovation Research Network (Open AIR) has attempted to address the gap between African entrepreneurs and innovation, through the collection of new evidence of African innovation in a range of settings across Africa. The research indicates that African entrepreneurs play an important role in the diffusion of economically useful skills, mainly through apprenticeships and learning on the job, and that innovative entrepreneurs successfully combine traditional knowledge with new, especially digital, technologies. On the basis of 12 case studies conducted by Open AIR between 2016 and 2018 in seven African countries, this chapter distils some of the central features of African innovative entrepreneurship. In particular, it expands on the following aspects: (a) the integration of modalities for skills development and training; (b) the rise of collaborative communities, and (c) the combination of traditional knowledge with new and emerging technologies. The chapter raises important questions about considering different forms of knowledge and learning, whereas currently African innovation ecosystems place high value on formal academic knowledge and give little social status or recognition to the value of practical skills. This must be addressed to avoid such a system reproducing the uneven spread of skills and competences, which may lead to (or exacerbate) more unequal societies.

Yu-Jen Chen and Richardson's chapter 'Understanding Cognitive Behaviours of Innopreneurs' [Chapter 8] argues for the importance of studying how individuals can be both more innovative and more entrepreneurial, given evidence of the direct and significant correlation between a country's innovativeness and the vibrancy of its entrepreneurship ecosystems. 'Innopreneurship' is the term that the authors use to describe the innovative undertakings that lead to successful entrepreneurship, and it is a term that has attracted increasing attention in recent years. However, the constructs of innovation and entrepreneurship are often studied in isolation rather than within a consolidated innopreneurial cognitive-behavioural framework based on empirical research. This chapter proposes an innopreneurial cognitive-behavioural framework based on input from 57 co-founders of innovative businesses within South Africa and beyond on the continent. It is proposed that by grasping the key underlying innopreneurial cognitive-behavioural components, policymakers and leaders in all sectors will be able to establish innovation ecosystem enablers that harness higher degrees of innopreneurial output. The proposition is that the innopreneurs being enabled will have the intuition, audacity, credulity, the resources and the training to discover and create new or re-applied innovations capable of disrupting the African economy while increasing employment, living standards, socio-political advancements and an inclusive socio-economic order.

Irurah et al. complete the volume with a conceptual chapter on 'Leveraging Neuro-phenomenology Insights from Neuroscience and Consciousness Studies towards Paradigm-shifting for Sustainable City Transitioning' [Chapter 9]. It is anchored around the acknowledgement that the escalating challenges facing humanity today clearly show that the incremental gains from our socio-technical innovations are not translating into expedited change at a rate fast enough for us to avert global crises such as climate change, loss of biodiversity or even socioeconomic inequalities. This chapter presents multidisciplinary scholarship anchored in architecture, while leveraging the insights from neuroscience and consciousness studies for innovation and prototyping towards tackling the prevailing inertia in paradigm-shifting, with specific focus on sustainable city transitioning. This is substantiated along three key themes: innovative multidisciplinary research approach, innovative multidisciplinary postgraduate curriculum, and prototyping of trans-disciplinary guided leadership skills for transitioning. A newly launched prototyping of the convergence towards smart- and sustainable-city transitioning for Mombasa, Kenya, is introduced as an emerging example. The chapter proposes the critical need to establish context-responsive neuroscience research labs in Africa where, at present, no meaningful or systematic research is happening in these rapidly-growing and rapidly innovating multidisciplinary domains.

RECOMMENDATIONS

The set of chapters purposefully covers wide and diverse ground on several levels. We conclude this project with seven recommendations following reflection on the contributions in this collection as well as the insights from the AIS dialogues to date (Adesida et al. 2018; Anahory et al. 2014).

This is a challenging period for the world, with the COVID-19 pandemic wreaking havoc on the global economy and health systems at the time of publishing. The pandemic has demonstrated clearly why African countries need to evolve a new approach to development management which places emphasis on innovation. While African countries have not suffered as much as countries in Europe, North America and Latin America, the economic impact on Africa is as devastating if not more, given the existing level of poverty on the continent before the advent of COVID-19.

First, **Africa needs to bet on innovation.** While there is a tendency now to blame everything on COVID-19, the reality is that it has only amplified and exposed the daunting hidden challenges faced by many. Innovation in all spheres of society is critical given the need to address a myriad of challenges facing the continent, from the lack of access to water, sanitation, energy, healthcare, transportation to the issues of governance and unemployment. In light of the issues, there is a need to rethink innovation within the African context so as to place emphasis on innovating and scaling up solutions to address Africa's perennial developmental challenges. While innovation for the sake of innovating may be exciting, it is important at this critical juncture in Africa that emphasis be placed on solving the real problems faced by the people.

Second, there is a **need for a greater sense of urgency on Africa's transformation,** given that reality for far too many people on the continent is dire. In many ways, Africa has become the face of global poverty. The situation will not get better unless there is rapid change. Africa's population is expected to double by 2050. Africa is the fastest growing region in the world and will account for about half of the total global population growth up to 2050 (UNDESA 2019). This could be a boon, as the rising working age population provides opportunity for economic growth. For the demographic dividend to materialize, however, the continent would have to make significant investments in the people, especially the education and health of the youth, while also creating the conditions for economic growth. Alternatively, rather than a boon, the continent could witness a demographic explosion. In the meantime, climate change is already impacting the continent in many severe ways.

There is no longer time for business as usual. Africa needs to act fast and strategically.

Third, Africa's transformation calls for **a bolder imagination about the future**. A key deficit today is a consistent, compelling narrative for a continent-wide transformative agenda. Despite the recent African Continental Free Trade Agreement (AfCFTA), a flagship project of the African Union's Agenda 2063 programme that came into force in 2021, the continent still lacks a bold agenda which captures the imagination of the population at large and which is capable of mobilizing all African stakeholders towards a common purpose. In the 1950s and 1990s, the rallying cry was independence and Pan-Africanism. By the 1980s, it was the agenda for industrialization with the Lagos Plan of Action (LPA). The LPA was derailed as a result of the structural adjustment programmes (SAPs) that were forced on African countries as part of the Washington Consensus. By the 1990s, the agenda was African Renaissance, which led to the creation of the New Partnership for Africa's Development (NEPAD) and the African Peer Review Mechanism (APRM). The fact is that not since the early 1960s has the continent had a truly shared and popular vision. Such a bold imaginative vision of the future could serve as the raison d'être and the rallying cry for a transformative agenda for the continent which is capable of mobilizing the people for change. The vision cannot simply be a continuation of the present status quo.

Fourth, it is imperative to **facilitate greater collaboration among the innovation system actors**. The national innovation system (NIS) framework highlights the importance of relationships among actors (government, industry, academy and communities) in building robust innovation ecosystems. For innovation to thrive, each actor must play their role effectively. The heroic narrative that innovation is the work of lone rangers is a myth. Importantly, innovation tends to be an incremental progress, with one building on the work of others.

The various actors including governments have crucial roles to play. Even in the advanced market economies, governments are engaged and play activist roles. Among the various roles that governments tend to play in the innovation ecosystem are funding primary research, creating a network of innovation supporting institutions, providing direct funding to companies in the form of grants, and helping mobilize actors and galvanizing them to achieve national objectives. However, the orthodox counsel to African countries is free markets. The free market ideology, which is not fully practised in the West, becomes in many cases the conditions for African governments to access international financing.

For Africa to build robust innovation ecosystems, all hands must be on deck and greater collaboration is a necessary condition. Given the unique circumstances of the continent, it is even noted that additional actors must be included and engaged in the innovation ecosystem, including civil society activists and the decision makers with the 'power to act' to direct resources to drive innovation in Africa.

Fifth, there is a need for **greater self-reliance**. For decades now, we have heard slogans such as African solutions to African problems. However, this has not been translated into practice in any significant way. The continent has not fully owned its problems and continues to rely on the international development industry with its army of consultants. This is partly the result of over-dependency on aid and the lack of an overarching vision and strategy by many of the countries on the continent. Ensuring greater self-reliance will require a change in approach and the way most of our countries manage the development process. It will also call for change in the educational systems in our countries, where focus must shift from teaching mainly to pass exams, to learning systems focused on acquiring skills for critical thinking, problem identification and problem solving. We must own our problems so as to ensure that we seize the opportunities to seek innovative solutions.

African countries must also find solutions to the challenge of financing, which calls for greater domestic resource mobilization. African countries cannot secure greater self-reliance if they are constantly relying on handouts, which mostly come with conditions. While innovations are happening in Africa, financing has become a binding constraint to scaling up innovation on the continent; many startups on the continent are stuck in the early stages due to lack of access to capital for growth and scaling up. Foreign Direct Investment (FDI) flows to tech startups on the continent have increased. However, the amount flowing into the continent remains quite limited when compared to other regions and needs. FDI into Africa tech firms tends to go largely to only a few countries and a limited number of firms. There is also the trend of investors requiring African firms to register in 'safer' countries in the West. The question being are these still African startups when their headquarters are in America or Europe and when all the consequential decisions are made outside of the continent? Mobilizing domestic resources to support innovation and the larger development agenda will require new approaches to enlarge the tax base, reduce corruption, and to reduce illicit flows.

It is crucial to incentivize the stakeholders to participate in funding innovation, and this can be encouraged via fiscal policies. It might also be necessary in some countries to levy an innovation tax that is fully dedicated to funding innovation activities. Crowd investment platforms could also be encouraged in African countries, as well as putting in place special programmes to attract the African diaspora as investors.

Sixth, **the future must be more inclusive with the promise of equitable opportunity** if sustained growth and transformation are to be achieved. We must aim to create an inclusive future in Africa countries in all dimensions. All citizens must have equal opportunities for self-development, rather than continuing to expand current forms of inequality, elitism and prejudice. This will not be easy. But it is the only sure way for the necessary transformation to happen and for it to be sustained. As such, inclusiveness must be a fundamental metric of the national development agenda across the continent. It provides the basis for stability and the necessary space for socioeconomic transformation. This calls for a people-centred development agenda, with a focus on the people's benefit and how to enhance the quality of life for all, ensuring freedom from poverty.

Seventh, **leadership is key**. Transforming Africa will require all hands on deck. But the leadership has a critical role to play. Leadership in this case is not limited to the political class; transformation of Africa will require distributed leadership across the various sectors and institutions. With respect to innovation, leadership is necessary at the various levels and in the different communities. The capacities required for broad-based inclusion, trans-local engagements, innopreneurial thinking, and radical paradigm-shifting require dynamic leadership. The continent will need leaders with the 'vision with agility' to drive innovation, as well as the creative entrepreneurs who can serve as the bridge between various communities and 'doers' that will make things happen. These will offer the foundations for robust innovation ecosystems that can offer enabling space for Africans to engage with the problems and solutions that Africa has.

BIBLIOGRAPHY

Adesida, O., Karuri-Sebina, G. & Afonso, T. (2018) *Africa Innovation Summit (AIS)—Kigali, 2018 Report.*

Adesida, O., Karuri-Sebina, G. & Resende-Santos, J. (2016) *Innovation Africa: Emerging Hubs of Excellence,* Bingley: Emerald Books.

Adner, R. (2006) Match Your Innovation Strategy to Your Innovation Ecosystem. HBR Spotlight, *Harvard Business Review,* April 2006. Accessed at: http://sjbae. pbworks.com/w/file/fetch/60084211/Adner_2006_HBR.pdf

Ahern, Jack, Cilliers, S. & Niemela, J. (2014) The Concept of Ecosystem Services in Adaptive Urban Planning and Design: A Framework for Supporting Innovation. *Landscape and Urban Planning* 125, 254–259. Available at https:// pdfs.semanticscholar.org/fd5e/bcca91c6d8e77224d70a095ceb9b6dcd1375. pdf

Anahory, P. & Adesida, O. (2014) *Africa Innovation Summit (AIS)—Cape Verde, 2014 Report.*

Block, Fred L. and Keller, M.R. (Eds.) (2016) *State of Innovation: The U.S. Government's Role in Technology Development,* New York: Routledge.

Gobble, MaryAnne M. (2014) Charting the Innovation Ecosystem, *Research Technology Management,* 57:4, 55–59. Accessed at: https://www.tandfonline.com/doi/pdf/10.5437/08956308X5704005?casa_token=6H76DF6ekmMAAAAA:J1_hqXsQMRWJ_26X5mKSoknFq3lxIS6XL7vo1pZb7nO1m36urNUiM4K7vGf_hDnahromyvGHGuXpgQ

Freeman, C. (2008) *Systems of Innovation: Selected Essays in Evolutionary Economics,* Cheltenham: Edward Elgar Publishing.

Lundvall, B. (2007) National Innovation Systems—Analytical Concept and Development Tool. *Industry and Innovation,* Vol. 14, No. 1, 95–119.

Lundvall, Bengt-Åke, Muchie, M. and Gammeltoft, P. (2003) *Putting Africa First: The Making of African Innovation Systems,* Aalborg: Aalborg University Press.

Mashelkar, R.A. (2012) On building an inclusive innovation ecosystem. Conference on Innovation for Inclusive Development, 21 November 2012, Cape Town. Accessed at: https://search.oecd.org/sti/inno/K_Mashelkar.pdf

UN Department of Economic and Social Affairs (UNDESA). *World Population Prospects 2019: Highlights,* New York: Population Division, UNDESA.UNECA (2011). *Economic Report on Africa 2011. Governing development in Africa—The role of the state in economic transformation,* Addis Ababa: UNECA.

2.

REINVENTING AFRICAN HEALTHCARE SYSTEMS

Yap Boum II

What counts in life is not the mere fact that we have lived... It is what difference we have made to the lives of others that will determine the significance of the life we lead. – Nelson Mandela

More than 40 years after its discovery, Ebola is now a curable disease. Two new treatments have proven to be highly effective just one year after the start of an Ebola outbreak in the Democratic Republic of Congo (DRC), a country that has now seen fourteen Ebola outbreaks since its discovery in 1976 near the Ebola river. During the outbreak that took place in West Africa from 2014 to 2016 and which resulted in more than 30,000 cases and 10,000 deaths, an effective vaccine was found that was later used in the DRC. Since then the COVID-19 pandemic has reached most African countries between February and March 2020 and has impacted African countries differently (Salyer, Maeda, Sembuche et al. 2021). During the last two years of the pandemic, and despite predictions most African countries have been resilient (Esso et al. 2021) and implemented local solutions to address this global crisis (Boum, Bebell, & Bisseck 2021).

The Ebola outbreaks and the COVID-19 pandemic highlight both the challenges of healthcare in Africa and the opportunities to rethink African healthcare systems, to achieve universal health coverage (UHC) in Africa, thereby ensuring no one is left behind.

Although the relationship between the spread of Ebola in particular and UHC is not obvious, the interaction between UHC and global health security (GHS) is clear. GHS and UHC are concepts that have been called 'two sides of the same coin', given their parallel aims of improving health outcomes (Wenham et al. 2019). GHS is about preventing and responding to infectious outbreaks and epidemics that pose a cross-border threat, while UHC is about people having access to healthcare. UHC promotes high immunization, access to healthcare and healthcare workers, which in turn supports the prevention and detection of outbreaks, as well as the response to outbreaks (Jimenez 2015). The UHC coverage index is measured based on reproductive, maternal, newborn and child health, non-communicable diseases (NCDs) and infectious disease control, and service capacity and access. Africa has a low coverage index of UHC, with the worst coverage index recorded in Sub-Saharan Africa (GHM 2018a), where most countries have a substandard UHC coverage index of ≤45 (Figure 2.1).

Despite delays in some countries, multisectoral investments are flowing to Africa. Yet there are enormous inequalities in these investments, and the healthcare sector is particularly lagging (Economist Intelligence Unit 2014). New technology is upgrading the continent through entrepreneurial start-ups, but healthcare still does not benefit enough from those innovations (Bastos de Morais 2017). This is affecting how countries are able respond to pandemics such as Ebola and other viral haemorrhagic fevers. Moreover, Africa faces the double burden of communicable diseases and NCDs, compounded by the fact that millions of Africans have no access to adequate healthcare. The continent is characterized by high levels of mortality and morbidity from preventable and/or curable communicable diseases, such as malaria, pneumonia and diarrhoeal diseases, as well as rampant NCDs, such as diabetes, hypertension, cancer, and trauma (GHM 2018a). Delays in getting access to adequate patient management also increase fatalities, especially for children suffering from malaria, for whom the first 24 hours of management are critical (Dondorp et al. 2010). Many patients choose to visit traditional healers before going to healthcare facilities, and risk getting infections and improper treatment during these visits (Peeters Grietens et al. 2012). Other patients spend a huge amount of time and money to reach hospitals when their illness could have been treated in the community (Sundararajan et al. 2015).

In the meantime, African presidents and officials are increasingly seeking healthcare in Europe and the United States. African citizens spend at least US$1 billion on medical tourism every year, leaving African healthcare systems in a poor state (Liedong 2017). Medical tourism is a result of weakened African health systems that cannot take care of the rich and the poor.

Innovation and research are the cornerstone of reinventing African healthcare, as shown by the latest finding of highly efficient treatments against Ebola virus disease in the DRC. The 2030 agenda for SDGs challenges the global health community to innovate in order to achieve a level of development that leaves no one behind (Zamora et al. 2018) gender and human rights in order to support member states in operationalizing their commitment to leave no one behind in the health

Figure 2.1: UHC service coverage index by country (2015)

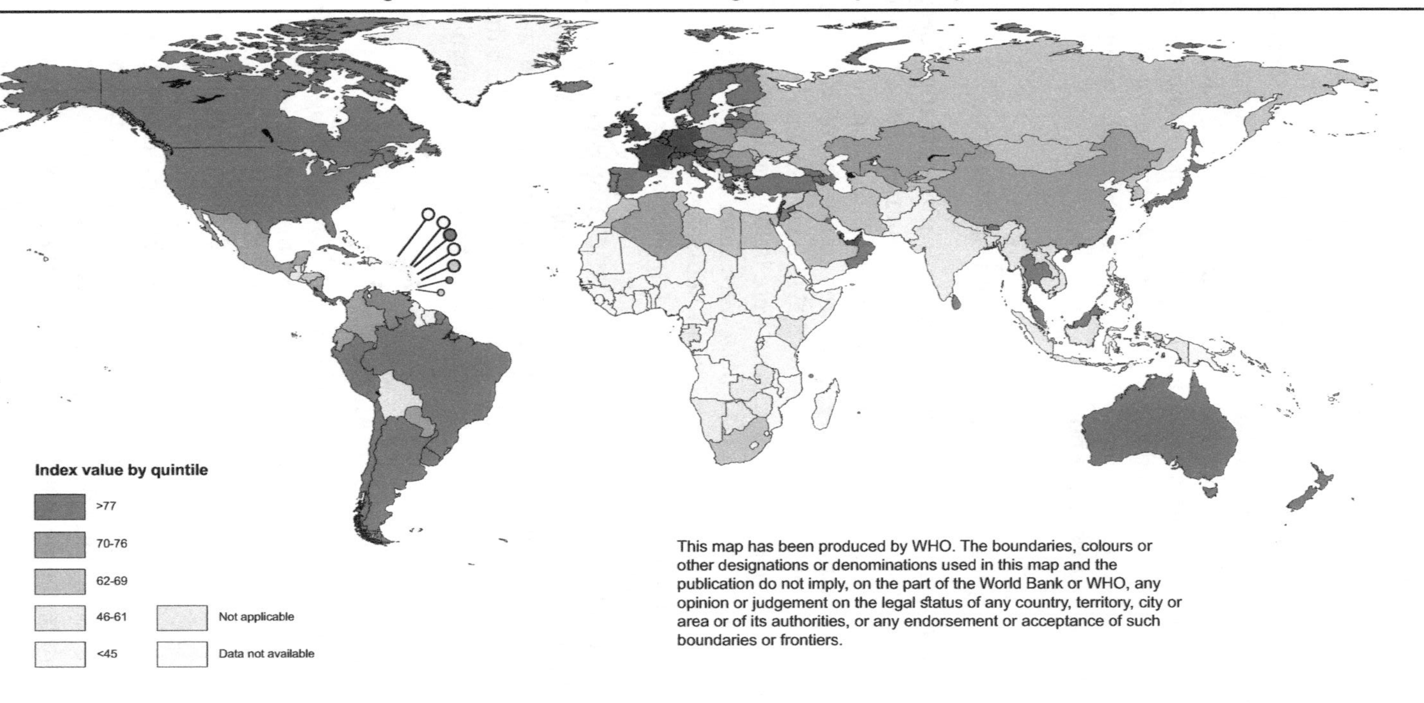

Source: WHO and World Bank (2017)

Sustainable Development Goals (SDGs). Innovation is commonly considered as technology, but it also includes other homegrown solutions, such as integrating African medicine into healthcare delivery. A conceptual framework for innovation in healthcare shows the interdependence between patients, healthcare practitioners/providers and technology as a catalyst (Omachonu & Einspruch 2010). This chapter presents some of Africa's health challenges, including the Ebola outbreak that recently affected the DRC in the provinces of Equateur and North Kivu. It then looks at some solutions already implemented in many countries and concludes by examining how developing these homegrown solutions within an African health innovation ecosystem can result in improved GHS and UHC across the continent.

HEALTHCARE CHALLENGES FOR AFRICAN POPULATIONS

Healthcare remains a challenge for most African countries, despite major health-sector improvements in some countries, such as Rwanda (Sayinzoga & Bijlmakers 2016). One in thirteen children in Sub-Saharan Africa die before the age of five, compared to one in 189 children for high-income countries. In 2015, of the 303 000 women who died due to pregnancy-related issues, 99% of them were in low- and middle-income countries and, shockingly, up to 66% were from Sub-Saharan Africa. Although the average life expectancy in Sub-Saharan Africa rose from 51 years in 2002 to 60 years in 2016, it remains low compared to life expectancy in North America (80 years) and Europe (78 years) (GHM 2018b). The likelihood of achieving the SDG 3 of good health and well-being for all by 2030 (UN 2015) seems dubious in the continent as a whole due to the various healthcare challenges. These include the burden of diseases, the lack of access to health services due to poor infrastructure and long distances, and the insufficient number of healthcare workers.

The burden of diseases in Africa

Disease surveillance and infection control are major challenges in Africa, given the public health emergencies facing the continent: outbreaks of Ebola, cholera, and meningitis (Green 2018); endemics, such as Lassa fever; and pandemics, such as HIV/AIDS (Tambo et al. 2018)90 deaths occurred representing 120% laboratory-confirmed case fatality. The outbreak has been imported into neighbouring country such as Benin, where 23 deaths out of 68 cases has also been reported. This study assesses the current trends in re-emerging Lassa fever outbreak in understanding spatio-geographical reservoir(s). Globally, two-thirds of

HIV/AIDs cases and HIV-related deaths are recorded in the region. The HIV burden is a two-fold epidemic because people living with HIV/AIDS are the most at risk of developing tuberculosis (TB), which accounts for 86% of HIV-related deaths, while countries such as South Africa are now facing emerging multidrug-resistant TB (Booysen et al. 2003).

Malaria, pneumonia and diarrhoeal diseases are responsible for most cases of under-five mortality in Africa (GHM 2018b). Despite massive investments to control malaria, in 2016 Sub-Saharan Africa was where 90% of malaria cases (and as many as 91% of malaria fatalities) occurred, with the majority of deaths being in children under five (Castellani et al. 2018). Figure 2.2 highlights the burden of infectious diseases that pose a huge public health problem for the continent.

Furthermore, the health system often 'forgets' the over one billion people who suffer from neglected tropical diseases (NTDs), such as Buruli ulcer (Mycobacterium ulcerans infections) and accidents such as snake bites. Yet NTDs may lead to disabilities, such as blindness and disfigurement, which have a huge impact on health, represent a socioeconomic burden, and have societal effects such as stigma and discrimination (Lamptey et al. 2013; Toutous Trellu et al. 2016).

Africa also has to deal with the burden of NCDs, such as diabetes, hypertension and cancer, which represent a rising epidemic – every year, 80 million people die as a result of NCDs. Of these deaths, 80% are recorded in low- and medium-income countries. And if nothing is done, NCDs will be responsible for 46% of African deaths in 2030 (GHM 2018a).

In addition to the above-mentioned challenges, antimicrobial resistance (AMR) appears to be a growing concern in Africa. However, the diagnosis of AMR has not been standardized in Africa, and the burden of AMR remains unknown in 40% of African countries (*The Lancet* 2022). Much still needs to be done.

Lack of access to healthcare

Epidemics, such as the DRC Ebola outbreak, can take months before announcements because of the lack of infrastructure such as roads. This creates healthcare 'deserts', where no healthcare structure is available or functional. For instance, the ninth Ebola outbreak in the DRC started in Ikoko Ipenge, a small village 15 hours away from Mbandaka. Between December 2017 and January 2018, some alerts of family and/or group deaths were sent from these villages, but only in April/May were the samples confirmed positive for Ebola. Similarly, the tenth Ebola outbreak, which was declared in Mangina early August, may have actually started – unknowingly – in May at the same time as the one in Itipo (Shuchman 2019).

Figure 2.2: Burden of infectious diseases in Africa

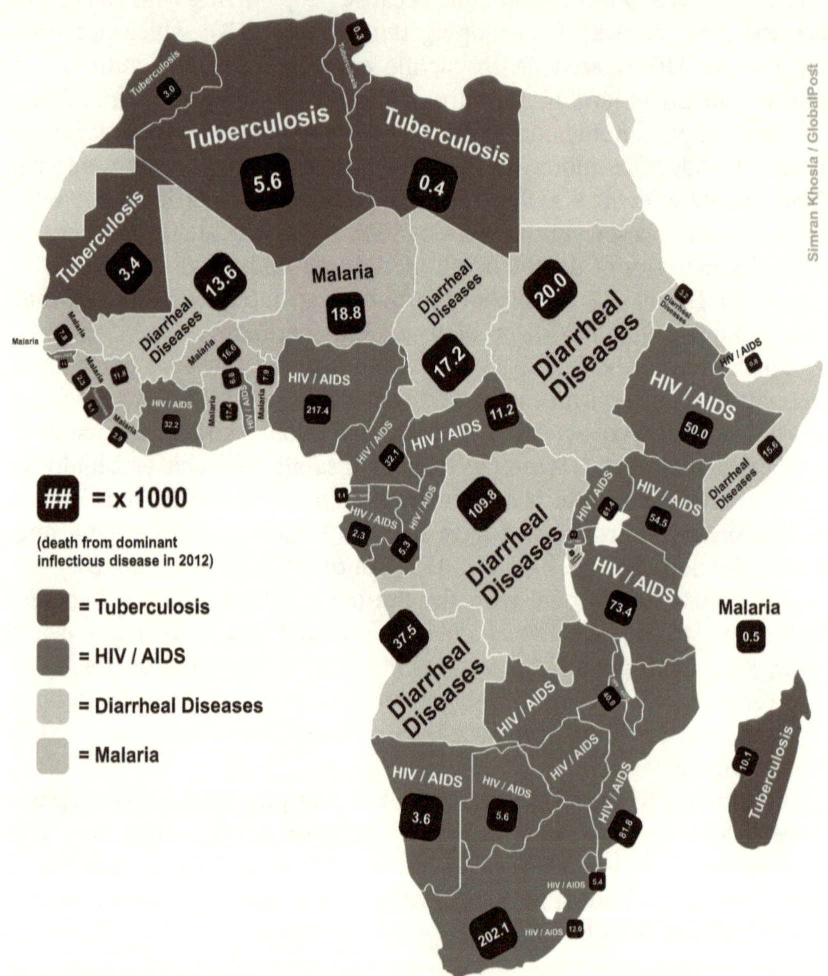

Source: Department of Health Statistics and Information Systems, WHO.

Other factors that contribute to the lack of access to healthcare include distance to facilities, quality of surveillance systems, availability of diagnostic tools and quality of health products. About 29% of the African population and 28% of African women of childbearing age lack access to healthcare facilities for emergency medical, obstetric and surgical care (Chavane et al. 2018). In most African countries, a fifth of the population live far away from emergency medical care, and people have to travel for over two hours to access medical facilities (Sundararajan et al. 2015).

Disease surveillance is suboptimal in many African countries, despite the fact that the early detection of infectious diseases can decrease the negative impact of an epidemic (Dakar 2017). In some villages, routine indicator-based and event-based surveillance is not effective, which makes early outbreak detection, investigation and response challenging. And even when an outbreak is detected and confirmed, appropriate diagnostic tools may not be available. For instance, in rural parts of Cameroon, the NTD Buruli ulcer is difficult to diagnose because samples from patients must be sent kilometres away to facilities capable of testing for and confirming the presence of the causative agent (Lamptey et al. 2013). And even when diagnostics tools are present, they may be fake, like other health products. More than 50% of the antimalarial drugs in Africa are either fake or of low-quality substances. In 2017, billions worth of fake drugs and tests were found in West Africa. Patients are wrongly diagnosed with fake tests and consequently treated for the wrong disease using fake drugs. As the symptoms of Ebola and malaria are similar (fever, headaches, joint pain), patients suffering from Ebola may be wrongly diagnosed as suffering from malaria, especially in an area where malaria is endemic, such as North Kivu in the DRC (Fitzpatrick et al. 2014).

Insufficient healthcare workers

The lack of investments in healthcare, especially in Francophone countries, means limited training of health professionals (Linnander et al. 2019) and a mismatch in the distribution of healthcare workers needed to cover the population. Despite bearing a quarter of the disease burden worldwide, Africa is home to only 3% of the world's health workforce (GHM 2018a). In Malawi, only 284 physicians are available in the public sector to meet the needs of a population of 17 million (Bastos de Morais 2017), while in Tanzania, up to 70% of the people live in rural areas but may never see a doctor because 69% of physicians are based in urban areas. Medical personnel are also targeted and even killed while providing care – for example, Dr Richard Mouzoko, an epidemiologist killed on 19 April 2019 in the DRC while supporting the Ebola response.

Lastly, because of sociocultural beliefs and language barriers, communities turn to African/traditional healers that treat the patient with African medicine as opposed to modern/Western/Chinese medicine (Sundararajan et al. 2015). Modern health professionals are scarce in the most remote areas and may be mistrusted, whereas African healers are present in most communities and integrated into many healthcare systems, for example in Rwanda (*Medical Futurist* 2018; WHO 2017). However, because of a lack of understanding, their practices are not integrated into a comprehensive healthcare system, which can create some challenges in patient management.

HOMEGROWN INNOVATIVE SOLUTIONS TO AFRICAN
CHALLENGES

The health challenges faced by Africa are not exclusive to the continent, but the context, culture and environment make them specific. For example, traditional medicine is a common practice in Africa but is mainly used by higher income groups in Europe and North America who can afford it because it is not reimbursed by insurance policies (Abdullahi 2013).

Strengthening health systems is a way to achieve both GHS and UHC. To address health challenges, the World Health Organization (WHO) has identified six core building blocks that make up a health system: (i) service delivery; (ii) health workforce; (iii) information; (iv) medical products, vaccines and technologies; (v) financing; and (vi) leadership and governance (Mounier-Jack et al. 2014). For Africa, innovative and homegrown solutions will be required to deal with the many health challenges and to make healthcare accessible to communities. Several innovative initiatives are being implemented in Africa that offer potential solutions to the challenges described in the previous section. These relate to information, technology and tools, and training.

Information: health data and research

An effective healthcare system is set up to ensure timely collection, analysis and dissemination of data on health outcomes and associated determinants (Jimenez 2015; Knapp et al. 2010). Health information systems are innovative tools used to store patient's electronic medical records, or to collect and analyse data used to inform policy-making and health management.

DHIS 2

The District Health Information System 2 (DHIS 2) is a revised version of DHIS, an open-source software platform that was originally developed in South Africa (Hazel et al. 2018) based on several frameworks (e.g., Health Metrics Network supported by World Health Organization. With DHIS 2, governments and health organizations are able to report, analyse and disseminate data for all health programmes, resulting in more effective management and monitoring, and improved communication. The DHIS 2 allows not only the routine collection of data but also for findings to be reported through readily available reports. It works as a national data repository, which can be accessed in multiple platforms through a browser and enables real-time national data analysis for decision-making. It has been identified as the preferred health management system in 30 developing countries (Dehnavieh et al. 2019).

Afyakit

Another information-related innovation is Afyakit, which was developed by Dr Frida Njogu-Ngongwe, to address the lack of data on challenges that affect health service quality. Health managers need information on health service quality in order to make decisions about allocating resources. Afyakit is a platform that provides actionable in-facility data to health-sector players across Sub-Saharan Africa. Health managers are able to co-create supervision tools that enable them to extract useful insights from supervision. Managers receive colour-coded dashboards that highlight problem areas and can then be aggregated at facility and administrative levels. Health facilities also receive detailed reports, so they can act on identified areas for improvement. The platform has been used in Nairobi and led to more efficient allocation of resources and improved quality of health services of services. The modular and scalable tools can be used in a wide array of health systems in many resource-limited countries.

The 4S Network

To promote GHS, the WHO developed the International Health Regulations, to improve disease surveillance and response to public health threats (Hazel et al. 2018). In many countries, health departments have recognized the importance of data for improving the effectiveness of limited resources. An important use of real-time data is seen in disease surveillance programmes, particularly for emerging infectious diseases and for the early identification and control of potential sources of disease dissemination. One such programme is the 4S Network, a sentinel influenza surveillance programme in Senegal, conducted by the Pasteur Institute of Dakar in partnership with the Ministry of Health. The programme uses tools to identify early unusual disease events that display influenza-like syndromes and other syndromes related to febrile diseases of public health interest, such as malaria, arboviruses and diarrhea (Dakar 2017). The use of such a system in the DRC would have resulted in earlier detection (and containment) of the Ebola outbreak.

Ebola vaccines and treatments

Research provided the tools adapted to the environment and the situation that were able to treat the Ebola vaccine. Many studies have taken place in several countries (including the USA, Switzerland, Gabon and Kenya) to assess the safety of the rVSV ZEBOV Ebola vaccine that targets the Ebola Zaire strain. In 2014/15, the vaccine was tested during the Ebola outbreak in West Africa and was found to be safe, efficient and effective (Henao-Restrepo et al. 2017; Juan-Giner et al. 2018). However, registration is a long way away. Although more than 160,000 people have already received the vaccine, it is still not licensed and can only be used as part of a very strict protocol that follows good clinical practices or as expanded access during an emergency, which is the case currently in the DRC (Boum 2018). The vaccination is administered using a 'ring' approach, whereby newly diagnosed and laboratory-confirmed Ebola patients are identified and people who they have been in contact with are located. These people and their contacts, who are often family members, neighbours, colleagues and friends, constitute the 'ring'. Frontline workers from the health area where an Ebola case has been detected also qualify to receive the vaccine (Henao-Restrepo et al. 2017). The vaccine has played a positive role in reducing the spread/severity of the disease in the DRC. However, the real breakthrough has come from a local Congolese doctor, Professor Jean-Jacques Muyembe, who dedicated his life to fight against Ebola. Since November 2018, four new therapeutics have been assessed in a randomized clinical trial to evaluate their safety and efficacy. The trial found that two out of four treatments, which are synthetic antibodies (mAb114 and REGN-EB3), saved roughly 90% of the patients who were newly infected. The study was conducted by an international research partnership co-ordinated by the WHO and co-sponsored by the US National Institute of Allergy and Infectious Diseases.

Technology and tools

Barriers to accessing health services include financial costs, lack of transport services, lack of local healthcare providers, intimidation by healthcare settings and incompatible service hours (Sundararajan et al. 2015). Technology and tools enable these barriers to be dismantled and communities to have access to better healthcare in spite of the limited resources. They include rapid diagnostic tests, mobile health (mHealth) tools such as telemedicine and mobile clinics and drones that could change the patient experience (Sim 2019).

Rapid diagnostic tests

Rapid diagnostic tests (RDTs) are essential tools for point-of-care diagnostics and early detection of numerous diseases. They provide a cost-efficient alternative to expensive and centralized diagnostic methods, such as polymerase chain reaction (PCR) or other serological tests requiring significant lab equipment. RDTs provide local communities with cheaper, faster and easier access to diagnostics and, as a result, treatment (Rasti et al. 2017). Their use in the Ebola response in Guinea and the DRC led to a timely identification and isolation of positive cases and better epidemiologic surveillance due to flexibility of use in the field conditions (Green 2018).

Multiplex immunochromatographic RDTs can simultaneously identify cases of co-infections in addition to cases of single infections, and so can be used for Ebola screening, as well as for detecting HIV and hepatitis B and C viruses. In 2016, they were able to diagnose chronic viral infections among pregnant woman in a sexual health centre in N'Djamena, Chad. The women were all referred to a medical health centre for biological monitoring and antiretroviral treatment (Oldach 2015, 2018). RDTs have a wide spectrum of use, are cost efficient, and enable local health centres to rapidly detect Ebola and other infectious diseases, thereby reducing the response time needed to fight them.

mHealth tools – telemedicine

Telemedicine can bring healthcare to communities, especially the most remote populations. Africa is currently home to 960 million mobile subscribers, representing an 80% penetration rate. The three countries with the highest rate of mobile-phone ownership are South Africa (89%), Ghana (83%) and Kenya (82%). Although the ownership rate in other countries, such as Uganda, may lag slightly (about 65%), African countries can leverage mobile technology to improve the quality of care, accessibility to healthcare services, and evidence-based decision-making. In 2016, nearly 40% of South Africans use the internet, and about 78% access it through mobile devices. The level of mobile ownership provides an opportunity to introduce and expand on telemedicine technology in Africa, leading to improved decision support, predictive analytics and care coordination (IFC 2016; *Medical Futurist* 2018; Omachonu & Einspruch 2010). The current COVID-19 pandemic has highlighted the positive impact of mobile health in Africa which needed to be sustained (Boum 2021).

The CommCare app is an example of an mHealth technology that has been implemented in rural areas of over 50 countries, including several African countries. It allows frontline community healthcare workers with limited literacy to record data and follow patients in multiple languages using their mobile phones. The app has been used to collect data on malaria, TB, HIV/AIDS, chronic diseases, maternal and child health, and Ebola. It improves the performance of community healthcare workers, as well as the quality of care, programme efficiency and community health outcomes. For example, in Nigeria, community healthcare workers using CommCare showed statistically significant improvements in their knowledge about human transmission of the virus, common symptoms, and whether or not Ebola fever is preventable. In the recent Ebola outbreak in DRC, this app would have made a huge difference in community engagement, which was one of the missing pillars of the Ebola response at the epicentre of the outbreak.

Technology enables health professionals to reach populations regardless of their location (Sim 2019), which is what companies such as iDocta in Cameroon, Amref in Kenya and Allodoctors in South Africa are doing. In Cameroon, iDocta recently launched a programme to build a network of iClinic and health professionals, so that the population can access healthcare services wherever they are. By using a mobile application and/or a phone call, a health professional is able to consult a patient physically or remotely (Boum 2018). Similarly, mobile health teams are able to reach communities and provide primary healthcare. One example is the Last Mile Health in Liberia, which in 2017 trained and deployed more than 2900 community healthcare workers and 350 clinical supervisors across 14 of Liberia's 15 counties (Kraemer et al. 2018).

In conjunction with community healthcare workers and qualified medical personnel, mobile clinics can be used for disease diagnostics, prevention (education and awareness, prophylactic medication), treatment and palliative care, all at the community's convenience (Kraemer et al. 2018; Mensah 2014; Economist Intelligence Unit 2014). Rapid diagnostics along with essential first-aid drugs could then be carried from the trucks on motorbikes and/or bicycles to the interior of the community, depending on how remote the area is. Many villages, such as Bokongo in the Equator region of the DRC, can only be accessed by motorbikes and bicycles because of the poor road network (Boum 2018).

Nevertheless, while these apps may appear as revolutionary agents, many countries still lack power and telecommunication – this is still the case in DRC, where the most recent Ebola outbreak resulted in the highest number of cases. Therefore, for these tools to have a much higher impact, an improved infrastructure will be required in order to reach far-flung communities.

Life-saving drones for vaccine delivery

Zipline is an American start-up that uses drones for blood deliveries to needy patients in rural areas of Rwanda (*Medical Futurist* 2018). In partnership with the Government of Rwanda, Zipline launches at least 50 drones daily to deliver blood products to 21 regional hospitals. Physicians order either by phone or online, and the blood is usually delivered within 30 minutes. The blood is used for cases of postpartum haemorrhage (PPH) and anaemia due to malaria, among others. PPH[1] is the leading cause of maternal mortality worldwide, and especially in Sub-Saharan Africa, as a result of challenges related to access to healthcare (GHM 2018b).

The Zipline model was recently used to stop the spread of Ebola, by delivering vaccines to remote places (Kitsita 2019). The vaccines were transported by helicopter from the major city to places that were unreachable because of distance or insecurity, and then by motorbike to the patient in the most remote places. In future, trained healthcare workers could receive vaccines/drugs delivered by drones directly to their health centre. For instance, drones could deliver antimalarial drugs to remote malaria-endemic villages in Africa, to quicken treatment. This would reduce the resources required to deliver drugs and increase access to healthcare (IFC 2016; *Medical Futurist* 2018).

Strengthening the health workforce

A decentralized healthcare system is more efficient at providing accessible, cost-effective and individualized care than a large centralized system. The exponential growth of digital and virtual health has made it possible to deploy advanced technology deeper into the community. Decentralizing healthcare can also take the form of training young scientists, local community healthcare workers (IFC 2016; Jimenez 2015; Kraemer et al. 2018), as well as traditional healers.

Training the scientists

Several programmes are already in place to train the next generation of African scientists. The National Institute of Health (NIH) and the Wellcome Trust recently established the Human Health and Heredity initiative in Africa (H3Africa), which provides financial support to African scientists and local institutions, to enable them to conduct basic research into the genomic and environmental bases of health issues prevalent on the continent, including pandemics. The pharmaceutical group Novartis is supporting scientific exchange through collaborating with H3-D, the first drug discovery and development centre in Africa. H3-D's aim is to train scientists from Ghana, Kenya, South Africa, Sudan and Zimbabwe to develop treatments that address widespread conditions in Africa (Jimenez 2015). Similarly, the Expanded Programme on Immunization Leadership and Management Programme (EPI LAMP) builds the leadership and management capacity required to achieve

---

1   PPH refers to the loss of more than 500 ml or 10005 ml of blood within the first 24 hours following normal vaginal or caesarean section delivery.

immunization (Linnander et al. 2019). Such training programmes need to happen all over the continent, regardless of the language, to ensure that non English-speaking global health practitioners are not left behind (Roca et al. 2019).

Training the healthcare workers

African countries could hugely improve access to healthcare by using a combination of medical doctors and professionally trained health-care workers who serve in their local communities. The three steps to increasing access to healthcare services are as follows (Bryan et al. 2010; Knapp et al. 2010).

- Hire local (preferably) women who have completed at least primary education and are literate.

- Compensate local healthcare workers with a country-specific financial amount.

- Focus on healthcare services that cover all essential needs but are manageable by the healthcare workers.

Support will include first aid, basic preventive and diagnostic services, the distribution of materials (for example, nutritional supplements or condoms) and essential curative care, as well as the monitoring (and occasionally the treatment) of chronic conditions. Importantly, the charges for these services must be low (Knapp et al. 2010) but cannot be free, so as to be sustainable (Kraemer et al. 2018).

African countries could manage the majority of the most critical clinical health conditions at the community level by adopting best practices and developing groups of paid local healthcare workers. Meeting this goal would require just one local health officer per every 1,000 to 1,500 people, at a cost of about US$1 a year per capita – a dramatic improvement over the status quo (Bryan et al. 2010). With such a system in place, any outbreak could be detected within three days and an alert from the central level raised. Had this system been in place, 30,000 cases of Ebola and 11,000 deaths could have been avoided in Liberia, Guinea and Sierra Leone between 2014 and 2015, as well as the recent deaths in the DRC.

Integrating African medicine

Many traditional medicines, especially from Asian countries, have been found to be effective. However, with more research, Africa could make great strides in developing African medicines. In the meantime, it is imperative to think about how to harvest medicinal plants without decreasing biodiversity or over-harvesting them (Abdullahi 2013).

It is important to consider and make use of the resources already available in our communities, to be culturally sensitive, and to integrate the context and realities of communities. Traditional healers are an inevitable healthcare option in most rural areas in African societies. According to the WHO, 80% of Africans resort to traditional medicine for treatment (Abdullahi 2013). In many African countries, when people think they may have malaria, one of their first actions is to visit a traditional healer (Sundararajan et al. 2015). Therefore, it makes sense to collaborate with traditional healers in order to reach the maximum number of people. Traditional healers were at the frontline of recent Ebola outbreaks in West and Central Africa, where many of them lost their lives (Green 2018; Boum, Kwedi-Nolna, Haberer & Leke 2021).

Traditional healers are not only a source of referrals but also offer potential solutions for treatment. Several African countries have formally integrated traditional healers into their healthcare system (Abdullahi 2013). A study conducted in Bankim, Cameroon found that traditional healers, if properly trained, were able to correctly recognize the NTD Buruli ulcer and to refer patients to the hospital for proper treatment (Peeters Grietens et al. 2012). In other studies conducted in Uganda, they were able to identify plants that can be used as sources of herbal remedies for malaria (Sundararajan et al. 2015). Traditional healers found that they earned more through collaboration than in the loss of referrals. Traditional leaders who are involved from the ground up in the fight against NTDs feel recognized and that their status is enhanced. This is essential for strengthening the health system and preparing for emerging diseases.

COLLABORATING TO DRIVE INNOVATIVE SOLUTIONS

This section examines the components of a health innovation ecosystem that could work for Africa – health innovation ecosystems are all about bringing together stakeholders with the aim of improving health and well-being, and improving resource efficiency.

Communication, promotion, collaboration and trust between community stakeholders and health personnel are essential to the fight against NTDs and surveillance of pandemics. The collaborative efforts of private-sector and public-sector stakeholders, and partnerships with like-minded organizations in the diaspora, are possible avenues to expand and improve the digitalization of African healthcare systems. The One Health approach is an example of multisectoral collaboration that strengthens GHS. One Health is a concept whereby information, tools, expertise and resources are integrated across sectors to tackle environmental challenges as well as human and animal threats to public health (Bryan et al. 2010; Knapp et al. 2010).

Despite the benefits of digitalizing healthcare in specific African countries, the challenges of sustaining these innovations are enormous. Primarily, it is because they have not been able to attract sufficient user numbers to allow them to make a significant impact on health and – crucially – make money at the same time. The biggest challenge cited by most health start-ups in Africa is attracting enough users (IFC 2016).[2] In addition, the growth of start-ups is constrained by the lack of supportive infrastructures, such as good connectivity to access high-quality data in real time (Dehnavieh et al. 2019).

Although some governments are becoming more supportive of local start-up ecosystems, most African countries rank low on the World Bank's Doing Business ratings (IFC 2016). When starting a business in Africa, some of the difficulties include having to go through several regulatory hoops, confusing and constantly evolving political and trading laws, and the high cost of moving money in and out of Africa – bank charges are high and using services such as Western Union can cost upwards of 15% (Jimenez 2015). Another challenge for start-ups is securing early-stage funding because of the lack of early-stage market validation capital. Therefore, there is an opportunity to develop multilateral organizations to raise funds that could help African innovations in healthcare systems to thrive. Organizations such as the African Academic of Science (AAS) are working towards building those ecosystems (IFC 2016; Omachonu & Einspruch 2010; Sayinzoga & Bijlmakers 2016). Adding to the hurdles is the citizen culture that underrates locally produced digital products and prefers international products. Furthermore, start-ups struggle to get access to digital gateways and application programming interface from established companies, which prevents penetration growth and scaling.

Given these challenges that hinder a potentially profitable improvement in healthcare delivery, it is important that partnerships be established to target the stakeholders involved. A global network of organizations and philanthropies supports healthcare initiatives, while many international partnerships with Africa recognize the importance of research and education in driving innovation and development (Rao 2017). For example, Aliko Dangote and the Bill and Melinda Gates Foundation, along with companies such as Vodacom, Novartis and IBM, are focused on three areas to improve the delivery of healthcare in Africa: leveraging digital technologies; improving knowledge, skills and

---

2   Available at https://www.ftc.gov/system/files/documents/public_
    events/200361/mehrotra_-_innovations_in_health_care_delivery_overview_
    and_framework.pdf

resources; and creating collaboration and consensus among key stakeholders. This will hopefully have a positive impact on the management of endemics and epidemics in Africa. Furthermore, multilateral organizations and development cooperatives can help channel funds from multiple governments to finance healthcare innovations in Africa (Rao 2017). The prospect of such collaborations offers some optimism for the future of Africa's healthcare.

For Dangote, a better healthcare system is the first step in breaking the cycle of poverty and disease, and he believes that '[e]veryone should have access to good health, no matter where they live. This is how we kick start a virtuous cycle of health, productivity, and prosperity.'[3] Dangote joined the Bill and Melinda Gates Foundation to support the polio eradication programme in Nigeria, and contributed by acquiring a vaccine carrier, a tool that saves costs in resource-poor settings such as those found in Nigeria (Rao 2017). If extended to the rapid control of pandemics such as Ebola, Marburg and other haemorrhagic fevers, response to the outbreak would be faster and more adequate. Research and technologies led by Africans will provide tools for improving the response to outbreaks.

However, transforming African healthcare system framework requires a new mindset and behaviour from all stakeholders, to ensure that the patient is at the centre of the system. Government and the private sector should motivate healthcare workers to provide high-quality care to the population by using pay – for performance contracts. Health professionals can also use technology to improve the quality of care, especially for patients who are difficult to reach. The introduction of telemedicine and mobile clinics will empower nurses and community healthcare workers and improve their patient management skills – they will not replace but will complement the existing system and the use of doctors.

African traditional medicine existed prior to colonization and is still used by a large proportion of the population. Therefore, traditional healers should be more integrated into the new African healthcare. Instead of being marginalized, they can be technologically equipped to serve as key stakeholders. The integration of traditional healers is crucial for diseases with a mystical perception among populations. It would reduce delay, increase adherence to biomedical treatment and protect people, as seen in recent Ebola outbreaks. This will improve the quality of care traditional healers provide to the community and ensure a real continuum between African and Western medicine in Africa, as it seems to be in Asia.

---

3   Sulaiman Philip, Africa can improve access to healthcare for all, *Brand South Africa*, 8 May 2017. Available at https://brandsouthafrica.com/africa-can-improve-access-healthcare Accessed 31 August 2022.

UHC is a target that could be achieved through a public–private partnership, where government provides infrastructure and promotes private investment to find innovative and homegrown solutions to address challenges faces by Africa. In return, private entities, diaspora and philanthropists could be involved in the operations to improve the quality of healthcare delivery ensuring that no one is left behind. Such a partnership would create an African environment ready for the transformation of healthcare, combining the use of community healthcare workers, telemedicine, mobile clinics, and traditional healers to provide affordable and quality healthcare services for all everywhere.

CONCLUSION

The fourteen Ebola outbreaks since 1976 in the DRC and the ongoing COVID-19 pandemic highlight the health challenges faced by Africa, as well as how they can be transformed into great opportunities to reshape the continent's health systems. Indeed, there is a need for country-specific solutions as no one-size-fits-all approach will succeed within a continent as diverse as Africa (Boum, Bebell & Bisseck 2021).

The high burden of diseases, coupled with the lack of infrastructure and trained healthcare workers, can be an opportunity to use technology and integrate traditional healers into the new African healthcare ecosystem and create better management of pandemics. Ideally, African healthcare systems should be brought to the community, not the opposite, with traditional healers and community healthcare workers playing a greater role in patient management and disease surveillance. These traditional and community health providers can be equipped with adequate training and technology tools to provide care to the population at the community level. Then, only the more severe patients will have to be referred to hospitals. This would limit not only the cost for patients but also the number of patients unnecessarily attending hospitals, where resources are usually limited, and where patients could be exposed to other serious infectious diseases.

Innovation and research are contributing to transform African healthcare. New vaccines, diagnostics and treatments against Ebola and COVID-19 are being used today as part of a workable response to fight these diseases. Similarly, drones and other technological innovations are being integrated in the health system to ensure no one is left behind. What is required is for the private sector, philanthropists and African diasporas to support initiatives that create innovative and homegrown solutions to the health challenges facing Africa (Figure 2.3). This will allow most African countries to reach UHC – only then will healthcare cease to be a privilege and become a human right, as it should be.

Figure 2.3: Re-inventing African healthcare

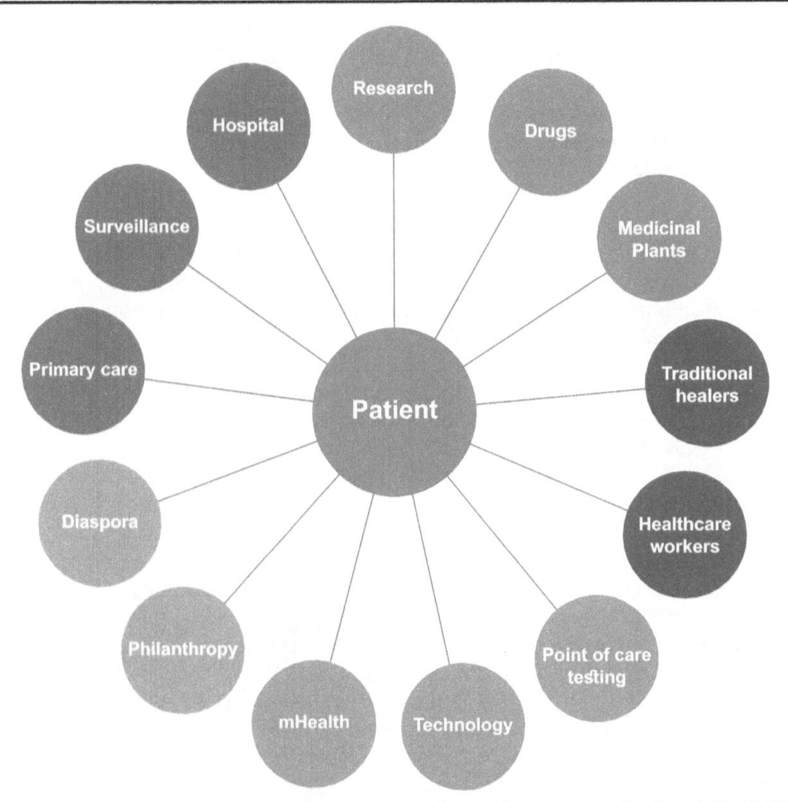

BIBLIOGRAPHY

Abdullahi, A.A. (2013) Trends and challenges of traditional medicine. *Africa Trends* 8: 115–123. Available at https://doi.org/10.4314/ajtcam.v8i5S.5

Bastos de Morais, J-C. (2017) Digital technologies can deliver better healthcare to sub-Saharan Africa. Here's how. World Economic Forum. Retrieved from https://www.weforum.org/agenda/2017/10/digital-paths-for-better-healthcare-in-sub-saharan-africa/

Booysen, F., Geldenhuys, J.P., Marinkov, M. (2003) The impact of HIV/AIDS on the South African economy: A review of current evidence. TIPS/DPRU Conference on The Challenge of Growth and Poverty: The South African Economy since Democracy, Johannnesburg. South Africa.

Boum, Y. (2018) Challenges of administering an Ebola vaccine in remote areas of the DRC. *The Conversation.* Retrieved from https://theconversation.com/challenges-of-administering-an-ebola-vaccine-in-remote-areas-of-the-drc-98181

Boum, Y., Bebell, L.M., & Bisseck, A.Z. (2021). Africa needs local solutions to face the COVID-19 pandemic. *Lancet.* Apr 3;397(10281):1238-1240. doi:

10.1016/S0140-6736(21)00719-4. Epub 2021 Mar 24. Erratum in: *Lancet.* 2021 Jun 19;397(10292):2336. PMID: 33773113; PMCID: PMC7990475.

Boum, Y., Kwedi-Nolna, S., Haberer, J.E., & Leke, R.R.G. (2021). Traditional healers to improve access to quality health care in Africa. *Lancet Global Health.* Nov; 9(11):e1487-e1488. doi: 10.1016/S2214-109X(21)00438-1. PMID: 34678184.

Boum, Y. (2021). Beyond COVID-19: scaling up and sustaining mobile health in Africa. *Lancet.* 2021 Nov 27;398(10315):1962-1963. doi: 10.1016/S0140-6736(21)02349-7.PMID: 34838171

Bryan, L., Conway, M., Keesmaat, T., McKenna, S. & Ben, R. (2010) Strengthening sub-Saharan Africa's health systems: A practical approach. Accessed 1 December 2018 https://www.mckinsey.com/industries/healthcare-systems-and-services/our-insights/strengthening-sub-saharan-africas-health-systems-a-practical-approach

Castellani, J., Mihaylova, B., Siribié, M., Gansane, Z., Ouedraogo, A.Z., Fouque, F., Sirima, S.B., Evers, S.M.A.A., Paulus, A.T.G., & Gomes, M. (2018) Household costs and time to treatment for children with severe febrile illness in rural Burkina Faso: The role of rectal artesunate. *Malaria Journal* 1–12. https://doi.org/10.1186/s12936-018-2526-8

Chavane, L.A., Bailey, P., Loquiha, O., Dgedge, M., Aerts, M. & Temmerman, M. (2018) Maternal death and delays in accessing emergency obstetric care in Mozambique. *BMC Pregnancy and Childbirth* 18: 1–8.

Dakar IP. (2017) Surveillance des fièvres: surveillance sentinelle syndromique au Sénégal (réseau 4S). Retrieved from http://www.pasteur.sn/activites_recherche/surveillance-sentinelle-syndromique-au-senegal-reseau-4s/

Dehnavieh, R., Haghdoost, A., Khosravi, A., Hoseinabadi, F., Rahimi, H., Poursheikhali, A., Aghamohamadi, S. (2019) The district health information system (DHIS2): A literature review and meta-synthesis of its strengths and operational challenges based on the experiences of 11 countries. *Health Information Management Journal*, 48(2): 62–75. https://doi.org/10.1177/1833358318777713

Dondorp. A.M., Fanello, C.I., Hendriksen, I.C.E., Gomes, E., Seni, A., Chhaganlal, K.D. et al. (2010) Artesunate versus quinine in the treatment of severe falciparum malaria in African children (AQUAMAT): An open-label , randomised trial. *The Lancet*, 376(9753): 1647–1657. Available at https://doi.org/10.1016/S0140-6736(10)61924-1

Esso L., Epée E., Bilounga C., Abah A., Hamadou A., Dibongue E., Kamga Y., Belinga S., Eyangoh S., Okomo M.C., Mounagué C., Tiwoda C., Mandeng N., Onana T., Mendjime P., Mahamat F., Mballa G.A.E., Boum Y. Cameroon's bold response to the COVID-19 pandemic during the first and second waves. *Lancet Infect Dis.* 2021 Aug;21(8):1064-1065. doi: 10.1016/S1473-3099(21)00388-1. PMID: 34331876; PMCID: PMC8318523

Fitzpatrick, G., Vogt, F., Moi Gbabai, O.B., Black, B., Santantonio, M., Folkesson, E., Van Herp, M. (2014) Describing readmissions to an Ebola case management centre (CMC), Sierra Leone. *Eurosurveillance*, 19(40): 1–6.

GHM (Global Health Metrics) (2018a). Global, regional, and national incidence, prevalence, and years lived with disability for 354 diseases and injuries for 195 countries and territories, 1990–2017 : a systematic analysis for the *Global Burden of Disease Study 2017*, pp. 1789–1858) https://doi.org/10.1016/S0140-6736(18)32279-7

GHM (2018b) Measuring progress from 1990 to 2017 and projecting attainment to 2030 of the health-related Sustainable Development Goals for 195 countries and territories : a systematic analysis for the *Global Burden of Disease Study 2017*, pp. 2091–2138. https://doi.org/10.1016/S0140-6736(18)32281-5

Green, A. (2018) Ebola outbreak in the DR Congo: lessons learned. *The Lancet*, 391(10135): 2096. https://doi.org/10.1016/s0140-6736(18)31171-1

Hazel, E., Wilson, E., Anifalaje, A., Sawadogo-Lewis, T. & Heidkamp, R. (2018) Building integrated data systems for health and nutrition program evaluations: Lessons learned from a multi-country implementation of a DHIS 2-based system. *Journal of Global Health*, 8(2): 1–5. https://doi.org/10.7189/jogh.08.020307

Henao-Restrepo, A.M., Camacho, A., Longini, I.M., Watson, C.H., Edmunds, W.J., Egger, M., Kieny, M.P. (2017) Efficacy and effectiveness of an rVSV-vectored vaccine in preventing Ebola virus disease: final results from the Guinea ring vaccination, open-label, cluster-randomised trial (Ebola ça suffit!). *The Lancet*, 389(10068): 505–518. https://doi.org/10.1016/S0140-6736(16)32621-6

International Finance Corporation (IFC) (2016) African homegrown innovation take off. *EMCompass* Note 7(September). Retrieved from www.IFC.org/ThoughtLeadership Note.

Jimenez, J. (2015) Three ways to improve healthcare in Africa. WEF Forum. Retrieved from https://www.weforum.org/agenda/2015/01/3-ways-to-improve-healthcare-in-africa/

Juan-Giner, A., Tchaton, M., Jemmy, J.P., Soumah, A., Boum, Y., Faga, E.M. Grais, R.F. (2018) Safety of the rVSV ZEBOV vaccine against Ebola Zaire among frontline workers in Guinea. *Vaccine,* September 2018. https://doi.org/10.1016/j.vaccine.2018.09.009

Kitsita, J. (2019) Ebola control: Ministry of Health launches first drone vaccine delivery program in DRC. Accessed 15 August 2019. https://crofsblogs.typepad.com/h5n1/2019/08/ebola-control-ministry-of-health-launches-first-drone-vaccine-delivery-program-in-drc.html

Knapp, T., Richardson, B. & Shrey, V. (2010) Three practical steps to better health for Africans. Accessed 11 October 2018. https://www.mckinsey.com/industries/healthcare-systems-and-services/our-insights/three-practical-steps-to-better-health-for-africans

Kraemer, J.D., Nyumah, J., Duokie, D., Rabinowich, J., Kanjee, Z., Downey, J. Dorr, L. (2018). A community health worker intervention to increase childhood disease treatment coverage in rural Liberia: A controlled before-and-after evaluation. *American Journal of Public Health*, 108(9): 1252–1259. https://doi.org/10.2105/ajph.2018.304555

Lamptey, I., Yeboah-Manu, D., Ampadu, E., Koka, E. & Ahorlu, C.K. (2013) Enhancing Buruli ulcer control in Ghana through social interventions: a case study from the Obom sub-district. *BMC Public Health*, 13(1): 1. https://doi.org/10.1186/1471-2458-13-59

Liedong, T.A. (2017) African politicians seeking medical help abroad is shameful, and harms health care. *The Conversation*. Retrieved from https://theconversation.com/african-politicians-seeking-medical-help-abroad-is-shameful-and-harms-health-care-82771

Linnander, E., Nolna, S.K., Mwinsongo, A., Bechtold, K. & Boum, Y. (2019) Reaching across the linguistic divide in management and leadership education. *The Lancet Global Health* 7(9), e1177. https://doi.org/10.1016/S2214-109X(19)30256-6

Medical Futurist (2018) Rwanda and the dreamers of digital health in Africa: Wakanda is real. Retrieved from https://medicalfuturist.com/digital-health-in-rwanda

Mensah, J. (2014) The global financial crisis and access to health care in Africa. *Africa Today* 60(3): 35–54.

Mounier-Jack, S., Griffith, U.K., Closser, S., Burchett, H. & Marchal, B. (2014) Measuring the health systems impact of disease control programmes: A critical reflection on the WHO building blocks framework. *BMC Public Health*, 14(1): 1–8. https://doi.org/10.1186/1471-2458-14-278

Oldach, L. (2015) Pioneering new diagnostics: Addressing challenges and implications for point-of-care testing in African settings. Retrieved from http://www.aslm.org/stay-informed/press-room/news-articles/pioneering-new-diagnostics-addressing-challenges-and-implications-for-point-of-care-testing-in-african-settings/

Oldach, L. (2018) Pioneering new diagnostics: addressing challenges and implications for point-of-care testing in Africa settings. Available at http://www.aslm.org/resource/pioneering-new-diagnostics-addressing-challenges-implications-point-care-testing-african-settings/ Accessed 15 August 2019.

Omachonu, V.K. & Einspruch, N.G., (2010) Innovation in healthcare delivery systems : A conceptual framework. *The Innovation Journal: The Public Sector Innovation Journal* 15(1): Article 2 (October).

Peeters Grietens, K., Toomer, E., Um Boock, A., Hausmann-Muela, S., Peeters, H., Kanobana, K. Ribera, J.M. (2012) What role do traditional beliefs play in treatment seeking and delay for buruli ulcer disease? – Insights from a mixed methods study in Cameroon. *PLoS ONE*, 7(5). https://doi.org/10.1371/journal.pone.0036954

Rao, P. (2017) Philanthropists join forces to fund Africa's cash-strapped health sector. Accessed 5 January 2019, from https://www.un.org/africarenewal/magazine/august-november-2017/philanthropists-join-forces-fund-africa's-cash-strapped-health-sector

Rasti, R., Nanjebe, D., Karlström, J., Muchunguzi, C., Mwanga-Amumpaire, J., Gantelius, J. Alfvén, T. (2017) Health care workers' perceptions of point-of-care testing in a low-income country – A qualitative study in Southwestern Uganda. *PLoS ONE*, 12(7): 1–31. https://doi.org/10.1371/journal.pone.0182005

Roca, A., Boum, Y. & Wachsmuth, I. (2019) Plaidoyer contre l'exclusion des francophones dans la recherche en santé mondiale. *The Lancet Global Health*, 7(6): e701–e702. https://doi.org/10.1016/S2214-109X(19)30175-5.

Salyer, S.J., Maeda, J., Sembuche, S., Kebede, Y., Tshangela A., Moussif, M., Ihekweazu, C., Mayet, N., Abate, E., Ouma, A.O., Nkengasong, J. (2021) The first and second waves of the COVID-19 pandemic in Africa: a cross-sectional study. *Lancet* Apr 3;397(10281):1265–1275. doi: 10.1016/S0140-6736(21)00632-2. Epub 2021 Mar 24. PMID: 33773118; PMCID: PMC8046510

Sayinzoga, F. & Bijlmakers, L. (2016) Drivers of improved health sector performance in Rwanda: A qualitative view from within. *BMC Health Services Research*, 16(1): 1–10. https://doi.org/10.1186/s12913-016-1351-4

Shuchman, M. (2019) Logistical challenges in the DR Congo Ebola virus response. *The Lancet,* 393(10167), 117–118. https://doi.org/10.1016/s0140-6736(19)30076-5

Sim, I. (2019) Mobile devices and health. *The New England Journal of Medicine* 381(10): 956–968. https://doi.org/10.1056/NEJMra1806949

Sundararajan, R., Mwanga-Amumpaire, J., Adrama, H., Tumuhairwe, J., Mbabazi, S., Mworozi, K., Ware, N.C. (2015) Sociocultural and structural factors contributing to delays in treatment for children with severe malaria: A qualitative study in Southwestern Uganda. *American Journal of Tropical Medicine and Hygiene* 92(5): 933–940. https://doi.org/10.4269/ajtmh.14-0784

Tambo, E., Adetunde, O.T. & Olalubi, O.A. (2018) Re-emerging Lassa fever outbreaks in Nigeria: Re-enforcing "One Health" community surveillance and emergency response practice. *Infectious Diseases of Poverty,* 7(1): 1–7. https://doi.org/10.1186/s40249-018-0421-8

The Economist Intelligence Unit (2014) The future of healthcare in Africa. Retrieved from https://www.janssen.com/emea/sites/www_janssen_com_emea/files/pdf/the_future_of_healthcare_in_africa_-_progress-challenges_and_opportunit.pdf

The Lancet (2016) Time for global political action on antimicrobial resistance. *The Lancet Infectious Diseases* 16(10): 1085. https://doi.org/10.1016/s1473-3099(16)30341-3

The Lancet (2022) Antimicrobial resistance collaborators. Global burden of bacterial antimicrobial resistance in 2019: a systematic analysis. *The Lancet* volume 399, issue 10325, p 629–655, February 12.

Toutous Trellu, L., Nkemenang, P., Comte, E., Ehounou, G., Atangana, P., Mboua, D.J. et al. (2016) Differential diagnosis of skin ulcers in a mycobacterium ulcerans endemic area: Data from a prospective study in Cameroon. *PLOS Neglected Tropical Diseases,* 10(4), e0004385. https://doi.org/10.1371/journal.pntd.0004385

UN (2015) Transforming our world: the 2030 agenda for sustainable development. Retrieved from https://sustainabledevelopment.un.org/content/documents/21252030 Agenda for Sustainable Development web.pdf

Wenham, C., Katz, R., Birungi, C., Boden, L., Eccleston-Turner, M., Gostin, L. Sridhar, D (2019) Global health security and universal health coverage: From a marriage of convenience to a strategic, effective partnership. *BMJ Global Health,* 4(1): 1–7. https://doi.org/10.1136/bmjgh-2018-001145

World Health Organization (WHO) (2017) *WHO country cooperation strategy at a glance 2014–2018*: Rwanda. World Health Organization, 51(2), 39–54. https://doi.org/10.1017/CBO9781107415324.004

Zamora, G., Koller, T.S., Thomas, R., Manandhar, M., Lustigova, E., Diop, A. & Magar, V. (2018) Tools and approaches to operationalize the commitment to equity, gender and human rights: towards leaving no one behind in the Sustainable Development Goals. *Global Health Action,* 11(1). https://doi.org/10.1080/16549716.2018.146365

3.

PAYING TEACHERS FOR PERFORMANCE: A TANZANIAN INNOVATION TO IMPROVE BASIC LEARNING

Youdi Schipper & Aidan Eyakuze

'Bakari is a good boy. He is eleven years old. He lives in Motomoto town. He lives with his mother, father, and sister. Bakari works hard at home. He also works hard at school.' This short story was part of an English language test that 17,105 Tanzanian Standard III students took at the end of their 2016 school year. Just 2% of these students could read the story fluently. In the same test, 60% of Standard III students could read a Kiswahili story, but only 12% could do basic multiplication. These skills are all part of the Standard III curriculum in Tanzania.[1] It illustrates how schooling is not the same thing as learning for too many students – and the need to look for innovations in education around the world, not just in Tanzania.

The test was part of KiuFunza, which is short for *Kiu ya Kujifunza* or Thirst for Learning, a programme initiated in 2013 and implemented by Twaweza East Africa[2] in collaboration with the government of Tanzania and other partners. The KiuFunza programme provides cash bonuses to early-grade teachers in an innovative teacher-reward scheme that aims to improve student learning levels – the central measure of success in an education system – through increased motivation, performance

---

1   Tanzania is one of many countries that report skill mastery (far) below expected curriculum levels. Such findings are part of what is now termed the global learning crisis – see the *World Development Report* (World Bank 2018) for an overview of descriptive evidence, literature, underlying mechanisms and effectiveness of a wide array of policies and reforms to address the problem.

2   Twaweza East Africa is a non-profit organization operating in Tanzania, Kenya, and Uganda, committed to enabling citizens to exercise agency, promoting governments to be more open and responsive, and improving learning for children.

feedback and task focus (Twaweza 2018). The innovation is that payment of the bonus is conditional on learning outputs, thus the label 'cash on delivery'.

Teachers are key actors in the learning process. In a sample of 109 low- to high-income countries, teacher salaries accounted for 74% of the education budget (UNESCO 2017). Keeping other factors constant, teachers can make a substantial difference in what students learn – and earn later in life (Chetty et al. 2014). Skills and motivation both matter for the effectiveness of teachers, but low- and middle-income countries often put teachers who have low subject and pedagogy mastery into classrooms. Most education systems offer teacher training, but many training programmes are not effective (World Bank 2018), while many countries do not have effective mechanisms in place for motivating, monitoring and managing teachers to achieve the best learning results for their students.

Like many other countries, Tanzania sets teacher goals in terms of inputs, such as the curriculum-based workplan and the time spent preparing and teaching. These system goals are set centrally, but administrative responsibility for schools is decentralized to local governments, which have limited capacity for school or class-level monitoring. As a result, teachers typically run a 'one-person shop', have few student-learning targets and little supervision or guidance on how to reach targets. In Tanzania, most teachers meet once per semester with the head teacher (their day-to-day manager), but external quality inspections are rare and usually do not address student-level learning. These issues are not specific to Tanzania but feature across education systems in low-income countries.[3]

A key input indicator that reflects motivation is whether or not a teacher is in the classroom during school hours. Estimates of teacher classroom absence range from 47% (World Bank 2014) to 65% and 59% among Standards I and III teachers respectively (KiuFunza 2015 and 2016 data).[4] Most of these absent teachers are at school but not in the classroom. Few teachers fear sanctions, such as being transferred or dismissed as a result of bad performance, while about 40% of lower grade teachers say they would not choose teaching again if they could start over.[5] These observations have led to an emerging sense in Tanzania that evidence is needed to inform new policies aimed at improving teacher performance. One of the leading ideas is teacher performance

---

3   For an in-depth discussion of learning and school systems, please refer to World Bank (2018).

4   Estimates from nationally representative studies using unannounced monitoring of primary school classrooms.

5   Findings based on KiuFunza teacher surveys.

pay. This chapter provides an account of the KiuFunza teacher incentive programme in Tanzania.

After discussing how a global and domestic innovation ecosystem produced ideas that affected the history of Tanzania's education sector, the innovation of teacher performance pay is described. The development of the practical design of the programme is then explored, followed by a discussion of the implementation of the second-phase incentive programmes and the programme's impact on student learning.

INNOVATION ECOSYSTEMS AND EDUCATION REFORMS
IN TANZANIA

An ecosystem is 'the complex of living organisms, their physical environment, and all their interrelationships in a particular unit of space' (*Encyclopaedia Britannica*). The term ecosystem is generally used as a figure of speech to describe a complex network or an interconnected system.

The innovation – teacher performance pay – is generated in a global education innovation ecosystem. This system can be thought of as a collection of international and local institutions, universities and research organizations, thinkers, conferences, policymakers, civil servants and administrators, and funders – each with their respective goals and interactions. The ideas generated in the global innovation ecosystem can have powerful effects through national systems.

One such impactful idea is Education for All (EFA), whose birth is typically placed at the 1990 UN conference on Education for All in Jomtien, Thailand. The idea of EFA – all children are in school – provided a powerful target and helped shape global landmarks, such as the Millennium Development Goals. EFA and its resulting ecosystem have had long-lasting positive effects on the numbers of school-age children going to school in low-income countries around the world. For example, in East Africa, the EFA idea translated into Universal Primary Education (UPE) legislation, which resulted in increased enrolment that put considerable pressure on the system, including student–teacher ratios. These effects have been documented for East Africa (Oketch & Rolleston 2007), Uganda (Grogan 2009) and Tanzania (Valente 2015).

The global trend of increased enrolments has led to concerns about the quality of education, although studies found no evidence that the introduction of UPE had *caused* major reductions in learning levels, despite substantial increases in enrolment (Lucas & Mbiti 2012; Valente 2015). Nevertheless, these concerns triggered two major strands of enquiry into learning: What is the level of learning or skills among children in country A compared to other countries? What reforms are needed to improve learning?

Comparing levels of learning or skills

New programmes have been developed to measure and document learning outcomes of students. Since 2000, the OECD Programme for International Student Assessment (PISA) has done a quarterly assessment of skills mastered by 15-year-olds in OECD countries. In non-OECD countries, civil society organizations have helped to put learning assessments in the public and policy discourse through innovative citizen-led learning assessment methods. Examples are the Annual Status of Education Report (ASER), implemented by Pratham in India since 2005 (www.pratham.org) and the Uwezo assessments, implemented by Twaweza East Africa in Tanzania, Kenya and Uganda since 2009 (www.twaweza.org). These measurement systems should be viewed as part of the broader innovation system, into which they feed data on the state of learning.[6] The *World Development Report* acknowledges the importance of learning assessments, as a necessary requirement for education systems to recognize the problem of learning (World Bank 2018). The idea that schooling does not equal learning in many school systems is one of the true innovations generated by learning measurement systems and the ecosystems surrounding them. Programmes such as ASER and Uwezo have focused on rigorous measurement and on communication, so that the learning results find their way into policy and general public audiences.

Turning schooling into learning

These measurement systems and findings have spurred research into policy reform, asking what can be done to turn schooling into learning. A large literature exists on interventions and policies aimed at improving learning, and much of the experimental evidence for low-income countries has been produced since 2000 (Banerjee & Duflo 2010; Glewwe & Muralidharan 2016; Kremer et al. 2013). The experimental evidence helps to answer the ambitious question of how to reorient systems of education, so that the focus is on learning rather than on schooling or enrolment (Pritchett 2013). This education-systems research agenda has found a home in RISE (Research on Improving Systems of Education, www.riseprogramme.org), a research programme that was launched in

---

6   ASER and Uwezo learning assessments are large-scale field surveys that use simple test tools, so that citizens can understand results and hold stakeholders accountable, voice complaints, and monitor performance (Eberhardt et al. 2015).

2015. The RISE research agenda includes measuring learning levels, the impact of specific interventions and policies, accountability and information in education systems, and, fundamentally, why certain policies are or are not chosen by actors in the education system bureaucracy.

Launched by President Kikwete in early 2013, Tanzania's Big Results Now (BRN) Programme was inspired by the centralized 'delivery units' and best practice principles used in the UK in the early 2000s and successfully applied in Malaysia. BRN sought to improve service delivery in six priority sectors (education, energy, agriculture, water, transport and resource mobilization) through strict prioritization consistent with resource allocation, performance management and effective communications. The BRN innovation focuses on management and execution ('getting things done') rather than a particular type of intervention and is interesting for several reasons.

- It arose out of dissatisfaction with the level of service delivery in various sectors, including the education sector, where the results of both regular examinations and the Uwezo learning assessments contributed to the sense of urgency – of the candidates who sat the 2012 Secondary leaving exam, 60% failed.

- The BRN 'package' was an idea imported from abroad.

- The individual elements of the BRN programme were selected in a consultative process with sector representatives, and some (but not all) of these were backed by scientific evidence.

- BRN had a system 'delivery' focus.

In 2016, the BRN Programme was disbanded. Despite several weaknesses, including a lack of strict prioritization (nine education priorities), overly detailed and rigid planning, and the structural issue of two competing line ministries, the programme provided impetus to improve learning outcomes (Todd & Attfield 2017). It was strictly centred on improving learning outcomes, influenced by the growing global and domestic focus on learning as the goal of education, but was less successful than EFA in generating the support required to sustain implementation. Nevertheless, the learning focus and 'delivery' are ideas that have survived BRN in Tanzania – the recent policy initiative, Education P4R, follows on several BRN initiatives, emphasizing learning and other output targets.

RISE Tanzania (RISE TZ) assesses the impact of ongoing reform and accountability initiatives in Tanzania, including the BRN school ranking initiative (Cilliers et al. 2019). A survey of BRN implementation (RISE TZ 2017) found some encouraging evidence, with all primary head teachers indicating that at least one staff member received training on the new 3R curriculum. The 'school ranking' accountability intervention was successful at the level of the District Education Officer (most were informed about school performance), but much less so at the level of the head teachers. RISE TZ provides a new platform (ecosystem) for evidence-based dialogue about reforms aimed at learning improvements in the Tanzanian education sector, including reform of the School Quality Assurance Framework (responsible for school inspections) and of the KiuFunza III teacher performance pay programme.

THE BENEFITS OF TEACHER PERFORMANCE PAY

Three broad families of interventions improve learning: pedagogy that matches teaching to students' learning levels; detailed guidance for teacher pedagogy; and improving school governance, accountability and incentives (Evans & Popova 2016; Glewwe & Muralidharan 2016; World Bank 2018). Teacher performance pay is one element of a range of policies that can improve governance and teacher incentives. These incentives include professional rewards, such as recognition, professional mastery; accountability pressure, such as the threat of dismissal and managerial pressure; and financial incentives, including bonus pay, pension and other benefits, and career path reforms (Bruns & Luque 2015).

Teacher performance pay offers several practical and political advantages.

- It is an incentive with no financial downside for teachers and is, therefore, politically easier to accept.

- It has a clear quid pro quo, i.e. cash for learning outcomes, and the desired outputs can be specified, linked to curriculum goals and compensated.

- Its cost compared to base salaries is typically low.

- It addresses a potentially huge waste of public money because of teachers not fulfilling contract obligations.

- It offers flexibility, as no long-term commitments are put into law.

- It achieves short-term impacts without having to recruit and train new teachers.

The fundamental innovation of teacher performance pay is that it recognizes and rewards learning outcomes, and communicates several incentive signals. The emphasis is on student-level learning and testing, externally measured learning outcomes, and measurements that have concrete consequences. It provides a platform to account for and provide feedback on teacher performance. With good communication, teachers' efforts become visible for managers and colleagues, as well as the teachers themselves, and will be talked about. And, of course, the financial reward focuses attention.

However, performance pay is also controversial. The main criticisms are that teachers may not have the capacity to increase the desired learning outcomes, or may be constrained by factors outside their control, such as low student attendance. Bonuses may cause jealousy among other colleagues in schools, or affect intrinsic motivation and trigger perverse effects, such as cheating or abandoning poorly performing students. However, many of these issues can be addressed by the incentive design. For example, in KiuFunza each individual student can earn the teacher a reward, so there is no gain from excluding a student.

Despite serious subject knowledge constraints (e.g. World Bank 2014) and imperfect subject mastery, teacher incentives appear to improve test scores. Bonus pay programmes in developing countries 'have produced more consistently positive results than in developed countries (especially the United States) to date' and so may be most productive in countries where other systems of monitoring and accountability are weak (Bruns and Luque 2015: 45).

In Tanzania, teacher supervision and accountability are weak, and learning outcomes fall far short of curriculum expectations. With a rapidly growing student population, the great challenge is to increase the ratio of well-qualified teachers to pupils. Teachers have fixed salaries and get paid, but they are dissatisfied and demanding pay increases. However, as increasing teachers' pay without any conditions does not improve learning (De Ree et al. 2017), education policymakers and researchers are experimenting with programmes that introduce modest elements of performance-linked pay, to improve the learning focus and motivation of teachers.

KIUFUNZA DESIGN HISTORY

Based on these arguments and evidence, in 2013 Twaweza East Africa started the KiuFunza programme, targeting teachers in Standards I, II and III in public primary schools across Tanzania. KiuFunza I (2013–14) had three experimental arms and a control arm:

- Capitation grants (CGs), whereby the full grants were transferred directly to school accounts, according to policy, for the purchase of educational supplies including textbooks.

- Cash on delivery (COD), where teachers were paid a bonus for every student with basic literacy and numeracy skills, plus a bonus for the head teacher based on students' pass rates.

- Combination, where CGs were transferred directly to schools for inputs, and performance payments were made to teachers and head teachers.

These interventions were chosen because they represent two very different policy choices: paying for inputs (CG) and paying for outputs (COD). The performance pay programme gives teachers a fixed cash reward of about $3 for each student who passes all basic skills tests in a subject. The three focal subjects for KiuFunza are Kiswahili, English and maths (arithmetic), and teachers can obtain the reward for each student for each subject.

The impact evaluation revealed the following:[7]

- With the CG, the funds went to the schools but did not result in improved learning outcomes in Kiswahili, English and maths. However, the funds did lead to an increase in spending on textbooks, food, scholarships and administrative expenses and a decrease in the likelihood of teachers reporting shortages of materials.

- Results for the COD intervention were mixed. Based on data from low-stakes tests, which are research tests in a small student sample that were not used to calculate the bonus amount, student test scores in treated schools were somewhat (but not significantly) higher than those in the control group. However, results were different when using data from high-stakes tests that was obtained from testing all students in a more formal test setting and used to calculate teacher bonuses. The impact on learning outcomes was significantly positive, with students in treated schools more likely to pass the Twaweza tests in maths (by 37%), Kiswahili (by 17%) and English (by 70%).[8]

- The combination intervention, delivering both CG and COD, had a significant and positive impact on learning outcomes in the three subjects. It had a greater effect than the sum of the individual effects of the CG and COD. One of the headline results was the complementarity between providing input- and output-based teacher incentives.

Twaweza communicated the results of the impact evaluation to government stakeholders and the press. Then, in 2015, the Tanzanian government announced the national implementation of a version of 'CG direct' from January 2016. This meant that schools would no longer

---

7   Detailed descriptions and findings are provided in a research paper, see Mbiti et al. (2019a).

8   As described in detail in Mbiti et al. (2019a) there is no reason to suspect that the difference is due to test irregularities, but rather to students being more aware of the test importance (a so-called test-day effect).

depend on district council payments but would receive CGs directly from central government. As a result, capitation grant receipts at school level became more predictable and uniform across the country. With this change, part of the KiuFunza I combined treatment is now in place, but these resources needed to be complemented by teacher incentives, as this combination results in improved learning outcomes that are comparable with the impact of other education interventions (Kremer et al. 2013). The design of the incentives also needed rethinking, as the KiuFunza I design set a high bar for bonus payment. Students had to pass a comprehensive set of skills from the national school curriculum, which proved to be a challenging threshold: in 2014, the mean share of students (across the three grades) passing this threshold was 53% for Kiswahili, 6% for English and 30% for maths. More generally, in bonus systems, setting an absolute bonus threshold that is neither too low nor too high is a challenge (Neal 2011).

Against this background, in 2015 Twaweza launched KiuFunza II (2015–2016), which provided teacher incentives only, with the understanding that central government would pay CGs directly to schools. For Twaweza, the question was what type of incentive design to implement. After discussions, two distinct performance pay designs were adopted for further testing: Stadi or 'levels', which is designed to pay for skills levels, and Mashindano or 'competitions', which is a 'pay for percentile' design proposed by Barlevy and Neal (2011).[9]

KIUFUNZA II IMPLEMENTATION

In 2015 and 2016, the two KiuFunza incentive programmes were implemented in a sample of schools across Tanzania (mainland), with each school receiving one of the programmes. Figure 3.1 shows the annual implementation cycle followed by KiuFunza district teams.

When teachers signed up for the programme, they provided their grade-subject assignment and account details. The teachers taught the curriculum during the year and, at the end of the year (November), the teams came back to test the skills mastered by the students. By early April of the following year, the teachers' bonuses were paid into their bank or mobile money account. Table 3.1 provides a summary of the KiuFunza interventions in 2015–16.

---

9 For background, descriptive statistics and impact measurement of the KiuFunza II programme, see Mbiti et al. (2019b).

To be able to finance and manage the project, Twaweza implemented the interventions in 11 districts only (Figure 3.2).[10] KiuFunza districts were sampled randomly from all districts in mainland Tanzania. Random sampling means that every school and student in mainland Tanzania had an equal chance to be selected for the study. It also meant that findings from KiuFunza would be nationally representative and provide

Figure 3.1: KiuFunza implementation cycle summary

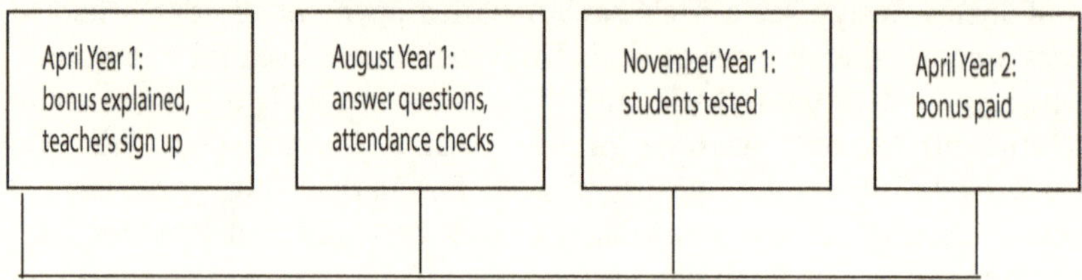

Figure 3.2: KiuFunza district sample map

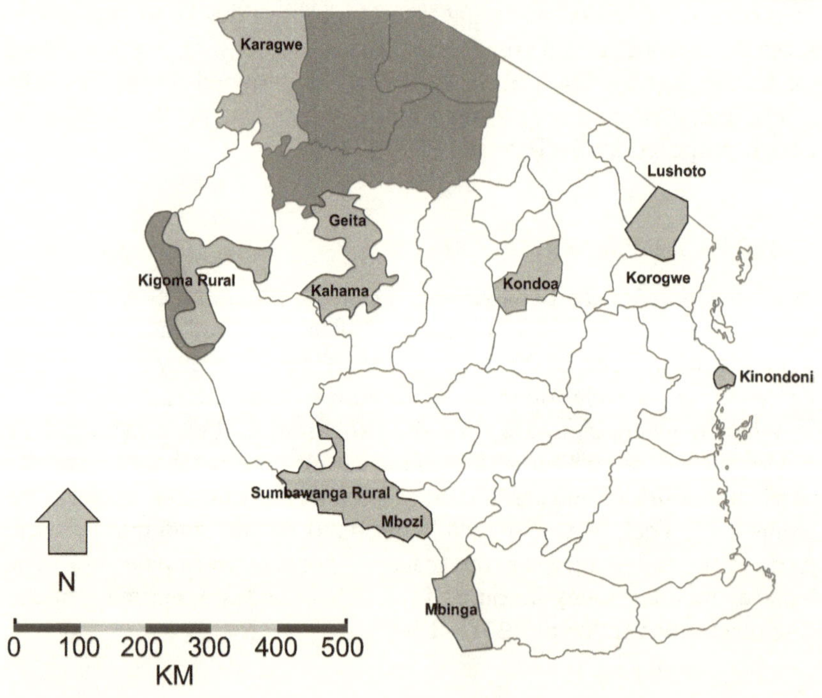

---

10 The selected sample included the following 11 districts (districts that split during the study period are still labelled as part of the mother district): Geita, Kahama, Karagwe, Kigoma, Kinondoni, Kondoa, Korogwe Rural, Lushoto, Mbinga, Mbozi, and Sumbawanga Rural.

relevant lessons for the whole education system in the country. Those districts with a higher number of primary school students had a greater chance of being in the sample.[11] In each district, 12 primary government schools were randomly selected, with half assigned the Stadi and half assigned Mashindano performance systems. In addition, the 'control arm' in each district consisted of ten other randomly selected schools that did not receive any financial flows or other support.

Table 3.1: KiuFunza key implementation numbers

	2016	2015
Number of schools participating (including pilot schools)	134 COD 60 control	133 COD 60 control
Standards with bonus	I, II and III	I, II and III
Topics tested	Kiswahili, Maths (English only in Standard III)	Kiswahili, Maths, English
Teachers		
Number of subject teachers	788	758
Number of head teachers	135	134
Students		
Number of students tested	65,643	51,580
Bonus money earned, totals		
Kiswahili	110,000,000	105,000,000
Maths	110,000,000	105,000,000
English	31,827,040 (only Std III)	105,000,000

Stadi and Mashindano incentives

Each incentive type is a separate intervention. The incentives are calculated based on test results at the stream level, and teachers are paid only for the streams for which they are responsible. The Stadi incentive rewards the absolute learning level a student has at a given moment – for example, the student can or cannot read words. The Mashindano incentive rewards learning improvements that are assessed relative to

---

11 The exception is Kigoma, which was selected on purpose for the implementation sample, as the district leadership had expressed early interest in the initiative. Kigoma was the training and pilot district and is not represented in the KiuFunza research sample. Similarly, two additional intervention schools were selected for piloting in Kinondoni.

other students who start at the same skill level – learning is measured at the end of the previous school year and at the end of the current school year.

In a Stadi school, teachers receive a bonus for every one of their students who passes a curriculum skill test according to the skills level. For example, a teacher of Kiswahili will earn a small bonus if a Standard 1 student can read syllables, a larger bonus if the student can read words, and an even greater bonus if the student can read a paragraph. The same applies to maths, where the skills tested include counting, recognizing numbers, telling which number is larger, adding up, subtracting, and multiplication and division in Standard 2 and 3.

In a Mashindano school, students are placed in one of ten national ability groups based on the previous year's test. Ability groups range from low level (cannot read anything, has no knowledge of numbers) to high levels (can read fluently, do math operations well). Each ability group typically has students from KiuFunza schools from all over the country – for example, a Standard 2 ability group for students who can read Kiswahili words but not sentences could have a student from Mbozi and a student from Geita. The progress of these students over the year is compared and rewarded. At the end of the year, students who did very well in their group receive a high ranking, which results in a high bonus for their teachers. The teachers' total payments are determined by the ranking of their students, and so teachers that move many of their students to the top of their national ability group earn a lot.

Mashindano may be more complex to understand than Stadi, but it is also fairer for the teachers, since students compete at their own level. This is not the case for Stadi, where teachers with higher-level students (often in urban schools) tend to earn more. However, Stadi pays for levels and so is easier to understand, while the slightly more complicated Mashindano design pays for value-added.

Feedback from the teachers

All the teachers in the Stadi and Mashindano schools agreed to participate and signed up for Twaweza's programme (one teacher declined at first but later changed her mind and asked to be registered). The implementation data also show that teachers made an effort to ensure that many children participated in the student tests.

At various points during the implementation, Twaweza asked teachers a set of questions to test their understanding of the programme, as they would not be able to respond without understanding it. The scores ranged from 62% to 91% correct, while trust in Twaweza to calculate and pay the bonuses in a transparent manner was high, at 95%. Teachers were also asked about performance pay programmes in general. Nine out of ten teachers (91%) teachers supported the idea of performance pay, and 63% of the teachers said that the government should include a performance-based bonus scheme in a future salary review, 37% said they preferred a flat increase.

THE IMPACT OF KIUFUNZA II

The implementation of the Stadi and Mashindano incentive schemes had an impact on both the money earned by teachers and the learning outcomes of the students.

Incentives paid to teachers

In 2016, the total budget for incentive payments for teachers and head teachers was TZS 251,827,040 (± US$120,000). The budget per subject increased to TZS 110,000 (US$53), up from the TZS 105,000 (US$50) per subject that was set in 2015. The budget was adjusted upwards for inflation, and the English incentive budget was adjusted downwards because English was removed from the Standard I–II curriculum during 2015. The remaining English incentive budget reflects the number of students in Standard III, and the incentive amount per student is equal between grades. As in previous years, head teachers received 20% of subject-teacher earnings.

Table 3.2 shows the incentive amounts earned in 2016 that were paid to teachers in April 2017. The two interventions have the same total per student budget, but the total Stadi budget is slightly higher because of a slightly higher total number of students.

Table 3.2: Incentive payments 2016 by programme

Incentive	Teachers	Head Teachers	Totals
Mashindano	97,966,883	19,593,377	117,560,260
Stadi	111,888,984	22,377,797	134,266,780
TOTAL	209,855,867	41,971,173	251,827,040

The average bonus for subject teachers was TZS 266,315 (TZS 209,855,867 divided by 788 early grade teachers), or US$127. This equals about 42% of the average net monthly teacher salary, which was TZS 637,790 (US$304) in 2016. Each teacher's bonus depended on how well their students did, and bonuses ranged from TZS 8,100 (US$4) to TZS 3.6 million (US$1,715), which is the equivalent of almost six months' salary.

Table 3.3 shows the distribution of the 2016 incentives over the 11 KiuFunza districts.

Table 3.3: Incentive payments 2016 by district

District	Teachers	Head Teachers
Geita	37,139,134	7,427,827
Kahama	16,461,657	3,292,331
Karagwe	14,946,439	2,989,288
Kinondoni	42,329,790	8,465,958
Kondoa	18,045,381	3,609,076
Korogwe Rural	13,368,905	2,673,781
Lushoto	13,785,074	2,757,015
Mbinga	9,674,692	1,934,938
Mbozi	18,253,712	3,650,742
Sumbawanga Rural	12,593,641	2,518,728
Kigoma	13,257,443	2,651,489
TOTAL	209,855,867	41,971,173

As Table 3.4 illustrates, the incentives paid to teachers varied according to programme (Stadi or Mashindano) and school setting (rural or urban). Teachers in rural schools typically did much better with Mashindano than with Stadi, because Mashindano rewards value-added gains within student groups of equal starting ability – rural schools outperformed urban schools by TZS 100 per student. In contrast, urban schools did better with Stadi, which rewards learning levels, because their students start at a higher level. School size is another factor that explains pay differences: urban schools are larger than rural schools, and so the average incentive payment is larger than the average rural payment, even for Mashindano, because the incentive pays for every student's achievements.

Learning outcomes

The research outcomes, which included student learning and teacher attitudes and practices, were measured in each school participating in the two incentive programmes (Stadi or Mashindano), as well as in each school in the control group. Mbiti et al. (2019b) found the following:

- The impact of the incentive on student learning is the equivalent to one-third of a year of schooling, added to the business as usual (i.e. without incentives) learning progress.

- Both types of programme improve learning outcomes. The Stadi (levels) incentive programme is easier to communicate and implement than Mashindano (gains).

- The learning impacts are 30–70% higher when using high-stakes test data for the teacher payments.

- There is no effect, negative or positive, on grades or subjects that are not tested or incentivized. This result implies teachers in incentivized grades did not reduce effort on non-incentivized subjects, nor did teachers in non-incentivized grades reduce effort.

Table 3.4: Average incentive pay by intervention and setting

	School setting		
Incentive type	Urban	Rural	All
Mashindano			
Payment per student tested (TZS)	5,020	4,323	4,416
Number of students per school	585	478	497
Average teacher bonus (TZS)	297,188	246,231	255,122
% of urban teacher bonus	100%	83%	86%
Stadi			
Payment per student tested (TZS)	6,227	3,885	4,275
Number of students per school	604	462	494
Average teacher bonus (TZS)	376,746	244,993	276,953
% of urban teacher bonus	100%	65%	74%

CONCLUSION

In Tanzania, schooling is expensive and government's expenditure on education is growing – between 2006 and 2014, education's share of the GDP grew from 4.6% to 5.9%. The largest share of the education budget is spent on teacher salaries, which makes sense, as teachers are the key to everyday learning in classrooms across the country. However, the way in which teacher contracts are currently written does not do justice to the goal of learning for all children. As in most other countries, teacher pay does not differentiate between the quality of teaching and learning that takes place, despite research showing substantial differences in teacher quality within schools. Having a good or a bad teacher affects the learning and lifetime incomes of students, but teacher quality differences are difficult to observe. In addition, a teacher's salary is based in large part on experience, and yet research shows that more experience does not correlate well with teaching effort and quality (apart from during the first years of a teacher's career).

In Tanzania, teachers are paid only for their time (input) and not for the learning (output) produced. This arrangement does not send the right signals to teachers about the value of their output, nor incite talented potential teachers to join the profession. Moreover, the widespread absence of teachers from classrooms shows that education administrators find it difficult to enforce the delivery of a full day of teaching in every classroom. Every day in classrooms across the country, large amounts of valuable instruction time are lost, putting children's learning and future welfare at risk.

The Twaweza implementation of incentive pay shows that introducing a modest salary component related to measured performance can inspire teachers to improve learning. Teachers respond to their efforts being acknowledged. Incentive pay sends a signal to all teachers that learning is the outcome that matters most; recognizes that some teachers put in more effort than others, and rewards that effort in a transparent manner; and provides feedback about performance through the payment and feedback reports. For now, Twaweza has only measured the incentive effects on teachers who are already employed, but incentive pay may well increase the quality of newly recruited teachers in the future.

A limitation of the implementation models tested so far is that they are not designed for scale. At the request of, and in collaboration with, the Government of Tanzania, Twaweza is setting up a follow-up study – KiuFunza III – that will implement a simpler version of the Stadi model, with a view to scaling up.

The key design principles of the KiuFunza III model are:
- A simple and robust incentive design, for ease of implementation, understanding and transparency.

- A well-communicated programme by government personnel.

- High-stakes testing and teacher bonus payments implemented by an independent entity.

This new model will be subjected to experimental testing, to assess whether the scalable model retains the learning impact demonstrated so far. The research will involve a quantitative impact analysis using an experimental design, coordinated by the RISE TZ research team (research working papers will become available through the RISE website, www.riseprogramme.org). Implementation will involve documenting the execution systems, field notes from implementers and meeting notes to provide a picture of what challenges are encountered.

Part of the challenge is likely to be the system integration or PPP (public–private partnership) aspect of KiuFunza III, where a civil society organization is now holding hands with the government in its implementation. Implementation will include getting civil servants to understand and appreciate the KiuFunza goals and instruments, and to pursue a common agenda. It will also involve getting access to the government data required to build the data infrastructure needed for performance pay. Moreover, reactions of education managers, politicians, KiuFunza teachers and other stakeholders must be taken on board.

Implementation reports and process documents will provide a description of the fortunes and challenges of the public private partnership. They will complement the quantitative impact evaluation to answer three questions: (1) Is the KiuFunza III performance pay model effective in raising learning outcomes (compared with business as usual)? (2) Looking at the impact per dollar (using the implementation costs), is the KiuFunza model a cost-effective way to achieve learning? (3) Is the public–private partnership model financially, practically and politically feasible?

BIBLIOGRAPHY

Banerjee, A. & Duflo, E. (2011) *Poor Economics: A radical rethinking of the way to fight global poverty,* New York: Public Affairs.

Barlevy, G. & Neal, D. (2012) Pay for percentile. *American Economic Review* 102(5): 1805–31.

Bruns, B. & Luque, J. (2015) *Great Teachers: How to raise student learning in Latin America and the Caribbean,* New York: World Bank Publications.

Chetty, R., Friedman, J.N. & Rockoff, J.E. (2014) Measuring the impacts of teachers II: Teacher value-added and student outcomes in adulthood. *The American Economic Review* 104(9): 2633–79.

Cilliers, J., Mbiti, I.M. & Zeitlin, A. (2019) Can public rankings improve school performance? Evidence from a nationwide reform in Tanzania. *RISE Working Paper* 19/027.

De Ree, J., Muralidharan, K., Pradhan, M. & Rogers, H. (2017) Double for nothing? Experimental evidence on an unconditional teacher salary increase in Indonesia. *The Quarterly Journal of Economics* 133(2).

Eberhardt, M.J., Hill, T. & Plaut, D. (2015). Assessing learning, achieving impact: A literature review on citizen-led assessments. A report from Results for Development Institute.

Encyclopaedia Britannica, https://www.britannica.com/science/ecosystem, accessed August 2019.

Evans, D.K. & Popova, A. (2016) What really works to improve learning in developing countries? An analysis of divergent findings in systematic reviews, *The World Bank Research Observer* 31(2), 242–270.

Glewwe, P. & Muralidharan, K. (2016) Improving education outcomes in developing countries: Evidence, knowledge gaps, and policy implications. *Handbook of the Economics of Education Volume 5.* Elsevier. pp. 653–743.

Grogan, L. (2009) Universal primary education and school entry in Uganda. *Journal of African Economies* 18(2): 183–211.

Kremer, M., Brannen, C. & Glennerster, R. (2013) The challenge of education and learning in the developing world. *Science* 340(6130): 297–300.

Lucas, A.M. & Mbiti, I.M. (2012) Access, sorting, and achievement: the short-run effects of free primary education in Kenya. *American Economic Journal: Applied Economics,* 226–253.

Mbiti, I., Muralidharan, K., Romero, M., Schipper, Y., Manda, C. & Rajani, R. (2019a) Inputs, incentives and complementarities in education: Experimental evidence from Tanzania, *Quarterly Journal of Economics* 134: 1627–1673. Available at https://doi.org/10.1093/qje/qjz010.

Mbiti, I., Romero, M. & Schipper, Y. (2019b) Designing effective teacher performance pay programs: Experimental evidence from Tanzania. Working Paper No. 25903, Working Paper Series. National Bureau of Economic Research. https://doi.org/10.3386/w25903.

Neal, D. (2011) The design of performance pay in education. *Handbook of the Economics of Education Volume 4,* 495–550.

Oketch, M. & Rolleston, C. (2007) Policies on free primary and secondary education in East Africa?: Retrospect and prospect. *Review of Research in Education,* 31 (1): 131–58.

Pritchett, L. (2013) *The Rebirth of Education: Schooling Ain't Learning,* Washington DC: Center for Global Development.

RISE TZ (2017) Monitoring the Big Results Now in Education Program. Report of the Tanzania Country Research Team. *Guide,* Georgetown University.

Todd, R. & Attfield, I. (2017) Big results now in Tanzanian education: Has the delivery approach delivered? Unpublished paper.

Twaweza (2018) Teacher incentives in public schools: Do they improve learning in Tanzania? KiuFunza impact briefing. February 2018, Twaweza East Africa, Dar es Salaam. Web link: https://www.twaweza.org/uploads/files/KiuFunzaIIResultsBrief-FINAL-web.pdf.

Twaweza (2017a) KiuFunza randomized evaluation: methodology and sample. Web link: https://twaweza.or.tz/uploads/files/KF%20methods%20(short).pdf.

Twaweza (2017b) KiuFunza II (2015–16) intervention endline test protocol. Web link: https://twaweza.or.tz/uploads/files/Twaweza%20KFII%202015-16%20Protocol%20Final.pdf.

UNESCO (2017) All education Staff compensation, primary (% of total expenditure). UNESCO Institute for Statistics, accessed through World Bank online data catalogue.

Valente, C. (2015) Primary education expansion and quality of schooling: Evidence from Tanzania. IZA Discussion Paper No. 9208. Web link: https://papers.ssrn.com/sol3/papers.cfm?abstract_id=2655157

World Bank (2014) Service delivery indicators: Tanzania (technical report), Washington DC: The World Bank.

World Bank (2018) *World Development Report 2018: Learning to realize education's promise.* Washington DC: The World Bank. Retrieved from https://elibrary.worldbank.org/doi/abs/10. 1596/978-1-4648-1096-1.

4.

INSURANCE AS AN EFFECTIVE DEVELOPMENT INSTRUMENT

Samuel Munzele Maimbo,
Pauline Anna Marie Delay & Shadreck Mapfumo

Insurance is a risk-mitigation tool that can have a significant impact on a country's growth. It also helps households manage risk, reducing poverty and improving resilience. This is why developing sustainable insurance markets is important for achieving the World Bank Group's twin goals of eliminating extreme poverty and boosting shared prosperity. Insurance is an instrument that allows a specific risk to be transferred from an individual, or group of individuals, to a third party that can handle the financial impact of potential loss. Insurance policies and products exist to protect individuals and companies from a wide variety of risks associated with events ranging from health issues to car accidents, loss of property, or death. Insurance can both help a country's economy grow and contribute to reducing poverty, including through mitigating the effects of climate change. However, although many insurance products are aligned with public policy priorities in Africa, several barriers need to be overcome to develop insurance markets and increase penetration in the region. One particular innovative insurance product is the weather-based index insurance, which is insurance linked to an index such as rainfall or temperature. Such a product can be an effective tool for increasing insurance penetration in Africa, provided insurance companies and regulators understand how to design and implement such a complex and labour-intensive product. Capacity building can be used as an effective tool to create sustainable insurance markets that provide innovative development solutions for African countries.

THE ROLE OF INSURANCE IN ECONOMIC DEVELOPMENT

Since the early 2000s, the concept of insurance as a catalytic tool for economic development has come into focus with the emergence of new types of tailored insurance products, such as catastrophe insurance and index insurance. By providing risk management and financial intermediation, the insurance industry contributes to economic development through the following channels (CENFRI & FSD Africa 2017):

- **Insurance protects corporate assets.** Insurance supports industry development, foreign direct investment, infrastructure, and trade, all of which are key to development in Africa. For example, insuring underlying assets supports industry development and allows for higher risk. Insurance also manages risk around the movement of goods, which facilitates trade, and promotes infrastructure and foreign direct investment by providing guarantees.

- **Insurance helps develop the credit market.** By protecting credit providers against the risk of default, insurance makes it possible to look at financing options that would otherwise have been deemed too risky. Thanks to insurance, credit providers can develop new products and target different population segments, thereby expanding the credit market. A strong correlation exists between insurance penetration and domestic credit to the private sector. Insurance is also 'adept at pricing risk', and so the 'presence of insurance skills [...] enables credit providers to extend credit on more commercially viable terms, making for a stronger credit industry' (CENFRI & FSD Africa 2017: 4).

- **Insurance helps fiscally constrained governments to free up resources** for productive investments. In Africa, governments tend to have high fiscal constraints. Insurance provides direct financial protection to both governments and individuals against high-impact events, such as natural disasters. This means that governments will have reduced liabilities if such events occur, freeing up public funds for other, more productive investments, and leading to more efficient and effective public finances.

- **Insurance helps mobilize long-term domestic capital** for strategic sectors of the economy. The insurance sector plays a key role as an institutional investor in capital markets by mobilizing domestic capital into long-term investments. This is especially important in developing economies that often suffer from a shortage of domestic capital.

While several academic studies (CENFRI & FSD Africa 2017; Chantarat et al. 2017; Gine 2009; Pollner 1999) explain the link between the insurance sector and economic development, empirical evidence on the direction of causality is limited. Only in the last decade have studies been published that offer evidence on the cause–effect relationship between insurance activity and economic growth, with most finding that 'insurance development has a positive effect on economic growth' (Lester 2014: 8). A 2006 World Bank review covering 56 countries supports this causal relationship, finding that both life and non-life insurance promotes several economic development outcomes. These include facilitating financial stability, promoting trade and commerce, mobilizing domestic savings, managing risk, serving as a complementary safety net, reducing or mitigating losses, and incentivizing risk-reducing behaviour (Arena 2006).

The impact of insurance on poverty reduction

Insurance is not only an effective risk-management tool at the macroeconomic and industry levels, but also an invaluable tool that helps households manage risk, thereby reducing poverty, improving resilience, and catalysing entrepreneurial activity.

Poor and low-income households are more exposed to greater risks than wealthier households and less equipped to deal effectively with these risks. Inadequate housing, poor or no access to sanitation and healthcare, and a reliance on a few assets for income are just some of the factors that put these households at risk of remaining or being pushed back into poverty in the event of a natural disaster or other adverse event. This represents a form of structural violence, which is an anthropological term used to describe how certain structures embedded in the political and economic order hurt certain groups of people, often perpetuating and exacerbating inequalities, and leaving them in a vicious cycle of poverty. Without access to insurance products, these households engage in a range of informal risk management techniques that are both inefficient and have a high cost to society, particularly to the poor. Insurance can have long-term benefits that go well beyond mitigating the immediate shock or event, enabling households to avoid radical measures such as selling income-generating assets or taking children out of school, and ultimately reducing or avoiding poverty in the face of adversity.

Climate change and catastrophic events

More than one-third of the world's poor live in multi-hazard zones, and low-income countries account for more than 70% of the world's disaster hotspots. The most vulnerable economies are also the ones most likely to suffer the most adverse effects of climate change, which threatens to push an additional 100 million people into poverty by 2030. Between 1995 and 2014, lower-income countries experienced 26% of storms and 86% of storm-related deaths (World Bank 2018). The international community is working on several climate- and disaster-risk insurance solutions aimed at reducing the humanitarian impact and helping poor and vulnerable groups to recover more quickly from natural disasters and catastrophic events. These include the Africa Disaster Risk Financing Initiative, which currently works with 19 countries in Africa to help them better manage their response to natural disasters. Solutions developed are tailored for the local context of the country concerned and include policies, instruments and strategies (such as Kenya's Natural Disaster Risk strategy, the first to be implemented in Africa), as well as safety nets that help rapidly distribute emergency assistance in case of a shock or disaster (Wesley & Piccio 2019).

The aim is also to enhance a country's preparedness and resilience to such events. The 2010–2011 earthquakes in Haiti and New Zealand illustrate the role that insurance can play in minimizing the adverse impacts of natural disasters on a country's economy. In 2010, both island countries were struck by magnitude 7.0 earthquakes with the epicentre near a major city – New Zealand also suffered subsequent earthquakes and a destructive aftershock in February 2011. The magnitude of damage in absolute terms was similar in both countries. However, the economic costs varied greatly: 126% of GDP in Haiti ($8.5 billion) compared to

Figure 4.1: Uninsured losses as percentage of economic losses (2007–16)

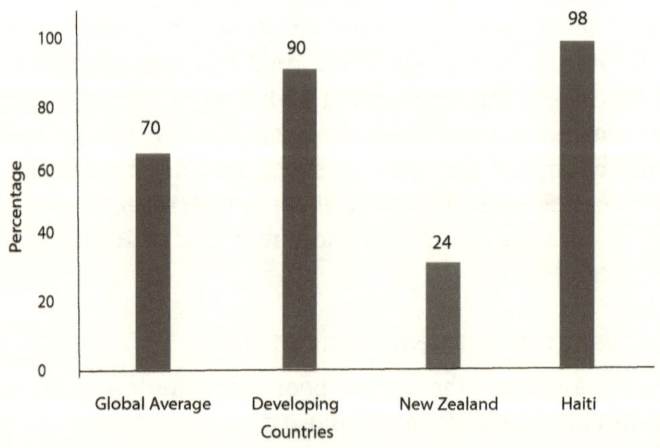

Source: Insurance Development Forum

18% of GDP ($31 billion) in New Zealand. This was because uninsured losses were much lower in New Zealand than in Haiti, as insurance covered and reimbursed 81% of the direct losses in New Zealand, but only 1% in Haiti (von Peter et al., 2012)[1].

As Figure 4.1 shows, uninsured losses, as a proportion of total economic losses, are much higher in developing and low-income countries than in middle- and high-income ones. Therefore, the insurance sector has a critical role to play in mitigating risks related to natural disasters and catastrophic events, including financial losses. Insurance interventions, at both country and household level, help reduce vulnerability to these events that are increasing as a result of climate change.

INSURANCE PENETRATION IN SUB-SAHARAN AFRICA

In Sub-Saharan Africa, insurance markets tend to be underdeveloped, and premiums vary from country to country, with South Africa recording by far the largest premium amount in the region, at over $45 billion (CENFRI & FSD Africa 2017). The development of insurance products is often linked to specific policy objectives. Boosting the penetration of insurance products in Sub-Saharan Africa has enormous potential to benefit economies, and thereby help countries to achieve these policy objectives.

Insurance and public policy

The insurance industry has evolved and matured considerably in developing and emerging economies, often to match specific policy objectives. One example is the development of appropriate insurance products to facilitate access to credit and increase productivity, including property, crop and livestock, as well as life and disability insurance. In Kenya, a successful insurance scheme was developed to insure farmers from the effects of severe drought on livestock. The Kenya Livestock Insurance Programme uses satellite data to assess the level of drought and, once a specific threshold is reached, makes payments to insured farmers that can be used to buy food and water needed to ensure their livestock survives.[2] Table 4.1 summarizes the link between policy objectives (related

---

1   Llull, E., Insurers' pledge to help developing countries on climate change, *The Financial Times*, 28 June 2016. Available at https://www.ft.com/content/04d57130-274d-11e6-8ba3-cdd781d02d89

2   Swiss Re, Successful Kenya livestock insurance program scheme scales up. Available at https://www.swissre.com/our-business/public-sector-solutions/thought-leadership/successful-kenya-livestock-insurance-program-scheme.html

to ending extreme poverty and boosting shared prosperity) and specific appropriate insurance products.

Table 4.1: Policy objectives and appropriate insurance

Policy Objective	Appropriate Insurance
Prevent old age poverty	Life insurance, especially endowment and annuity policies [a]
Enable protection of (productive) assets	Property/catastrophe insurance for households and enterprises
Facilitate access to credit to increase productivity	• Property, crop, and livestock insurance • Life/disability insurance
Protect citizens and migrants (especially when vulnerable)	• Life, health, and accident insurance • Crop and livestock insurance • Work injury compensation insurance • Motor vehicle third-party liability insurance • Professional, environmental, and product liability insurance
Increase road safety	Motor vehicle third-party liability insurance
Increase workplace safety	Work injury compensation insurance
Improve citizens' health	Health insurance
Strengthen business	• Inland marine insurance [b] • Trade credit insurance • Fidelity bonds • Surety bonds
Reduce dependency on foreign capital for investments	Life insurance and annuities
Broaden and deepen capital markets	• Life insurance and annuities • Deposit insurance • Financial guarantee insurance • Banker's blanket bond insurance
Protect the budgets of national and subnational governments	• Sovereign risk transfer • Public–private partnerships for health/life/crop/livestock (micro) insurance

Notes:

a. Life insurance products provide both income replacement after premature death (term policies) and a long-term savings instrument (endowment policies). Life insurers also provide annuity policies, where the insurer makes regular payments to the insured until their death.

b. Broadly defined, inland marine insurance is a type of property insurance that covers goods or materials that are frequently transported to different locations.

Housing insurance is a good example of an insurance product that is aligned to a policy objective. Housing represents the main asset of the poor in most developing countries and so plays a key socioeconomic role. By 2030, an estimated three billion people will need new housing and basic urban infrastructure, as by then the global population will have reached 8.5 billion, of which almost 60% will be living in urban centres (UN 2016). A nuanced framework has been developed for discussing the links between property market development and insurance. It points to several insurance products that can help property market actors across the value chain assume more productive risk, including 'political risk insurance, advance loss of profits insurance, credit insurance, construction insurance and commercial property insurance, among others' (Msulwa et al. 2018: 22). The range of products available in the property development market directly contributes to the ability to deliver affordable housing for the poor, which is at the forefront of the global development agenda.

A growing market for insurance

Despite the alignment between public policy priorities and insurance products, insurance coverage remains stubbornly low in developing economies, where around 80% of adults do not have access to any form of insurance – in 2015, gross premiums hovered at just over 1% of GDP for both life and non-life insurance (Swiss Re 2016). In Africa, total insurance premiums in 2017 were at 3% of GDP according to Swiss Re Institute, compared to a worldwide average of 6% of GDP (Swiss Re 2018). Such low coverage indicates that existing insurance markets need to be made more robust and inclusive.

The global insurance market is growing, albeit slowly, particularly across emerging markets and developing economies. In Sub-Saharan Africa, insurance penetration rates are low (2.9%) but are expected to rise in the long-term, thanks in large part to a growing middle class with a rising disposable income. Many countries, such as Ghana and Rwanda, are developing new health insurance programmes as a move toward universal healthcare. Leading the way is microinsurance, which is designed to enable low-income populations to access various types of insurance (including life, health, property, and index insurance). It is changing the insurance space and increasing the customer base for many insurance companies, including major insurers such as AIG and Munich Re. While microinsurance products can be packaged with other financial services, which reduces the operating cost, increasingly they are being sold as a standalone product using mobile technology. For example, in Kenya, MicroEnsure sells its microinsurance products through mobile money provider M-PESA, making it both affordable and accessible to its customers (KPMG 2017; Lloyds n.d.).

Over the past decade, the insurance industry has embraced innovation, moving away from traditional insurance products to new, innovative, risk-sharing instruments that meet the needs of new markets in developing countries. These new types of insurance – index insurance, renewable energy insurance, microinsurance, insurance pools, and sovereign insurance for catastrophe/disaster risk reduction and pandemics – contribute directly to sustainable development (UNEP 2015). Some initiatives include Munich Re's Climate Insurance Initiative (MCII) and the World Bank Group's partnership with Swiss Re for the Pandemic Emergency Financing Facility (PEF).

Nevertheless, challenges persist, such as a lack of trust in the ability of insurers to settle claims sufficiently and effectively, concentrated distribution channels, and the need to streamline long-term contracts. These challenges must be addressed, so that the insurance market can continue to develop in the region. Long-term contracts in particular have become a challenge in the microinsurance sector. Although many microinsurance customers have long-term income, such income tends to be irregular (for example, a small trader or a family receiving remittances from abroad), which makes drafting a standardized contract for premium payments difficult. This challenge is especially pronounced in Sub-Saharan Africa, where informal economic activity is the largest in the world, averaging 40% in low-income countries and 35% in middle-income countries (Medina et al. 2017).

Fundamental constraints in the development of inclusive insurance markets in Africa

The future evolution of insurance markets is changing, and the less-developed insurance markets today are unlikely to replicate the more advanced markets of yesterday. Technology and other factors are driving pockets of growth, but barriers to market development can undermine even promising market potential and market drivers, such as increased income levels – 43% of Africans are expected to be part of the middle or upper classes by 2030 (Signe 2019). In addition to low-income and low-wealth levels, these barriers include regulatory constraints, knowledge and skills shortages, and product distribution issues.

- **Regulatory constraints**. Until recently, insurance was not considered an industry that presents potential systemic risks to the economy. However, in many developing markets, the regulatory and legal framework governing the insurance sector is weak, allowing customers to be treated poorly and unsustainable insurance firms to operate. This erodes public trust and confidence, which is a prerequisite for insurance markets to grow – the insurance business can be characterized as a promise to indemnify or protect policyholders in case of a loss, which requires high public trust.

- **Knowledge and skills shortages**. These shortages exist on both the supply and demand sides and need to be addressed to grow the insurance market in Sub-Saharan Africa. On the demand side, the very concept of insurance (of pooling risk, paying premiums and making claims) is neither well known nor well understood in many markets because of the low levels of financial literacy across Sub-Saharan Africa. Programmes need to be designed and implemented that will help the potential customer base build this knowledge. On the supply side, capacity building among regulators and local industry representatives is also needed to enable and empower them to drive market development.

- **Product distribution issues**. Traditional insurance companies can be reluctant to serve lower-income markets or develop products that meet the needs of consumers in developing countries. This is mostly because of the costs associated with innovation and distribution, as well as a perceived absence of economies of scale. Data and technology are fundamentally changing the way insurance companies operate and how consumers interact with financial products. However, a lot more work needs to be done, so that the power of new technologies in product development and distribution can be leveraged to better serve low-income markets and help advance economic development in Sub-Saharan Africa.

THE ROLE AND IMPACT OF RISK MODELLING CAPACITY-BUILDING PROGRAMMES

The challenge is how to create sustainable insurance markets in Africa, i.e. markets that uphold quality and profitability, meet the specific needs of the region, and contribute to poverty reduction and economic growth. Insurance providers are starting to move away from traditional insurance products and towards innovative risk-sharing measures, such as index insurance, that can be effective tools to help reduce extreme poverty and boost shared prosperity. However, the insurance industry must have the necessary knowledge and skills required to create, promote, and evaluate such products, which can have a direct impact on creating sustainable insurance markets in Sub-Saharan Africa.

Motivation for decision tools

As discussed, sustainable insurance products are needed in order to develop inclusive insurance markets that will advance economic development. Quality and profitability are the two main components of product sustainability that must be addressed. To meet quality standards, an insurance product must meet client expectations and satisfy consumer protection guidelines. Given the low levels of financial literacy and high level of consumer mistrust pervasive in Africa, it is important to put in place a strong consumer protection framework that includes transparency, choice, redress, and privacy (Lester 2009). Profitability measures should be aimed at protecting shareholders and avoiding bankruptcies, and also protecting the insurance market.

Unsurprisingly, quality and profitability are not always perfectly aligned. High-quality insurance products should provide adequate compensation to policyholders when they make a claim. However, if such insurance coverage is too expensive, policyholders may be encouraged to retain some of the risk and only transfer it in specific cases, such as catastrophic events. To ensure a healthy balance between product quality and profitability measures, insurance practitioners should apply a rigorous process called the Product Sustainability Appraisal Tree (PSAT) when developing new products. The PSAT helps the insurer measure risk retention and transfer levels, and communicates these to their customers to ensure that they fully understand how much risk they are retaining (i.e. how much they would be responsible for themselves if an adverse event occurred) and how much they are transferring to the insurer. The PSAT also provides a framework for insurance companies to measure product profitability, which is important because the insurer must be able to demonstrate that a product is profitable to be able to continue to offer it in the market. The responsibility for selecting and setting product quality and profitability metrics lies with the board of directors and management of insurance companies. Regulators also have an interest in the efficacy of these metrics and need to be especially vigilant that these metrics are met in order to develop strong and stable insurance industries in African countries.

Index insurance: An innovative and inclusive risk-sharing solution

In Africa, most agricultural land is rainfed, and many regions are vulnerable to climate shocks, such as drought, flooding and irregular rainfall. To limit their losses in any given year, smallholder farmers often invest very little in their land, which leads to reduced yields and contributes to food insecurity. While insurance can be a good risk management tool for these farmers, the traditional insurance market largely fails to meet their demand for affordable insurance. Index insurance provides an innovative and more efficient solution for these farmers to protect their crops against losses and the subsequent loss of income. Mitigating weather-related risk is also an important precondition to providing credit, stimulating investment in farming, and increasing productivity among the millions of smallholder farmers who make up 70% of Sub-Saharan Africa's population (AGRA 2018) and produce up to 80% of the food consumed in the region.[3]

Weather-related events, such as droughts and floods, affect large numbers of farmers at the same time. In Sub-Saharan Africa, where agriculture is the predominant industry, these adverse weather events affect a disproportionate number of families, making it difficult or impossible for insurers to assess the losses of each individual party, especially in remote, difficult-to-access areas. Compounding these difficulties is the widespread lack of adequate transportation infrastructure. In these situations, regular indemnity insurance – where the insurance company sends an assessor to evaluate each claim – becomes unattractive for the insurer, being both logistically challenging and too expensive. In addition, the potential revenue from each farmer is too small for traditional indemnity insurance to be financially viable for insurers, as smallholder farmers usually insure a relatively small value, of up to $100 (Mapfumo et al. 2017).

Weather-based index insurance allows insurance companies to pay out claims for a hazardous event to a large number of farmers at the same time, based on specific weather-related indices. For instance, if rainfall fails to meet a given level for a specific season, this would indicate a loss of yield for farmers and trigger a payout by the insurer for the affected insured farmers. With index insurance, insurance companies do not need to send adjusters on field visits, which is not feasible when a high number of claims occur at the same time, often in difficult conditions e.g. following a hurricane or flood. Instead, losses can be assessed using real-time data (e.g. from satellites) and individual payouts automatically calculated based on deviations from a proxy – for example, wind-speed during a storm or typhoon, or rainfall over a specific period (Mapfumo et al. 2017). This is an efficient way to provide coverage that does not rely on individual assessments to process claims.

Index insurance uses publicly available data, including satellite data, to assess whether claims should be paid out to a large number of

---

3 Karuku, J., Smallholder farming the surest route to African growth, *Mail & Guardian*, 19 June 2014. Available at https://mg.co.za/article/2014-06-19-smallholder-farming-the-surest-route-to-african-growth

insured parties. This makes index insurance a viable, affordable risk management solution for smallholder farmers in Sub-Saharan Africa who cannot afford the premiums that come with traditional insurance. In addition, index insurance helps these farmers to enter the formal financial sector and access credit.

Yet, despite its great potential for smallholder farmers, insurers in Sub-Saharan Africa rarely offer index insurance, which is a relatively new product that is complex and labour intensive. This is because they lack the knowledge and technical capacity to develop sustainable index insurance products that are both profitable for them and helpful for smallholder farmers. The World Bank Group's Global Index Insurance Facility hopes to change this and is working towards building sustainable index-insurance markets to help strengthen the financial resilience of the poor against the impact of climate change and natural disasters. Alongside providing grants to help insurance companies cover the often prohibitive product development costs, the World Bank Group provides high-level training to insurance professionals. This enables them to acquire the skills they need to create new and innovative index-based insurance products, which are expected to increase insurance penetration to rural and low-income markets in Africa. These trainings have led to two important market developments in Nigeria and in Zambia.

The Case of Nigeria: August 2017 Results

Drought can spell disaster for the over 60% of Nigerians who rely on agriculture for their livelihoods. Without tools such as insurance to help mitigate their risk, these smallholder farmers are left vulnerable to climate shocks and the inevitable loss of income that follows. In the past, the difficulty of accessing agricultural insurance products meant that the vast majority of smallholder farmers and their families were not protected against catastrophic losses – and erratic weather patterns, droughts, floods, and other extreme weather-related events made it difficult or impossible to move away from their precarious state. For years, only the government-owned Nigerian Agricultural Insurance Corporation offered agricultural insurance. And the only product was traditional indemnity agricultural insurance, which had limited success in the low-income market because of its high administration costs and consequently high premium costs. Therefore, farmers were unlikely to use such insurance products to protect their crops and themselves against financial losses when a bad season occurred, which left the agricultural sector vulnerable.

Over the last few years, private sector insurance companies have been applying for – but failing to secure – licences to offer index-based agricultural insurance products to help farmers manage their risks. Like most African insurance regulatory bodies, the Nigerian regulator lacked the additional capacity needed to evaluate or approve these new and innovative products and, as a result, requests for licensing were delayed or rejected. The regulator needed to develop new skills and a strong technical understanding of weather-based index insurance.

The World Bank Group's Global Index Insurance Facility (GIIF) is a multi-donor programme that 'facilitates access to finance for smallholder farmers, micro-entrepreneurs, and microfinance institutions through the provisions of catastrophic risk transfer solutions and index-based insurance in developing countries',[4] to help improve their resilience to climate change and weather-related disasters. In collaboration with the African Reinsurance Corporation (Africa Re), the World Bank Group organized technical training specifically targeting African insurance regulators and CEOs of insurance companies. The objective was for participants to understand the function and benefits of weather-based index insurance, including how insurance companies can design profitable products, and how regulators can evaluate and ensure the quality of these products. As climate change will have disproportionate negative effects in Sub-Saharan Africa, the insurance industry also needs to understand the specific implications of climate change. Therefore, the training covered topics ranging from the concepts of index insurance and the importance of risk modelling for decision-making, to risk metrics for product quality evaluation, product pricing, market potential analysis, and the value of insurance for financial institutions. Participants also learned about the importance of risk transfer, which is where a specific type of risk is transferred from either a group or an individual to a third party who can handle the financial impact of the loss (Mapfumo et al. 2017), and the role of the insurance company's risk management committee in ensuring that the PSAT is effectively implemented.

The training resulted in a greater understanding of the function and benefits of weather-based index insurance and an active application of PSAT principles by the regulator and insurers. As a direct consequence of this training, the regulator's technical team now actively evaluates insurance products for quality and profitability. This should lead to more consumer confidence in the sector, an increased outreach, and a large profitable market for the insurers. By 2018, the National Insurance Commission (NAICOM), the Nigerian regulator, had issued five licences to private insurance companies for agriculture insurance, to enable them develop index insurance products. Four of these companies issued policies to about 15,000 farmers for the July–October season in 2017 and

---

4 See https://www.ifc.org/wps/wcm/connect/industry_ext_content/ifc_external_corporate_site/financial+institutions/priorities/access_essential+financial+services/global+index+insurance+facility

32,000 farmers for the 2018 season, helping them manage their risk and giving them access to bank loans and guarantees.

After another training for insurance professionals, NAICOM announced its intention to issue licences for weather-based index insurance to 15 additional companies, with the aim of insuring millions of households in the next two to three years, thereby unlocking access to finance and protecting farmers against the effects of climate-related shocks. In 2019, NAICOM had licensed a total of 12 private insurance companies to offer index insurance and, as of June 2019, seven companies were offering index insurance products to their customers.

One of Africa's major reinsurers, Africa Re, provided capacity to the four insurance companies involved in the 2017 season index programme. In partnership with the GIIF, Africa Re also sought to increase insurance penetration to smallholder farmers, by providing an incentive protection to participating companies. This protection would allow the companies to reduce the uncertain loadings on the original premiums charged to farmers, making them more affordable. The incentive protection programme was based on a stop-loss protection facility, which in essence focuses on the loss experienced during the crop season.

These capacity-building and knowledge-enhancement efforts have borne fruits, as the 2018 season saw an increase in requests for reinsurance capacity from additional insurers in the Nigeria market – in a recent survey in August 2022 undertaken by the IFC and NAICOM, 26 insurance companies expressed their desire to receive in-depth capacity building and reinsurance support; this is happening at a time the market is now offering insurance to over 650,000 smallholder farmers (up from 15,000 in 2017). This shows that capacity-building initiatives have been – and continue to be – a critical tool that allows the insurance industry in Nigeria to learn about and apply new solutions to their business, helping the industry to grow and the farmers to protect their livelihoods.

The Case of Zambia: November 2017 Results

For Hashit Patel, CEO of Mayfair Insurance Zambia, the main roadblock to developing index insurance products was convincing his board of directors of its profitability, which is the main factor that insurance companies consider when developing and rolling out new products. As mentioned earlier, index insurance is very expensive to design, especially when insurance companies lack the internal capability to design and price index-insurance products, so that they have to use the services of international product development specialists. However, as weather-related damages affect a large population at the same time, index insurance is much more cost-effective than indemnity insurance because it pays out benefits based on transparent and objective data, rather than costly field visits. It is a more efficient (and thus affordable) risk management tool, and the processes of signing up for a policy and of receiving a payout are simpler and quicker than traditional insurance. In Zambia, the agricultural sector employs 48% of the working population (World Bank 2018). Risk management can contribute to reducing poverty in rural areas by providing a source of income even in the event of a bad season. Index insurance can be an effective risk management solution, as it meets both the regulator's quality standards and the insurance company's profitability measures that are key for the adoption of any insurance product.

Patel and Martin Libinga, the Zambia insurance regulator, attended the same World Bank Group-led training as the Nigerian regulator, where they were able to gain a solid understanding of index insurance and its potential for growth in Sub-Saharan Africa. Armed with this technical knowledge – including product design and pricing – and decision-making skills, Patel returned to Zambia, where he successfully convinced the Mayfair's board to expand their agricultural insurance business. A performance-based grant from GIIF, to help with the initial set-up cost, gave Mayfair an incentive to invest their own capital. With the help of the insurance regulator, Mayfair also convinced the Government of Zambia to bundle index insurance with an input subsidy programme offered by the government to farmers. This public–private partnership allowed Mayfair to underwrite index insurance to cover 900,000 farmers in time for the November 2017 season, an encouraging result given that Zambia's population in 2018 was estimated at around 17 million. After the 2017 season, over 412,000 farmers qualified for payouts. In 2019, around one million additional farmers were insured, and around 216,000 farmers were to receive payouts following a second season of drought in the country.

CONCLUSIONS

Both case studies demonstrate how capacity building can have a positive impact on the creation of sustainable insurance markets in Sub-Saharan Africa. Long-term sustainability will require insurance companies and other stakeholders to develop local product-design capacity, making them more cost-efficient (they will not have to rely on international product design services). They will also be able to use their local knowledge and insights to develop and offer innovative products that are specifically suited to Sub-Saharan African markets.

Insurance is increasingly recognized as an effective development instrument that contributes to both accelerating economic growth and reducing poverty. Insurance provides financial protection for low-income households and micro, small, and medium enterprises; it builds resilience in communities, helps mitigate the risks of natural disasters, mobilizes savings, and accelerates long-term investment into strategic sectors; it frees up fiscal space on national balance sheets and sustains the efforts of development policy agendas, such as food security and housing market development. Given the multi-dimensional benefits of the insurance sector, it is crucial that the international development community and governments prioritize the development of a strong insurance sector as part of their financial sector development agenda.

Several demand-side and supply-side barriers need to be addressed to develop sustainable insurance markets in Sub-Saharan Africa. Demand-side barriers include affordability (or price), income and wealth level, lack of trust in insurers, and low levels of financial literacy, while supply-side barriers include regulations, high transaction costs, and inadequate technical abilities. Regulations and government policies must be enablers, not barriers, to insurance market development, which means building the capacity of regulators to evaluate different and innovative insurance products. Risk-modelling capacity building should also target insurance companies, to ensure that the collective behaviour of insurance companies and regulators leads to the development of sustainable products and markets.

To achieve enduring results, governments, insurers, and development partners need to collaborate and drive synergies, to ensure that insurance serves all segments of society. By supporting insurers to capitalize on the technological trends reshaping the industry, households and businesses across all economic segments will have access to quality and affordable insurance, and governments will have a unique opportunity to leverage insurance to advance a wide range of development objectives.

BIBLIOGRAPHY

Alliance for a Green Revolution in Africa (AGRA) (2018) *Annual Report 2018,* p.9. Available at http://agra.org/ar-2018/wp-content/uploads/2019/07/AGRA-Annual-Report-2018.pdf

Arena, M. (2006) Does insurance market activity promote economic growth? A cross-country study for industrialized and developing countries. *Policy Research Working Paper 4098,* Washington DC: World Bank.

Baraka, M, Loots, C., Hougaard, C. & Bennett, E. (2018) *Strong Foundations: A framework for assessing the role of the insurance sector in property market development,* Cape Town and Nairobi: CENFRI (Centre for Financial Regulation and Inclusion), FSD Africa, and DFID (UK Department for International Dvelopment). Available at https://cenfri.org/wp-content/uploads/2018/06/Strong-foundations_Cenfri-FSDA_June-2018-1.pdf.

CENFRI (Centre for Financial Regulation and Inclusion) and FSD Africa (2017) *Funding the Frontier: the link between inclusive insurance markets, growth, and poverty reduction.* Available at https://cenfri.org/documents/microinsurance/2017/Funding%20the%20frontier.pdf.

Chantarat, S., Mude, A.G., Barrett, C.B. & Turvey, C.G. (2017) Welfare impacts of index insurance in the presence of a poverty trap. *World Development 94* (June): 119–38.

Gine, X. (2009) The promise of index insurance. *Finance and PSD Impact March, No. 3.* Washington, DC: World Bank. https://openknowledge.worldbank.org/handle/10986/11835.

KPMG (2017) *Microinsurance in Africa.* Available at https://assets.kpmg.com/content/dam/kpmg/za/pdf/2017/08/microinsurance-in-africa.pdf

Lester, R. (2009) *Consumer Protection Insurance,* Washington DC: The World Bank. Available at http://siteresources.worldbank.org/EXTFINANCIALSECTOR/Resources/282884-1242281415644/Consumer_protection_Insurance.pdf

Lester, R. (2014) Insurance and inclusive growth. *Policy Research Working Paper 6943.* Washington DC: World Bank. Available at https://openknowledge.worldbank.org/bitstream/handle/10986/18830/WPS6943.pdf?sequence=1.

Lloyds (n.d.) *Insurance in developing countries: exploring opportunities in microinsurance.* Washington DC: Lloyds.

Mapfumo, S., Groenendaal, H. & Dugger, C.D. (2017) Risk modeling for appraising named peril index insurance products: a Guide for Practitioners. *Directions in Development Series.* Washington, DC: World Bank.

Medina, L., Jonelis, A. & Cangul, M. (2017) The informal economy in Sub-Saharan Africa: size and determinants. *IMF Working Paper WP/17/156.*

Msulwa, B., Loots, C., Hougaard, C., & Bennett, E. (2018) *Strong Foundations: A framework for assessing the role of the insurance sector in property market development.* Centre for Financial Regulation & Inclusion, Johannesburg.

Pollner, J.D. (1999) Using capital markets to develop private catastrophe insurance. *Viewpoint: Public Policy for the Private Sector, Note No. 197.* Washington DC: World Bank.

Signe, L. (2019) Africa's emerging economies to take the lead in consumer market growth. *Brookings.* Available at https://www.brookings.edu/blog/africa-in-focus/2019/04/03/africas-emerging-economies-to-take-the-lead-in-consumer-market-growth/ Accessed 3 April 2019.

Swiss Re Institute (2018) *Total Insurance Penetration – premiums as a % of GDP.* Available at http://www.sigma-explorer.com/

United Nations (UN) (2016) *The World's Cities in 2016 Data Booklet.* [Online] http://www.un.org/en/development/desa/population/publications/pdf/urbanization/the_worlds_cities_in_2016_data_booklet.pdf

United Nations Environment Programme (UNEP) (2015) Insurance 2030: Harnessing insurance for sustainable development. *Inquiry Working Paper 15/01.* Geneva: United Nations Environment Programme.

Von Peter, G., von Dahlen, S. & Saxena, S. (2012) Unmitigated disasters? New evidence on the macroeconomic cost of natural catastrophes. *BIS Working Papers No 394.* Bank for International Settlements.

Wesley, H. & Piccio, L. (2019) Across Africa, disaster risk finance is putting a resilient future within reach. Available at https://blogs.worldbank.org/nasikiliza/across-africa-disaster-risk-finance-is-putting-a-resilient-future-within-reach Accessed 1 October 2022.

World Bank (2018) Disaster risk management. Available at http://www.worldbank.org/en/topic/disasterriskmanagement/overview Accessed 22 July 2019.

5.

INNOVATIVE APPROACHES TO SUSTAINABLE HOUSING IN FOUR AFRICAN CITY-REGIONS: LESSONS FOR POST HABITAT III POLICY ENVIRONMENT

Ntombini Marrengane, Liza Cirolia, Kareem Ibrahim,
Deena Khalil, Margot Rubin, Taibat Lawanson & Omar Nagati

Innovation systems (IS) are often explored narrowly in the context of technological terms (Hanna 2016; Binz & Truffer 2017). However, IS can be conceptualized in broader terms and applied to Africa's structural transformation (Adesida et al. 2016). This chapter focuses on urbanization, which is radically shifting the development trajectory of the African continent. The world's 100 fastest urbanizing cities are in Africa – cities in this region are growing at 5% per annum, faster than any other region globally (UN-Habitat 2014). By 2040, it is estimated that 50% of the continent's population will be classified as urban (UN-Habitat 2010; Kariuki et al. 2013). These figures take on a more urgent meaning when juxtaposed with the seemingly intractable problems facing Africa's urban centres, such as insufficient access to decent shelter, the need for livelihoods, aging infrastructure and limited social protection. As the African continent enters its urban age (UN-Habitat 2008), what is needed is research to support policy formulation. And, more specifically, what is needed is urban research that centres IS ecosystem concepts within conversations about urban management.

This chapter draws from a larger comparative report on the four largest African city-regions, which are comprised of interdependent clusters of cities and towns in a single functional area, that explored a range of socioeconomic and built environment challenges. The attention is on the practices in place in these city-regions and the opportunities for IS. In doing so, the pressures and challenges in the continent's largest conurbations are identified, together with the critical areas for policy adjustment, while examining the innovations that have been adopted to govern and the extent to which an IS thinking can be applied beyond a technological focus. This chapter explores the linkages between IS theoretical grounding for new urban governance approaches. Moving away from the notion of cities purely as sites of innovation, it examines how IS can be used as a lens into the architecture of these city-regions with the purpose of creating opportunities for adaptations that align with the global drive for sustainable and resilient cities.

WHY CITY-REGIONS?

In a globally interconnected world, the rapid growth of African cities means more than an increased number of households and an expanding skyline. It also indicates, in select cases, a physical expansion combined with attributes that can yield productive clusters with the potential to connect to the global economy. These cities then become sites of social reproduction and new paradigms for political construction (Jonas & Moisio 2018; Pillay 2004). The catalytic economic activity observed in these urban spaces can create conditions for a functional and productive urban environment. However, these transitions are not automatic; they are the combination of increased economic activity, population and public investment in the built environment (Turok & McGranahan 2013). The ways in which these investments unfold take on greater importance in a policy environment influenced by global commitments such as Agenda 2030 (UNGA 2015) and the New Urban Agenda (NUA) (UNGA 2016), which foreground the potential of urbanization to support the development of an equitable, inclusive and sustainable global community. The NUA expressly positions the city-region as a mechanism to 'support the development of sustainable regional infrastructure projects that stimulate sustainable economic productivity, promoting equitable growth of regions across the urban-rural continuum' (UNGA 2016: 26). The equitable growth needed to address urban poverty and inequality is not optional. The New Climate Economy (NCE) recognises that effective responses to critical issues, such as resource scarcity and inequality, are not 'nice-to-haves' in growing urban centres but rather prerequisites to developing sustainable cities (NCE 2015, 2016, 2018). These requirements present both challenges and opportunities when positioned next to the critical factors evident in many African city-regions, such as unemployment, poverty, low levels of skills and rapid growth (Götz & Schäffler 2015).

Given the pressing nature of urbanization, what is the link between city-regions and innovations? Over the past decade, policy and academic research on the conditions in African cities has shifted radically. Until recently, the scholarship on cities and city-regions was based on the geographies of the global north (McFarlane 2010), while cities and city-regions of the global south (when considered) were represented as underdeveloped, poverty-stricken, and the locus of inequality, violence, and slums (Beall et al. 2014; Roy 2009; Davis 2006). However, more contemporary research reveals that the global south's cities and city-regions are in fact not only coping with a range of challenges, but also offering new paradigms for transforming the economic and political trajectories of the nation-states in which these city-regions are embedded.

What is striking about the contemporary literature is its emphasis on the flow of goods, services, people and information rather than on the physical manifestations of urban agglomerations (Castells 1996; Hall 2009). The discourse has expanded, as scholars and practitioners grapple with notions of governance and, at times, artificial arrangements used in the administration of these complex urban regions (Dittgen & Demissie 2017; Lawanson 2016; Nelles 2013; Tadamun 2016). The city-region is centred as an economic vehicle that both links nation-states and positions cities as important actors in regional and global economies (Greenberg 2010; Parilla & Trujillo 2018; Robinson 2002; Scott et al. 2001; Topham 2005).

In defining innovation as the evolution of institutions and systems, this chapter attempts to highlight contributions based on the experience of the four city-regions, as part of the larger conversation on innovation in the African context (Muchie 2016). In doing so, evidence is offered for the argument that 'cities and urban regions are not just mere containers for innovative activities – but actively involved in the generation of new ideas, new organizational forms and new enterprise' (Florida et al. 2017: 87). Urbanization is fundamentally changing the trajectory of the African continent, and it is crucial to reflect not only on the challenges but also on the experimentation taking place.

The four city-regions were chosen because they are the largest on the continent and offer an opportunity to examine the shared urban development and management challenges in functional city-regions.

- Addis Ababa, Ethiopia (AACR)

- Cairo, Egypt (CCR)

- Gauteng, South Africa (GCR)

- Lagos, Nigeria (LCR)

The focus on the emerging architecture of Africa city-regions reflects the existing fragmented and inefficient governance arrangements at work in many primate and secondary African cities. These cases also reveal how, in addition to managing the unrelenting pace of urbanization, urban policymakers must reconsider how informality and the growing demand for housing can be used as catalysts rather than viewed as problems to eradicate. The slow pace of governance adjustments in a dynamic environment highlights a need for new and imaginative thinking about urban management systems.

The chapter examines the institutional, political, and material realities influencing different city-region approaches to informality and affordable housing delivery, which are two key and interlinked challenges to urban development and management. It looks at to what extent the current city-region governance arrangements lend themselves to innovation processes and policies in the management of informality and delivery of adequate shelter.

DEFINING A CITY-REGION

An agreed definition of city-regions is elusive, in part because a city-region's actual spatial footprint and the extent of economic functions do not necessarily coincide with clear administrative boundaries (Dittgen & Rubin 2016). The city-region can be understood in three different ways:

- As a physical place – an urban formation firmly embedded in space whose clear edges are, however, often difficult (if not impossible) to define. A city-region often correlates with the province in which it is located, but parts of it can extend well beyond provincial boundaries to include areas that are highly dependent on economic opportunities located in the core. Apart from a purely geographic spatial interpretation, city-regions can also be framed through flows and systems that overlay or relate to physical space, such as road or water networks, proximity, travel distance, settlement patterns, transport, logistics corridors, firm networks and commuter patterns (Van Huyssteen et al. 2009).

- As a political project and/or the ideal of enhanced cooperative governance – highlighting the need for provincial and municipal authorities to improve collaboration. The aim of better internal cooperation has been largely informed by the ambitions of authorities to achieve a better global ranking and to enhance a competitive and comparative advantage with the outside world.

- As an academic proposition – mobilizing particular concepts around city-regions, such as new regionalism, new institutionalism, agglomeration economies (relative advantages and disadvantages), circulation and trade theory (Dittgen & Rubin 2016).

For the purposes of this chapter, the city-region is defined as 'a combination of territorial units' located at the subnational level and organized around 'a core city linked by functional ties to a hinterland'

(Rodríguez-Pose 2008: 1027). The nature of the linkages and the precise jurisdiction of the city-region are spatially and temporally dependent.

To identify the relevant lessons that city-regions can share requires drawing comparisons that are based on a sound understanding of their differences and similarities. Using data from global repositories such as the World Bank, a silhouette of urban data on the city-regions was constructed (Table 5.1).

Table 5.1: Comparative table on population, density, growth rate and structure

	Gauteng city-region (GCR)	Cairo city-region (CCR)	Lagos city-region (LCR)	Addis Ababa city-region (AACR)
Population	13.2m	19m	16–23m	3.5m
Population density	675 persons/ km^2, Joburg 2,900 persons/km^2	19,376 persons/km^2	2,500 persons/km^2 Lagos City 6,871 persons/km^2	5,165 persons/km^2
Growth rate	2.7%	2–3%	4–5%	4.8%
Structure	No formal structure – cities or province.	No official structure – three governorates	State data	Charter City – special city status in the Constitution

Source: Compiled by the authors.

The data in Table 5.1 offers a useful context to understand some of the basic similarities and differences among the city-regions.

- Cairo and Johannesburg have similar economies and structures.

- City-regions tend to have populations of more than ten million people, although Addis Ababa is closer in size to regional hubs, such as Nairobi and Dar es Salaam, than the other city-regions.

- City-regions tend to be densely populated, although Gauteng has by far the lowest population density.

- City-regions have very different growth rates and governance structures. This substantially affects the types of interventions needed and available.

Building on Healey's (2009) argument that context matters and cannot be simply transplanted from northern to southern geographies, the following section presents the realities of evolving city-regions in Africa, and the variations in governance arrangements, institutional and spatial configurations.

CITY-REGION CASE STUDIES

Gauteng city-region

The Gauteng city-region (GCR) sits in Gauteng, South Africa's smallest but most densely populated province, which arose in the late nineteenth century gold rush. Today, it accounts for 1.5% of South Africa's land mass and 25% of its population (Stats SA 2019). Between 2001 and 2011, the province's population grew by an annual average of 2.68% (GPG 2016). The province's population is expanding both naturally and as a result of migration to the region, mostly because of a perception of better work opportunities both from within (34.5%) and outside (9.5%) South Africa. According to Stats SA (2019), the province's population was 14.7 million in 2018. The GCR is variably defined, with the most narrow definition including the City of Johannesburg Metropolitan Municipality, City of Tshwane Metropolitan Municipality, Ekurhuleni Metropolitan Municipality, Sedibeng District Municipality and West Rand District Municipality.

The 1996 Constitution outlines the governance arrangements for all levels of government in South Africa, articulating the roles and responsibilities of each branch and sphere of government. These arrangements include the devolution of power to local government as seen in the GCR, which comprises numerous local authorities and a single provincial authority. Functions meant for local government cannot be taken away, but national and provincial government can add functions to local government (Steytler 2005). The three metropolitan municipalities that make up the majority of the GCR are single-tier municipalities with their own elected legislative councils and executive powers vested in a mayor appointed from the majority party in council. Key municipal functions include municipal planning, municipal health (mainly clinic services), municipal public transport, building control, sports and recreation, water and sanitation, electricity reticulation, municipal roads, and street trading (RSA 1996).

At the same time, the Constitution gives provinces exclusive competency over a limited number of areas (e.g. ambulances, roads, and recreation) but assigns concurrent competency with national government

Figure 5.1: GCR administrative boundaries (local and provincial) overlaid with conceptual view based on functionality

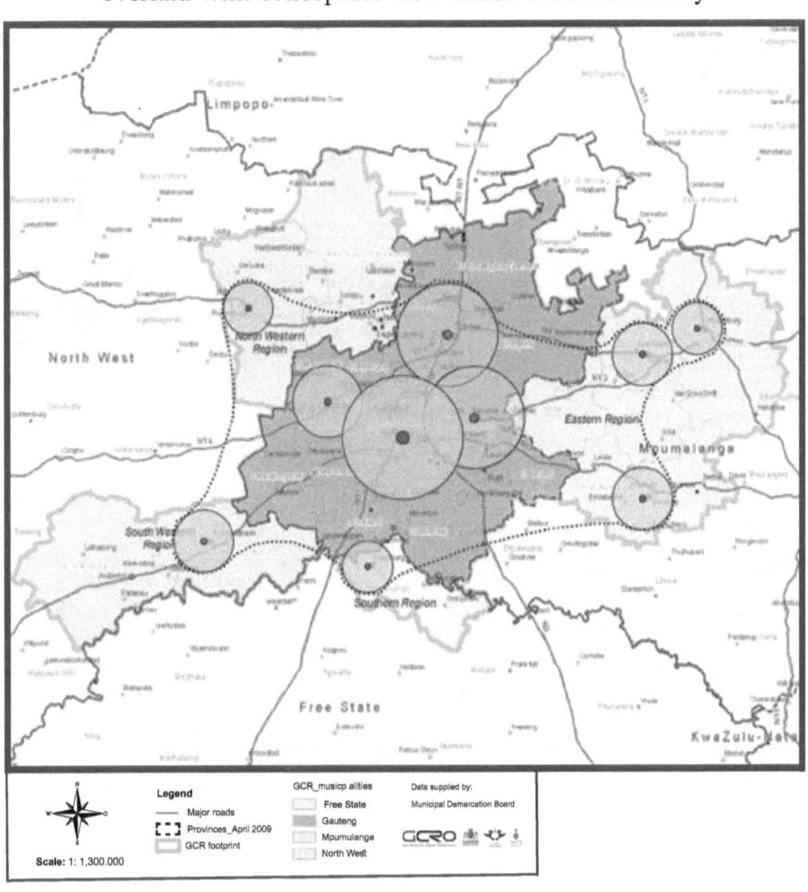

Source: Mubiwa & Annegarn (2013: 5).

over a far wider domain, including education (excluding universities), housing/human settlements, health services, welfare services, environmental management, and public transport (RSA 1996). Provincial government is largely funded by grants from national government, with the bulk of provincial budgets going to health and education. Although the Constitution outlines many of the municipal functions, some are not clearly defined (Steytler 2005), while having concurrent functions shared by both the province and municipalities creates ambiguity and contributes to friction between the spheres of government. Although the idea of a city-region has purchase across the different spheres of government, the approach to governance has been pragmatic and has focused on cultivating cooperation around the National Development

Figure 5.2: Gauteng city-region (GCR) governance structure

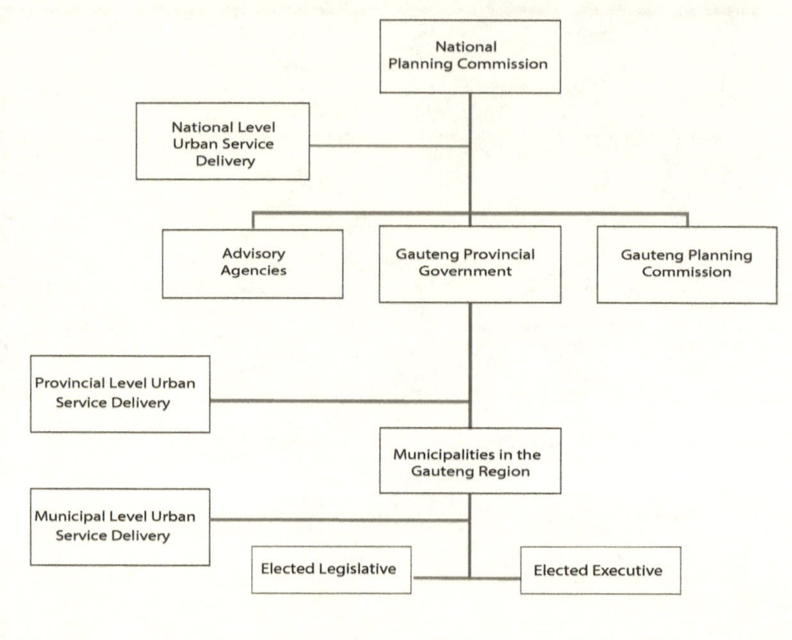

Plan (NPC 2016) and its priorities. In taking incremental steps towards cooperation, the GCR has put into practice the call by the NUA to develop a shared vision and enhance coordination (UN-Habitat 2016).

Cairo city-region

The Cairo city-region (CCR) has a population of more than 25 million (about a quarter of Egypt's population) and is Egypt's largest urban area (UNDESA 2019). It has grown incrementally from a small town to what is now Egypt's economic, political, administrative, and cultural capital. The CCR is made up of independent settlements that developed during various Islamic dynasties and, over time, merged into a single urban entity (AlSayyad 1991). However, no single definition of the CCR exists (UN-Habitat 2011). Estimates of the size of the CCR range from 3,133 km^2 to 4,367 km^2 (Figure 5.3). Part of the difference is the result of the different criteria used when defining the territory (GOPP 2012; UN Habitat 2016; UNDESA 2019).

Figure 5.3: Map of Greater Cairo

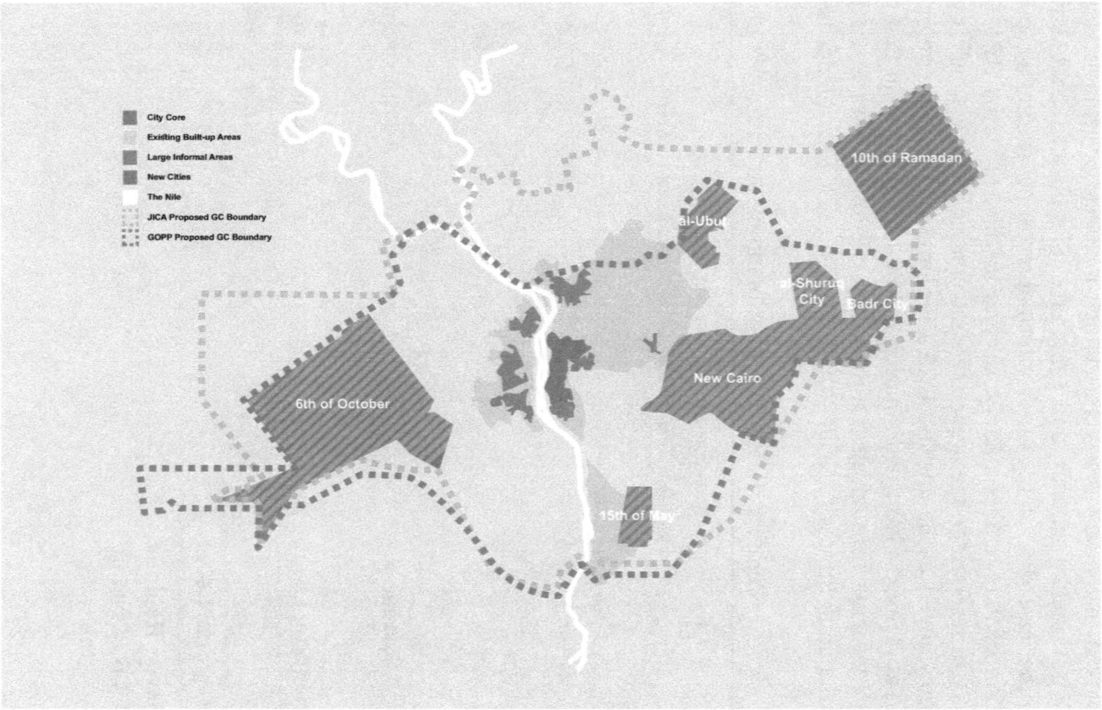

Source: © TCID.

Despite the lack of agreed physical boundaries, the CCR is the economic hub of Egypt, producing 31% of the country's economic output (GOPP 2012). The CCR is also home to 83% of all foreign establishments, as well as most incoming private and public investment and business (Sims 2010). Like many economies, most of the CCR's workforce is employed in the services sector, which includes government administration, financial services, and commerce. Significantly, and similar to the other case studies, the CCR's informal sector constitutes a significant portion of its overall economy, despite its 'illegal' status (UN-Habitat 2016). In response to the unplanned and chaotic growth, which is widely acknowledged as hampering CCR's regional and global competitiveness, government launched a national decentralization plan that covers the city-region through its 'Cairo Future Vision: Greater Cairo Urban Development Strategy' (GOPP 2009). The Future Vision intends to make

Figure 5.4: The Egyptian planning structure

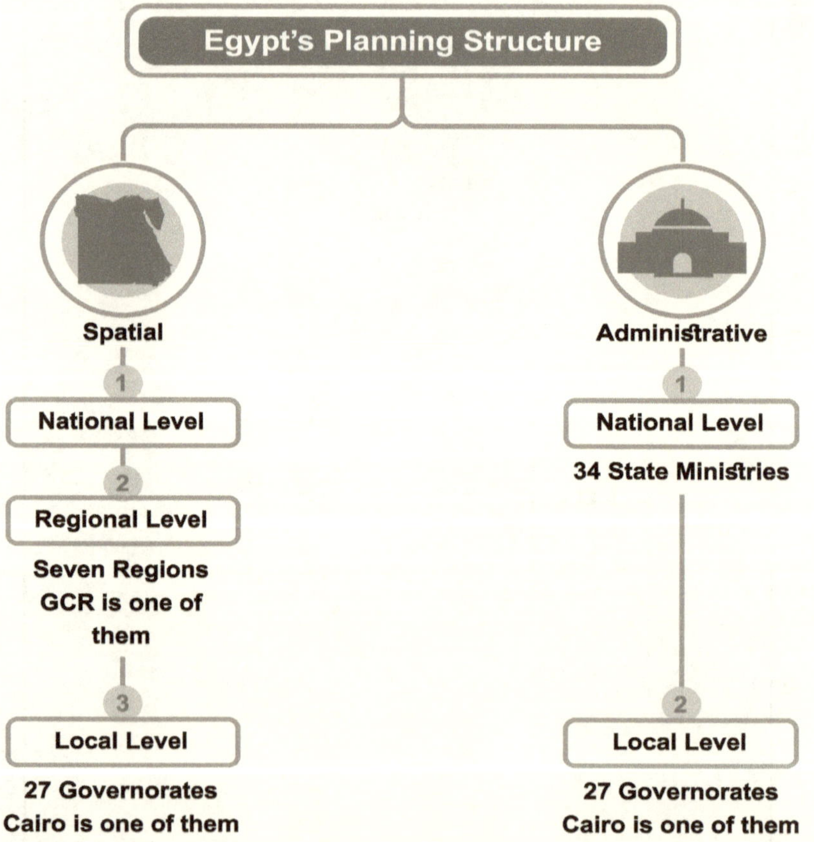

Source: © TCID.

Figure 5.5: The Governorate entities in the Egyptian local administration

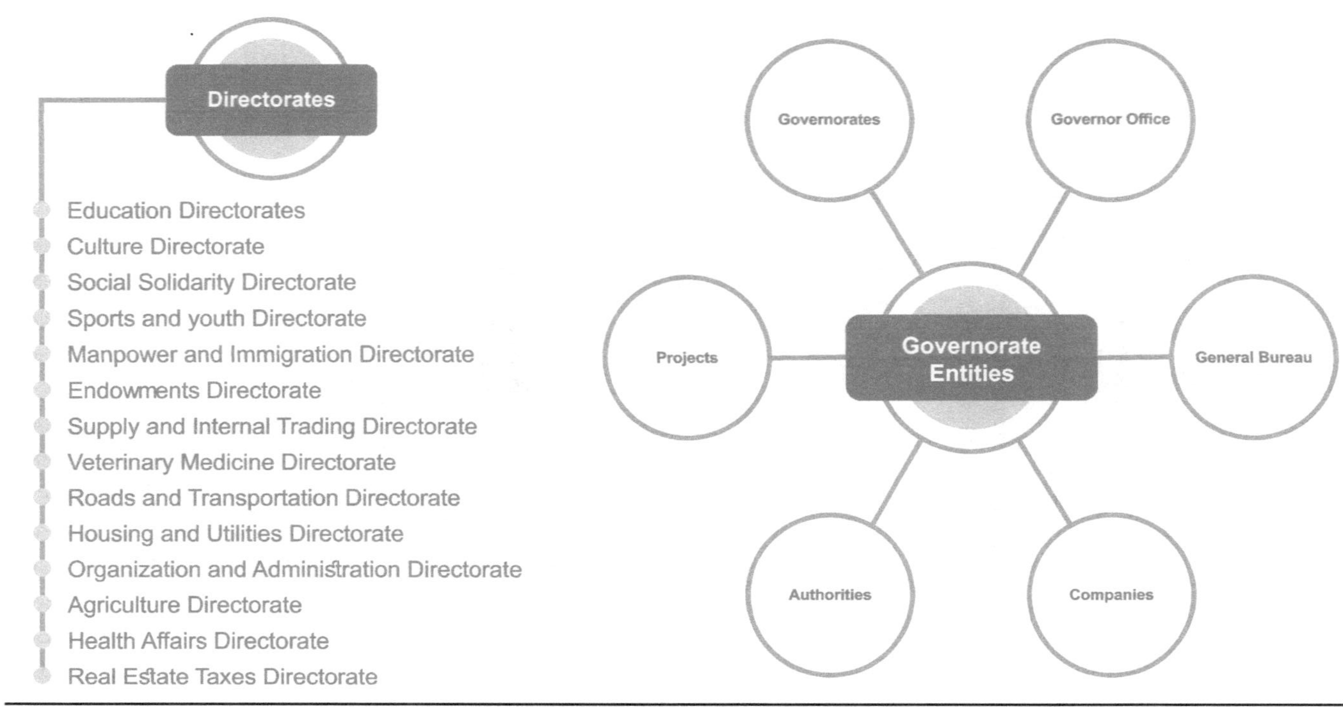

Source: © TCID.

huge capital investments in developing new urban communities outside of Cairo, under themes such as the 'smart village', the 'medical city', and the 'government district'. Aimed at attracting people and private investment to these areas, and thus reducing the city's population, the belief is that the city could then gradually be improved through further investments in heritage, green spaces, pedestrian mobility routes, and other 'quality of life' projects:

> The [Greater Cairo Region] needs to encourage new development centres outside its borders to attract population, redistribute population within its borders, direct GC [Greater Cairo] future population growth to its new urban communities, provide a better standard of living for all segments of residents, and meet the requirements of expected change in the population's consumer patterns (Ministry of Housing, Utilities, and Urban Communities, 2012: 46).

The development strategy for the CCR, as contained in the Cairo Future Vision, is to invest in and focus on the knowledge economy (GOPP 2009). This plan aligns with the region's growing information technology industries, spurred by the presence of many leading Arabic-language software companies in the CCR.

As Figures 5.4 and 5.5 show, the governance arrangements for the CCR are complex. The structure incorporates 31 districts and three separate local-level governorates: Cairo, Giza and al-Qalyubiyya. Although these governorates are administratively independent of one another, they are physically intertwined, function together as one urban core, and abide by the same legislation. The highly centralized nature of Egypt's public administration is clearly reflected in local governance (Nada 2014), with local administration systems primarily run by officials appointed by central government (Sims 2014). One example of this is the administration of the seven new satellite cities located within CCR. The New Urban Community Authority (NUCA) administers the cities, although the cities are located within a governorate with urban management capacity.

According to Law No. 59 of 1979, NUCA manages the new cities but, once they are developed, their administration should be transferred to the corresponding governorate (NUCA, nd). However, such transfer of power is yet to happen. The expanding and fragile network of agencies tasked with service delivery in the CCR is an example of the disconnect between the global compacts that promote urban sustainability and the challenge of moulding a local governance ecosystems that can meet that goal.

Figure 5.6: Lagos city-region

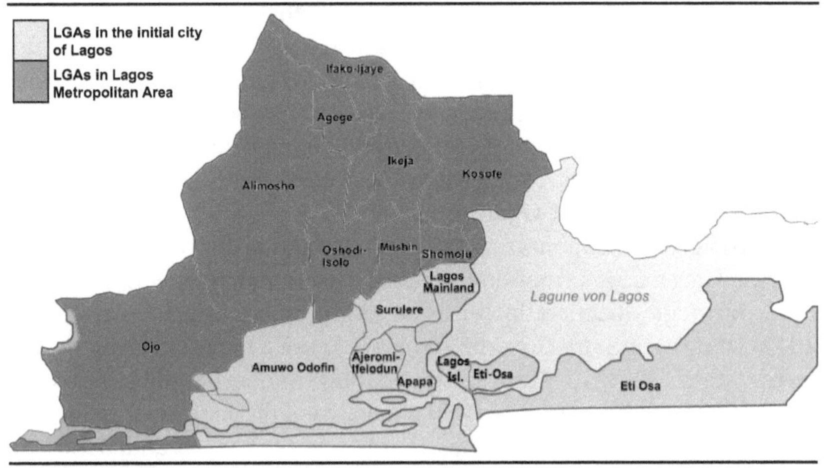

Source: Creative Commons.

Lagos city-region

The Lagos city-region (LCR) is arguably the fastest-growing city in Africa, although its exact population is disputed. According to the last interim census, its estimated population is about nine million people (National

Figure 5.7: Lagos city-region (LCR) governance network

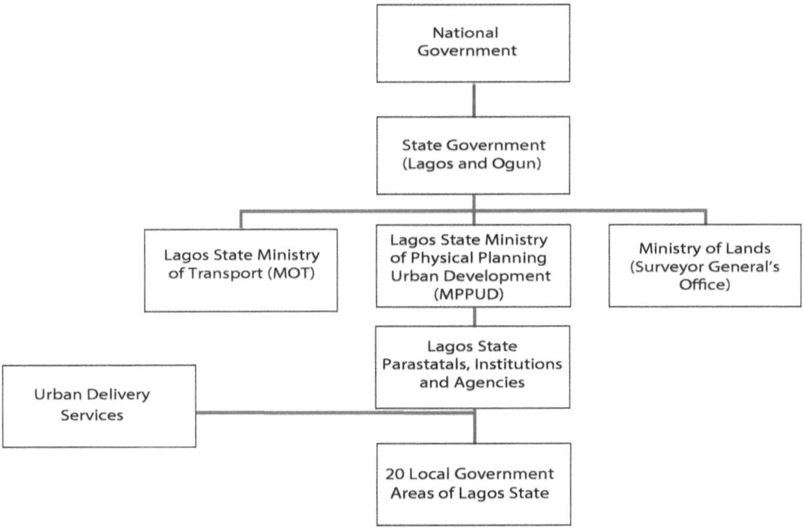

Source: Filani (2012).

Population Commission 2007), while other federal and international sources estimate the population to be between 14 and 17 million residents (UN 2016). The territory recognized as the LCR is also ambiguously defined. At its smallest, it covers 16 urban local authorities (Lagos Metropolitan Area). However, researchers and policymakers often include the entire territory of Lagos state, which contains an additional 41 local council development areas, as well as peri-urban settlements in the adjacent state of Ogun.

The Lagos Metropolitan Area alone accounts for 7% of Nigeria's GDP and over 50% of national manufacturing employment. Given the LCR's strategic location in terms of shipping, rail and flight (Filani 2012), the Lagos State Government aims to raise manufacturing's share of the state's GDP to 40%, by developing and expanding industrial zones. Although historically cast in a negative light because of crime and lagging infrastructure, Lagos has more recently been branded Africa's

Figure 5.8: Proposed LCR governance structure

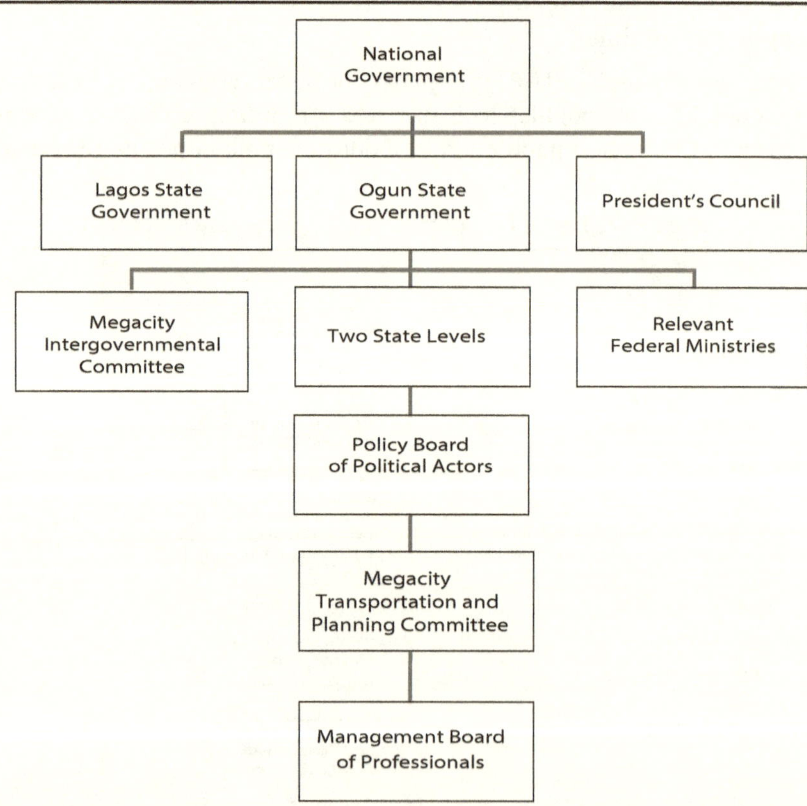

Source: Filani (2012).

'Big Apple', with the 'One Lagos' campaign showing how the LCR views itself as a hub of Nigerian and urban culture. By encouraging entrepreneurism and foreign investment, the LCR has taken steps to expand its economic options beyond the oil industry (Walt 2014; Filani 2012). Critically, unlike the city-regions discussed earlier, Lagos does not have a regional city government. The governance structure of the functional area of the LCR differs in important ways from (for example) Cairo. The Nigerian Constitution recognizes three distinct levels of government – national, state, and local government – each with defined spheres of jurisdiction and constitutional functions. However, under the current governance architecture, some of the LCR's functional areas are not formally recognized, making it difficult to effectively deliver basic services. This fact complicates the comparison between the four regions and is also emblematic of the different regulatory and policy regimes across the continent. Such inconsistency is not limited to concept of city-region and makes learning from regional practices challenging.

Addis Ababa city-region

The Addis Ababa city-region (AACR) differs in several key respects from the other three city-regions discussed. First, it is significantly smaller, with a population of 3.5 million, of which over 90% is concentrated within a 10-km radius of the city centre (Voukas & Palmer 2012; Gebeyehu & Takano 2007). Yet its population also represents nearly a quarter of Ethiopia's total urban population (DFID 2015). And, despite its relatively modest population, the AACR is one of the world's fastest growing cities, with a 2015 growth rate of 4.8% (DFID 2015). This is interesting, as Ethiopia remains predominantly rural, with less than 20% of the population in cities (KPMG 2017). Known as the 'diplomatic capital' of Africa, the AACR is home to the African Union and the United Nations Economic Commission for Africa. The AACR is designated as a 'city-state' and is also one of two charter cities in Ethiopia (DFID 2015; Goodfellow 2015) – a charter city is an urban jurisdiction whose governing system is defined by the city's own charter document rather than by the federal state. Therefore, instead of being officially called a city-region, the city of Addis Ababa is referred to as a 'charter city', 'city-state', or 'Metropolis (capital) city' (DFID 2015; Goodfellow 2015; NCE 2015). This is also because in Ethiopia, 'region' refers to the country's nine states and two charter cities which make up the jurisdiction. The precision about nomenclature is important, as Ethiopia's Constitution outlines Addis Ababa's special status, stating that both regional authorities and charter cities have the right to self-governance. As such, the Addis Ababa City Government does not fall under any federal authority and enjoys a significant degree of self-rule and autonomy. Unlike other Ethiopian cities, which are required to report to their respective federal authorities, Addis Ababa City Government is accountable only to the Ministry of Federal Affairs (DFID 2015).

The policy literature on Addis Ababa consistently notes high levels of local government authority in comparison to many cities in Africa (DFID 2015; Jones et al. 2015). However, since 1991 and the overthrow of Ethiopia's military regime, Addis Ababa has, like other city-regions presented here, had the opportunity to create its own political, institutional and legal frameworks. This is particularly notable because political power in Ethiopia is mostly highly centralized, with local governments

Figure 5.9: Urban services management in Ethiopia

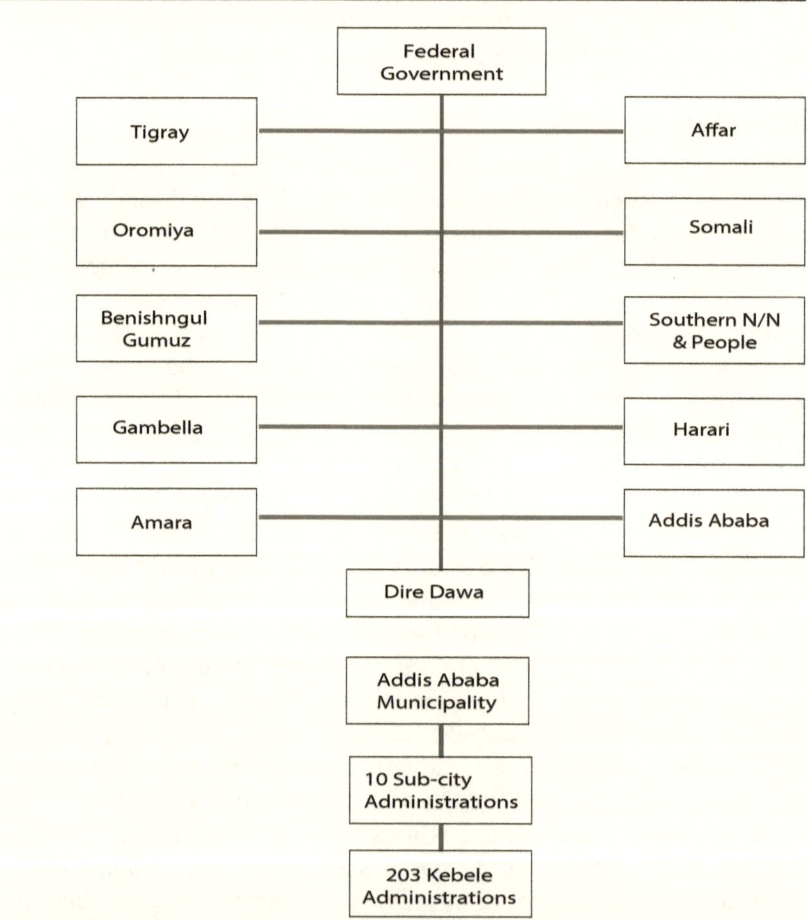

Source: World Bank Baseline report on solid waste management in Ethiopia.

Figure 5.10: Map of the Addis Ababa Metro Region

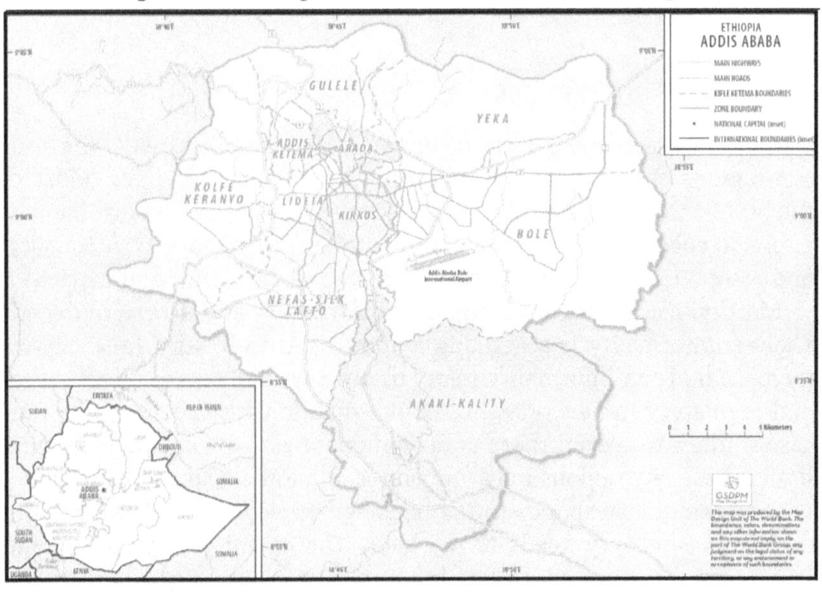

Source: World Bank (2015).

tending to represent the central government, rather than local communities (UN-Habitat 2008). Administratively, the core of the AACR, Addis Ababa is made up of ten *woredas* or 'sub-cities', which are administrative jurisdictions consisting of groups of *kebeles*, or lower-level administration (Goodfellow 2015).

Over the past 15 years, the AACR has experienced rapid economic growth, largely due to high levels of public-sphere investment in infrastructure and land development (Clapham 2018; World Bank 2015b). Despite this growth, the AACR has a higher unemployment rate and a lower economic growth rate than other urban areas in Ethiopia, suggesting that it could be losing its primacy (World Bank 2015b). As foreign investment concentrates on securing access to Ethiopia's agricultural (and other) exports in the medium- and long-term Ethiopia's secondary towns and cities are also growing (Lamson-Hall et al. 2019). Leveraging and guiding this trend is the Growth and Transformation Plan (GTP), a national government's polycentric growth strategy that encourages the growth of secondary cities. The GTP's agenda is investment in secondary cities, particularly in manufacturing, and could prove very successful. However, it is important to note that, internationally, investment in secondary cities rarely has a substantial impact on the primary cities. During the GTP's first three years, Ethiopia's already robust industrial sector registered an average growth rate of 16.7%, with much of this growth concentrated in Addis Ababa.

CITY-REGION CHALLENGES

Despite carrying the mantle of engines of national growth, the four city-regions share numerous urban development challenges. Most of the problems stem from fragmented governance systems, which hamper efforts to cohesively address migration, urbanization, poverty, inequality, and resource scarcity (e.g. constraints on budgets, land, and capacity).

Most critical are **the challenges of informality and access to decent shelter**. Informality is a defining feature of African cities (and city-regions). The term informality refers to practices outside of a city's legal and regulatory frameworks, but its presentation varies among the four case studies. However, there are commonalities. For example, informality in these city-regions may function as a parallel (and often interwoven) system that responds to the housing, employment, transportation, and service-delivery needs of the poor. The extent of informality and how the state views and treats informality are both key to understanding city-regions. The challenge of how to 'plan with' and 'plan for' informality in African cities is examined below, with a particular focus on informal settlements.

Relative to the other three city-regions, the GCR has comparatively few challenges with informality, owing in part to massive investments in state housing made possible through the post-apartheid redistributive programmes aimed at providing housing for previously disadvantaged communities. Yet despite these investments, 19% of the GCR population still resides in informal settlements, which are dominated by single-storey structures, and 7.8% in 'backyard' accommodation. Therefore, with over 800,000 people living in what is considered inadequate accommodation in need of better options, informality will remain an issue for the foreseeable future.

Similarly, informal settlements are a key challenge for the CCR. With over 67% of the population estimated to live in informal areas (Sims 2010), informality is the norm rather than the exception for CCR's urban population, which is anticipated to reach 30 million by 2050 (GOPP 2009). Over three decades of increased housing costs have forced millions of low- and mid-income Egyptians into informal housing. Here informal housing takes the form of multi-storey dwellings, represents around 40% of the built-up area (Sims 2010) and accommodates 60–70% of the CCR's total urban population. The combination of unaffordable alternatives and concentrated settlements on the banks of the Nile has had consequences:

- Policies focusing development on mega-housing projects and new cities catering to wealthier groups are partly responsible for the lack of legal access to land and infrastructure for low- and mid-income groups. This has resulted in high vacancy rates in the CCR (as well as other Egyptian cities), with 25% of Cairo's housing units vacant (32% in Giza) according to data extracted from the national census (CAPMAS 2006).

- In the absence of affordable housing, hundreds of thousands of people resort to creating a housing alternative by extending the urban fabric on to neighbouring agricultural land or squatting on state-owned desert land on the city periphery. The government has largely ignored these illegal expansions, which have resulted in unsafe settlements.

In the Lagos city-region (LCR), the proliferation of informal settlements is one of the most enduring spatial manifestations of poverty and urbanization (Morakinyo et al. 2012). The city of Lagos has expanded from its original lagoon setting to encompass a vast expanse of mostly low-rise developments, including as many as two hundred different slums (Gandy 2006). Over two-thirds of the population live in informal settlements, with inadequate access to infrastructure facilities and urban services (World Bank 2006). Informality in the LCR is not limited to shelter but includes transport and other businesses that currently employ 50–70% of the population despite unsupportive regulatory frameworks.

In contrast, the AACR's informality is concentrated in one sector. In the AACR, informal accommodation has become a defining feature of city centre and surrounding peri-urban areas (DFID 2015). According to some estimates, nearly 80% of residents live in informal accommodation in urban areas (World Bank 2015). Not all informal housing is inadequate (World Bank 2015a) nor is all government-developed housing adequate, with some of these latter developments having gradually merged into 'slums' (World Bank 2015). At least part of the explanation is the difficulty in accessing land through the complicated land lease system. However, without the capacity to redesign the allocation system at local government level, demand continues to outstrip supply (DFID 2015).

STEPS TOWARDS INNOVATION

As demonstrated, the political and economic environment is significantly different across the city-regions. However, the city-regions have marshalled a range of responses that follow a similar pattern. Although the city-regions may have different approaches to managing shelter provision and informality, some of their creative responses to the growing housing demand offer ideas on ways to push the boundaries of existing policy options.

Promoting affordable housing

In South Africa, Gauteng has made impressive strides in addressing the need for affordable housing, most directly by developing affordable mortgage housing for households in the 'gap market'. The Finance Linked Individual Subsidy Programme (FLISP) is a state guarantee system for people in the low- to middle-income sector. Using its policy tools, the state has forced commercial banks to sign the Finance Charter, which commits them to give loans to households in lower-income categories. Aside from these financial instruments, there has also been support at city and provincial level for well-located mixed-income and mixed-use housing developments in partnership with private developers. All housing market price points are catered for within the developments, which are aimed at addressing housing provision as well as social and economic integration. The GCR also intends developing inclusionary housing instruments as an additional way of providing well-located affordable housing and advancing better land-use value-capture instruments.

Upgrading informal settlements/building new cities

In the CCR, the state has mixed two different approaches. Initially, in 2008, the central government established the Informal Settlements Development Fund (ISDF) in response to the continued migration and expanding informal settlements. The purpose of the ISDF (2013) was to upgrade informal settlements in urban areas after first mapping geologically unsafe sections of the city. However, the ISDF's policies contributed to the continued growth of informal areas. After completing the mapping in 2013, the state shifted its strategy for informal areas to relocating public housing projects in neighbouring satellite cities and, in 2014, created the Ministry of Urban Renewal and Informal Settlements (MURIS). Under MURIS, housing provision was centred on 'human-oriented' development. With input from civil society and independent practitioners, a new vision was forged for providing adequate shelter. The outcome was an approach that prioritized in-situ development over relocation and the disruption of residents' livelihoods. However, one year later, the Ministry was dissolved for undisclosed reasons. In a climate of political instability, the state has not indicated any significant shifts in policy and continues to work with civil society to formulate options to meet the urban housing demand. Tangible results that can be adequately evaluated are not yet available, due to the early stages of the new administration. The state is simultaneously continuing to plan the delivery and construction of new cities in order to deconcentrate the core of the CCR. These new cities have been under construction for over thirty years but have not achieved the target populations because high rents and housing costs make them unaffordable to most low- and middle-income households. Despite this record of failure, the state has also launched plans for a new capital city 60 km outside of Cairo to accommodate the private sector, public administration authorities and to decrease Cairo's current density (Aljazeera News 2015).

Encouraging homeownership

In terms of housing provision, the LCR adopted an approach that focuses on a Home Ownership Mortgage Scheme (HOMS). Inaugurated in 2014, the Lagos HOMS is a government initiative specifically designed to address the challenges of the housing deficit and low home-ownership rate, by providing accessible mortgage finance to encourage and support home ownership among first-time buyers. The project targets the working population, particularly those either working in the formal sector or who can show evidence of regular income and pay an upfront deposit, followed by ten years of monthly instalments. Lagos HOMS provides a mortgage facility at an interest rate of 9.5%, which is considerably lower than the prevailing market rate of 20–22%. Beneficiaries are expected to pay 30% equity and the remaining 70% in equal instalments over ten years at 9.5% interest. Within a period of about one year (between February 2014, when the project was officially inaugurated, and May 2015, when there was a change of government), Lagos HOMS had completed 1,126 housing units; and another 7,000 units in different categories were at varying stages of completion, with expected completion within two to three years (Agunbiade & Olajide 2016). As of May 2015, 630 people had been selected, through a combination of qualification and a lottery, to be part of the programme. However, not a single housing unit has been allocated to date, and construction activities have also slowed down.

Transforming informal, unplanned settlements

In the AACR, the city government is attempting to address its shelter crisis by developing projects to transform informal and unplanned settlements into high-density, mixed-use hubs. The redevelopment is aligned to a master plan that includes the scaled relocation of informal settlements and their residents. Most of these programmes involve relocating residents who currently reside on the redevelopment land (DFID 2015). Recognizing the need for housing in rapidly urbanizing areas, the government introduced an ambitious programme aimed at developing the country's urban housing ownership market (World Bank 2015). In 2006, Addis Ababa was the first city to introduce the Integrated Housing Development Programme (IHDP), which promotes the mass-scale production of 'condominium housing'. In the project's first phase, the state built over 170,000 units in Addis Ababa, and another 50,000 units per year are planned for the second and current phase (World Bank 2015). As the city-state must cover the cost of infrastructure, services and part of the top-structure construction, the national government facilitated bank development loans to Addis Ababa as bridge finance. The state then offered subsidies both for the construction of the housing (development finance) and for mortgages (end-user finance) (World Bank 2015). The development finance opportunities offered by the programme contributed to improving the local construction sector (Ministry of Works and Urban Development 2008). However, one challenge is that the IHDP is not able to cater to the needs of its target group of low-income households: 'lower-income households may find even the smallest and most-subsidized condominiums unaffordable' (World Bank 2015: 32). Another challenge is that the condominium housing developers receive land through direct allocation, and so are not incentivized to use urban land efficiently (World Bank 2015).

PATTERNS EMERGING FROM THE CITY-REGIONS

All the city-regions face the challenges of affordability and the need to find creative ways to address the problem of housing, in which challenges of informality and infrastructure combine. A pattern across all four cases is the focus on homeownership and new-build development. However, given the land constraints and the need for flexibility and responsiveness that poorer households rely on in order to survive, such an approach is not that useful and (in the case of GCR) reinforces existing paradigms.

Another pattern is the appetite for resolving governance issues by creating new entities and generating new plans without learning from the costly mistakes of the past. The CCR is the best example of this practice. Critically, the four city-regions do not engage effectively with informality generally, and informal shelter in particular. By and large, the city-regions act unilaterally to clamp down on unauthorized housing construction and the unregulated expansion of settlements. However, this is an opportunity that is being missed, given that a significant portion of their population is informally housed – as much as 60–70% in the case of the CCR (Sims 2010). If city-regions and by extension national governments have truly committed to the NUA vision of promoting inclusive and sustainable cities with space for all, then these approaches must be reconsidered (UN-Habitat 2016).

This section has provided some insight into the governance landscape in the continent's fastest-growing urban centres and pointed to the pressures for city-regions to position themselves as globally competitive and well managed. The opportunity to learn from these city-regions comes from looking at the patterns of response, whether successful or not. In this way, it is possible to gauge the space for new conceptions of governance and innovation within existing political and fiscal limits. While this perspective is not as compelling as the Africa rising narrative or 'best practice', it does say something important about the value of generating and testing new ways to meet local development goals while aligning with global compacts. These deliberate steps towards innovation, while at the same time seeking to actively manage the urban challenges at hand, bring into focus what Adesida et al. (2016: 362) refer to as 'incremental innovation'.

CONCLUSION

African city-regions are transforming how urban management is conceived and implemented in the 21st century. This research, into Cairo in Egypt, Addis Ababa in Ethiopia, Lagos in Nigeria and Gauteng in South Africa, illuminates both the starkly different urban realities and the common need for sustainable solutions. The urban settlements, which form the core of each city-region, are a dynamic and unordered collection of residential, industrial and commercial spaces that resist attempts to manage expansion and regulate growth. Instead these settlements continue, as they have for decades, to expand and extend the urban footprint without the sanction of the state. In this context, the emerging and established governance institutions must consider new ways to harness urban growth and demographic shifts for the creation of sustainable and resilient cities.

In reimagining the future of this continent, these case studies make clear that policy and practice must evolve if the development dividend is to be realized in a sustainable way that leverages urban growth. Just as there is no one architecture among the cases presented, it is important to keep in mind that broad principles for instilling innovative policy frameworks may be more useful than creating entities in a weak governance environment without constitutional mandates, political authority or financial autonomy.

Practically, the findings suggest that the development and effective management of city-regions are less about developing a new sphere of government and more about:

- **Cross-boundary dynamics**: City-region dynamics must be engaged, meaning the real structure and flows of land markets, labour markets, movement systems, and the economy. Unfortunately, much of the research into city-regions does not take these dynamics seriously.

- **Building appropriately scaled operational entities**: While planning for city-regions is important, it is crucial to develop entities that can operate across municipal boundaries and respond to flexible 'functional' changes. This is particularly true when implementing large-scale developments.

- **Confronting deeply political and territorial challenges**: In all cases, city-regions are highly political entities because of the complex and deeply territorial nature of urban politics and sub-national investment. In African cities, city-regions are often tied to national political objectives, as well as local complexities. When grappling with city-regions, careful attention should be paid to their political nature. Addis Ababa is an interesting case where such care was not taken, resulting in violence and conflict.

- **Coordinating/advising the investment of large-scale infrastructure**: In many cases, the city-region is the best (and maybe only) scale for delivering large-scale urban infrastructure. This is particularly true when seeking to break from the path of dependency.

The cases offer learning material rather than how-to instructions. However, the value of these lessons should not be underestimated, and much can be gained from learning what not to do, coupled with the reassurance that new approaches being developed are more appropriate.

- **Informality**: The removal of people living in informal settlements and their forced relocation are insufficient for engaging with the reality of unmet need for shelter in these cities. That said, the more humane approach to informal settlements – incremental and in-situ upgrading – is under threat from the mega-projects approach. Cairo's ghost towns (i.e. vacancy issues) and the general lack of success of newly built towns on the continent offer cautionary tales about the utility of large-scale new-town developments.

- **Affordable housing**: It goes without saying that affordable housing is a critical issue in all city-regions. Lagos's HOMS programme offers subsidized interest rates, while Gauteng focuses on an upfront capital subsidy. Neither of these address the lower income segment of the urban population, which find themselves without the means to engage with the formal financial sector. However, if global compacts such as the NUA and the SDGs are to have purchase, the urban poor (who have the biggest unmet need for urban housing) must be engaged, lest they be left to continue building their shelters on the edge.

Innovation System literature acknowledges the complexity of innovation and the limitations faced by single entities trying to build and develop new ways of solving problems (Talmar et al. 2018). The same can be said for governing, developing and sustaining urbanizing spaces on the African continent. Old paradigms that do not acknowledge the interdependency at play within an urban governance ecosystem will continue to recreate the same urban challenges. The heterogeneous approaches to providing adequate shelter and inclusion in the economic life of these territories are all dynamic and fertile ground for new practices and innovation. What has yet to emerge is the boldness needed to bring all urban actors to the table. Until this happens creative solutions to the region's most critical development challenges will remain elusive.

BIBLIOGRAPHY

Adesida, O., Karuri-Sebina G. & Resende-Santos, J. (2016) Introduction. In O Adesida, G Karuri-Sebina & J Resende-Santos (ed.) *Innovation Africa,* Bingley: Emerald. Available at https://doi.org/10.1108/978-1-78560-311-220151001

Agunbiade, E.M., & Olajide, O.A. (2016) Urban governance and turning African cities around: Lagos case study. Partnership for African Social and Governance Research (PASGR) Working Paper No. 019.

Aljazeera News (2015) Egypt plans new capital adjacent to Cairo. Available at https://www.aljazeera.com/news/2015/03/egypt-plans-capital-adjacent-cairo-150314014400946.html

AlSayyad, N. (1991) *Cities and Caliphs: On the genesis of Arab Muslim urbanism,* New York: Greenwood Press.

Beall, J. & Goodfellow, T. (2014) Conflict and post-war transition in African cities. In S.Parnell & E Pieterse (eds.) *Africa's Urban Revolution,* London: Zed Books.

Binz, C. & Truffer, B. (2017) Global innovation systems: A conceptual framework for innovation dynamics in transnational contexts. *Research Policy* 46(7): 1284–1298.

Central Authority for Public Mobilization and Statistics (CAPMAS) (1981). *The Census Annual Book,* Cairo: Government of Egypt.

Central Authority for Public Mobilization and Statistics (CAPMAS) (2006) *Egypt National Census,* Cairo: Government of Egypt.

Castells, M. (1996) *The Information Age: Economy, Society and Culture. Volume 1: The rise of the network society,* Oxford; Malden, MA: Blackwell.

Clapham, C. (2018) The Ethiopian developmental state. *Third World Quarterly* 39(6): 1151–1165.

Davis, M. (2006) *Planet of Slums.* London; New York: Verso.

de Satgé, R. & Watson, V. (2015) African cities: Planning ambitions and planning realities. In World Bank, *Addis Ababa, Ethiopia: Enhancing urban resilience,* Washington DC: IBRD.

DFID (2015) *Ethiopia case study*. Available: http://pdg.co.za/wp-content/uploads/2015/09/DfID-Harnessing-Land-Values-Report-1.7-Ethiopia-Case-Study-20150908.pdf

Dittgen, R. & Demissie, A.A. (2017) Own ways of doing: national pride, power and China's political calculus in Ethiopia. Occasional Paper, South Africa Institute of International Affairs. Available: https://www.africaportal.org/publications/own-ways-of-doing-national-pride-power-and-chinas-political-calculus-in-ethiopia/

Dittgen, R. & Rubin, M. 2016. Comparative research on African city regions – lessons for the Gauteng City Region. Unpublished working paper.

Filani, M.O. (2012) *The Changing Face of Lagos: From vision to reform and transformation,* Ibadan, Nigeria: Cities Alliance.

Florida, R., Adler, P. & Mellander, C. (2017) The city as innovation machine. *Regional Studies* 51(1): 86–96.

Gandy, M. (2006) Planning, anti-planning, and the infrastructure crisis facing metropolitan Lagos. In M Murray & G Myers (eds.) *Cities in Contemporary Africa,* New York: Palgrave Macmillan.

Gebeyehu, M. and Takano, S.E., 2007. Diagnostic evaluation of public transportation mode choice in Addis Ababa. *Journal of Public Transportation, 10*(4).

Goodfellow, T. (2015) Taxing the urban boom: Property taxation and land leasing in Kigali and Addis Ababa. ICTD Working Paper 38. Brighton: ICTD.

GOPP (2009) Vision of Cairo 2050 within a National Vision of Egypt. Presentation. Retrieved 30 October 2016 from https://cairofrombelow.files.wordpress.com/2011/08/cairo-2050-vision-v-2009-gopp-12-mb.pdf

GOPP (2012) *Greater Cairo: Urban development strategy,* Cairo: Ministry of Housing and Urban Communities.

Götz, G. & Schäffler, A. (2015) Conundrums in implementing a green economy in the Gauteng City-Region. *Current Opinion in Environmental Sustainability* 13: 79–87.

GPG (Gauteng Provincial Government) (2016) *Gauteng spatial development framework 2030.* Johannesburg: GPG.

Greenberg, S. (2010). The political economy of the Gauteng city-region. Occasional Paper, Gauteng City-Region Observatory Johannesburg.

Hall, P. (2009) Looking backward, looking forward: The city region of the mid-21st century. *Regional Studies* 43: 803–817.

Hanna, N.K. (2016) *Mastering Digital Transformation: Towards a smarter society, economy, city and nation.* Bingley: Emerald.

Healey, P. (2009) In search of the 'strategic' in spatial strategy making. *Planning Theory and Practice* 10: 439–57.

ISDF (Informal Settlements Development Facility) (2013) *Development of Slum Areas in Egypt,* Cairo: ISDF Publishing.

Jonas, A.E & Moisio, S. (2018) City regionalism as geopolitical processes: A new framework for analysis. *Progress in Human Geography* 42(3): 350–370.

Jones, P., Franklin, S., Daredia, M & Zenebe, S. (2015) *Addis Ababa: A policy narrative,* Washington, DC: IBRD. Available at https://collaboration.worldbank.org/servlet/JiveServlet/previewBody/20827-

Kariuki, R., Bakalian A.E., Lall, S., White, R., Parby, J.I., Huang, C., Wheeler, S., Gracia, N.L., Dasgupta, B., Mukim, M & Shi, T. (2013) Harnessing urbanization to end poverty and boost prosperity in Africa : an action agenda for transformation (English). Africa Region Sustainable Development Series, Washington DC: World Bank. http://documents.worldbank.org/curated/

en/710431468191672231/Harnessing-urbanization-to-end-poverty-and-boost-prosperity-in-Africa-an-action-agenda-for-transformation

Keller, E.J. and Mukudi-Omwami, E., 2017. Rapid urban expansion and the challenge of pro-poor housing in Addis Ababa, Ethiopia. *Africa Review*, 9(2), pp.173–185.

KPMG (2017) *Economic snapshot H2, 2016 of Ethiopia*. Accessed 14 February 2017, https://home.kpmg.com/content/dam/kpmg/za/pdf/2016/10/KPMG-Ethiopia-2016-Snapshot.pdf, accessed on 14 February 2017.

Lamson-Hall, P., Angel, S., DeGroot, D., Martin, R. and Tafesse, T., 2019. A new plan for African cities: The Ethiopia urban expansion initiative. *Urban Studies, 56*(6), pp.1234–1249.

Lawanson, T. (2016) Governing Lagos in the urban century: The need for a paradigm shift. In F Hoelzel (ed.) *Urban planning processes in Lagos: Policies, laws, planning instruments, strategies and actors of urban projects, urban development and urban services in Africa's largest city,* Abuja & Switzerland: Heinrich Boell Stiftung Nigeria/Fabulous Urban.

McFarlane, C. (2010) The comparative city: knowledge, learning, urbanism. *International Journal of Urban and Regional Research* 34(4): 725–742.

Ministry of Housing, Utilities, and Urban Communities (2012) *Greater Cairo urban development strategy*.

Ministry of Works and Urban Development (2008) *Integrated housing development program of the Federal Democratic Republic of Ethiopia*. African Ministerial Conference on Housing and Urban Development AMCHUD II, Abuja, Nigeria 28–30 July 2008.

Morakinyo, K.O., Ogunrayewa, M.O., Koleosho, B.O. & Adenubi, O.O. (2012) Urban slums as spatial manifestations of urbanization in sub-Saharan Africa: A case study of Ajegunle slum settlement, Lagos, Nigeria. *Developing Country Studies* 2(11): 1–10.

Mubiwa, B & Annegarn, H. (2013) Historical spatial change in the Gauteng City-Region. Occasional Paper. Johannesburg: Gauteng City-Region Observatory.

Muchie, M. (2016). Towards a unified theory of pan-African innovation systems and integrated development. In O Adesida, G Karuri-Sebina & J Resende-Santos (eds.) *Innovation Africa: Emerging hubs of excellence,* Bingley: Emerald.

Nada, M. (2014): The politics and governance of implementing urban expansion policies in Egyptian cities. *Égypte/Monde arabe* (11): 6.

National Population Commission (2007). *National census provisional results*. Federal Republic of Nigeria, Abuja: National Population Commission.

NCE (New Climate Economy) (2015) Seizing the global opportunity. Available at https://newclimateeconomy.report/2015/

NCE (2016) *The sustainable infrastructure imperative: Financing for better growth and development,* Washington & London: NCE.Available at https://newclimateeconomy.report/2016/misc/downloads/

NCE (2018). *Unlocking the inclusive growth story of the 21st century: Accelerating climate action in urgent times,* Washington & London: NCE. Available at https://newclimateeconomy.report/2018/

Nelles, J. (2013) Cooperation and capacity? Exploring the sources and limits of city-region governance partnerships. *International Journal of Urban and Regional Research* 37(4): 1349.

NPC (National Planning Commission) (2011) *National Development Plan*: vision for 2030. Pretoria: NPC.

NUCA (New Urban Communities Authority) (nd) 6th October City. Available from http://www.newcities.gov.eg/english/New_Communities/October/default.aspx

Parilla, J. & Trujillo, J.L. (2018) The international competitiveness and connections of African cities: Profiling South Africa's Gauteng City-Region. In I. Adeleye & M. Esposito (eds.) *Africa's Competitiveness in the Global Economy,* Cham: Palgrave Macmillan.

Pillay, U. (2004) Are globally competitive 'city-regions' developing in South Africa? Formulaic aspirations or new imaginations. *Urban Forum* 15(4): 340–364.

Robinson, J. (2002) Global and world cities: A view from off the map. *International Journal of Urban and Regional Research* 26(3): 531–554.

Rodríguez-Pose, A. (2008) The rise of the 'city-region' concept and its development policy implications. *European Planning Studies* 16(8): 1025–1046.

Roy, A. (2009) The 21st-century metropolis: New geographies of theory. *Regional Studies* 43(6): 819–830.

South Africa (RSA), Republic (1996) *The Constitution of the Republic of South Africa, Act 108 of 1996.*

Scott, A., Agnew, J., Storper, M. & Soja, E. (2001) Global city-regions: An overview. In A Schott (ed.) *Global city-regions: Trends, theory, policies.* Oxford: Oxford University Press.

Sims, D. (2010) *Understanding Cairo: The logic of a city out of control,* Cairo: American University in Cairo Press.

Sims, D. (2014) *Egypt's Desert Dreams: Development or disaster,* Cairo: American University in Cairo Press.

Stats SA (Statistics South Africa) (2019). *Mid-year Population Estimates 2019,* Pretoria: StatsSA.

Steytler, N. (2005) Local government in South Africa: Entrenching decentralised government. In N Steytler *The Place and Role of Local Government in Federal Systems,* Johannesburg: Konrad-Adenauer-Stiftung.

Tadamun. (2016). Mapping Spatial Justice in the Greater Cairo Region. *Tadamun: The Cairo Urban Solidarity Initiative.* Retrieved from https://issuu.com/87709/docs/mapping-spatial-injustice.

Talmar, M., Walrave, B., Podoynitsyna, K.S., Holmström, J & Romme, A.G.L (2018) Mapping, analyzing and designing innovation ecosystems: The ecosystem pie model. *Long Range Planning* October 2018.

Topham, S. (2005) Building Gauteng as a globally competitive city-region strategy document. Unpublished.

Turok, I & McGranahan, G. (2013) Urbanization and economic growth: the arguments and evidence for Africa and Asia. *Environment and Urbanization* 25(2): 465–482.

United Nations (2016) *The World's Cities in 2016.* New York: United Nations.

UNDESA (United Nations Department of Economic and Social Affairs, Population Division) (2019) *World Urbanization Prospects: The 2018 revision* (ST/ESA/SER.A/420). New York: United Nations.

UNGA (United Nations General Assembly) (2015). Transforming our world: the 2030 agenda for sustainable development. Available at: https://www.refworld.org/docid/57b6e3e44.html

UNGA (2016) New urban agenda: Quito declaration on sustainable cities and human settlements for all (71/256).

UN-Habitat (2008) The State of African Cities 2008: A Framework for Addressing Urban Challenges in Africa (Nairobi: UN-Habitat)

UN-Habitat (2010) The State of African Cities 2010: Governance, Inequality, and Urban Land Markets. Nairobi, Kenya: UN–HABITAT.

UN-Habitat (2011) Cairo: A city in transition. Cairo: UN-Habitat Regional Office for the Arab States.

UN-Habitat (2014) The State of African Cities 2014: Re-imagining Sustainable Urban Transitions. Nairobi: UN Habitat.

UN-Habitat (2016) The first Egypt urban forum 2015. Cairo: UN-Habitat Regional Office for the Arab States.

Van Huyssteen, E., Oranje, M., Robinson, S. & Makoni, E. (2009) South Africa's city-regions: A call for contemplation... and action. *Urban Forum* 20(2): 175–194.

Voukas, Y. & Palmer, D. (2012) Sustainable transportation in East Africa: The bus rapid transport evolution in Addis Ababa, Ethiopia. Cooperation for Urban Mobility in the Developing World (CODATU) XV Conference: The role of urban mobility in (re)shaping cities, 22-25 October 2012 in Addis Ababa, Ethiopia. Available at http://www.codatu.org/wp-content/uploads/Y.-Voukas-D.-Palmer-ARTICLE-Codatu-XV-2012-EN.pdf

Walt, V. (2014) Lagos, Nigeria: Africa's big apple. *Fortune.*

World Bank (2006) Project Appraisal Document on a Proposed Credit in the amount of SDR 138.10 Million (US$200.00 Million Equivalent), to the Federal Republic of Nigeria for the Lagos Metropolitan Development and Governance Project, World Bank, Washington DC. Available at www.worldbank.org.

World Bank (2015a) Addis Ababa, Ethiopia: Enhancing urban resilience, Washington, DC: IBRD DFID (2015) Ethiopia case study. Available: http://pdg.co.za/wp-content/uploads/2015/09/DfID-Harnessing-Land-Values-Report-1.7-Ethiopia-Case-Study-20150908.pdf

World Bank (2015b) *Ethiopia Urbanization Review: Urban institutions for middle income Ethiopia,* Washington, DC: IBRD.

6.

INNOVATIVE GOVERNANCE SYSTEMS – KENYA, RWANDA AND THE IMPLEMENTATION OF AFRICA'S AGENDA 2063 THROUGH THE AfCFTA

Martin Mbaya, Robert Mudida & Brian Omwenga

'The task now is to ratify the African Continental Free Trade Area and the Protocol on the Free Movement of Persons, so that they may come into force as soon as possible. Let's use the momentum we have gained to push forward with the other Agenda 2063 flagship projects that we have committed ourselves to in the first Ten-Year Implementation Plan.' – AU Chairman and Rwanda President Paul Kagame's statement at the closing ceremony of the AfCFTA Business Forum in Kigali, Rwanda, 21 March 2018.

'Africa should build her digital knowledge base and engage on this basis to ensure that any development of disciplines in e-commerce must have a development content that advances the future of Africa's Integration and Industrialization Agenda in the digital economy in line with the Africa Union vision 2063.' – Kenya President Uhuru Kenyatta speaking at the inaugural UNCTAD Africa Ecommerce Week in Nairobi, Kenya, 11 December 2018.

Achieving Africa's ambitious Agenda 2063 will require a continental, multi-sectoral innovation ecosystem, such as the African Continental Free Trade Area (AfCFTA)[1] – a free market anchored by new institutions (or those yet to be established) whose success depends on the free movement of people across traditional borders. This free movement of goods and services is supported by logistics, payments

---

1 Several resources provide greater detail on Africa Agenda 2063 and the AfCFTA, and their connection to the eight AU-recognized Regional Economic Communities, the linkages to broader African integration efforts from the Lagos Plan of Action to TFTA, and to broader global efforts on trade – Brexit, America First, One Bridge One Road and WTO (Juma 2011; Juma & Mangeni 2018; Mugabe 2011; Ismael 2016).

and dispute resolution. Most importantly, the AfCFTA is envisioned as a digital, free-trade area that is effectively an ICT innovation ecosystem.

In March 2018, 44 African countries signed the AfCFTA agreement at a business forum hosted in Kigali, Rwanda. Two months later, Kenya, Rwanda and Ghana, with the support of their respective legislatures, were the first three countries to deposit the instruments of ratification to the AfCFTA. This was an important step in the agreement's implementation.

Using the AfCFTA to achieve Agenda 2063 requires governance systems that are innovative, inclusive, integrated and supportive of the Fourth Industrial Revolution. Such governance systems need to be structured to maximize the provision of public goods underpinned by a social contract, be aligned with systems of innovation, and embrace the Sustainable Development Goals (SDGs). This chapter highlights the experience of Kenya and Rwanda, two countries that have established governance systems for promoting ICT innovation and actively support the AfCFTA.

The successful implementation of the AfCFTA lies in 'creating and designating regional economic communities as the building blocks for continental economic integration' (Mangeni & Juma 2019: 30). Through their membership of overlapping Regional Economic Communities (RECs), such as the Common Market for Eastern and Southern Africa (COMESA) and the East African Community (EAC), Kenya and Rwanda have the catalytic potential to 'operationalise a continent-wide digital system' through the AfCFTA (Mangeni 2018: 31). Within the EAC, the two countries have actively explored ways to collaborate in the areas of technology, infrastructure, tourism and education. Both countries have been globally praised for their innovations in the technology sector: country-wide mobile money in Kenya and city-wide free internet access in Rwanda. These innovation successes have in turn extended to the governance realm. Kenya has played an important global leadership role in establishing and championing the SDGs, both at a multilateral level through the UN and domestically through its Vision 2030 development blueprint; while Rwanda has distinguished itself as a post-conflict nation that used traditional innovations for successful national reconciliation, and embraced various transformations that have improved its global competitiveness. However, both countries have struggled with social inequality, and Kenya has struggled with electoral malpractice, corruption and social cohesion.

The chapter examines three case studies of innovative governance systems at national and sub-national level with strong linkages to the rest of the ICT innovation ecosystems: Kenya's devolution through the revenue-sharing formula and improved service delivery through the Huduma

Centres, and Rwanda's experience with the National Umushyikirano Council. Both countries have in place ICT policies that are based on clearly defined problems and supported by strong implementation efforts through well-evaluated projects and programmes. Their experience illustrates good practice in implementing projects and explains their willingness to extend their successes to the AfCFTA.

The ICT innovation ecosystem in Kenya and Rwanda is described through a 'sectoral system of innovation' model that comprises eight inter-linked pillars (or nodes). One of the pillars is 'ICT governance and leadership', and its policy implementation is viewed using a three-part framework: 'interests, implementation and institutions' that enables the seamless analysis of a governance system using a paradigm that spans public policy and innovation. The chapter concludes by proposing a policy recommendation on continental knowledge flows that optimizes linkages between an innovative governance system and other pillars in an ICT innovation ecosystem. The recommendation is applicable at different levels of government and can be harnessed by leaders and citizens to transform the African continent through a thriving multi-sectoral innovation ecosystem such as the AfCFTA.

KENYA AND RWANDA AS EXAMPLES OF INNOVATIVE
GOVERNANCE SYSTEMS

The three case studies from Kenya and Rwanda highlight the optimization of institutions and ICT sector ecosystem linkages. They show how innovative governance systems can improve support to – and engagement with – citizens. Kenya's revenue-sharing formula illustrates how a governance system can optimize public participation, by enabling citizens to communicate through web- and SMS-enabled mobile phones during the budget deliberation process, while the Huduma Centres case study shows how the availability of reliable data connectivity may ensure access to service delivery. In the case of Umushyikirano, social media and media broadcast play an important role in facilitating communication between government institutions and citizens. Viewed collectively, the strong linkages between each governance system and the rest of the ICT innovation ecosystem at a national level represent a scaling opportunity at a regional and continental level.

Devolution of revenue sharing in Kenya: Optimizing interests and ICT Sector ecosystem linkages

In Africa, one of the most contested issues in politics is revenue sharing in federal systems, combined with devolution. In the 1990s, Kenyan citizens began demanding constitutional review, against the background of a global wave of democratization and constitutional reform that followed the collapse of the Soviet bloc in the late 1980s and the post-Cold War realignment of geopolitical relations. This led to the spread of liberal ideas on state organization, which challenged the ideology of the developmental state that had been prevalent among the African elite since independence. One consequence was the opening up of the political space for internal dialogue in most African countries, which led rapidly to pressure for constitutional reform, and in Kenya resulted in the promulgation of a more devolved Constitution in 2010 (Mudida 2015). The Constitution allows for participatory budgeting, which first took root in Brazil and then throughout Latin America, especially during the period 1990–2005.

Chapter 12 of the 2010 Constitution of Kenya lays out detailed principles and elaborate procedures for making decisions about public finances.[2] In making decisions about sharing resources, the Constitution requires policymakers to consider the views of the public and the principle of equity, which is made explicit in Article 202(1): 'Revenue raised nationally shall be shared equitably among national and county governments.' The annual budget process must include public participation: (i) when the decision about the division of revenue between national and county governments is made; and (ii) when Parliament makes its decision about the executive's proposed budget. Funding for counties is singled out as a decision that particularly requires broad participation (Lakin & Mudida 2015). Additional principles include: choices should be deliberative and not left to any one institution; democratic choice should be partially constrained by detailed technical guidance; and decisions should be frequently reviewed and revised.[3]

In overhauling the way in which resources are shared across the country, the Constitution took the power away from the executive and created new bodies, including the Commission on Revenue Allocation (CRA) and the Senate. Under the previous Constitution, Permanent Secretaries were the Accounting Officers in charge of all monies allocated to the ministry – they cascaded the budget to grassroots through authorities to incur expenditure (AIEs) issued directly to the district heads in the regions. This changed with the enactment of the new Constitution, and the 47 counties took charge of their budgeting process. It was an important governance innovation in how devolution is

---

2   This section draws on Lakin J (2015) "The Values of Money" in Ghai and Ghai, Editors, *National Values and Principles of the Constitution,* Katiba Institute.

3   J. Lakin and R. Mudida (2015) Sharing Resources Fairly: The evolution of Kenya's revenue sharing formula, 2012–2015, International Budget Partnership and Strathmore Business School Case Study.

implemented to optimize the interests of citizens. The decision about how much money to give counties involves two key decisions that must take into account the principle of equity: (i) how much of the total national pot to give to the two levels of government (the 'vertical' share), and (ii) how much each individual county gets of the total given to the counties' level of government (the 'horizontal share'). Factors that should guide the horizontal share include developmental needs, fiscal capacity and incentives for counties to optimize their own revenue collection, as well as 'economic disparities' and 'affirmative action in respect of disadvantaged areas and groups'. Further enshrining the equity principle is the creation of the Equalisation Fund (Chapter 12) that channels a small fixed share of annual revenues to marginalized areas in order 'to bring the quality of those services [roads, water, electricity and health] in those areas to the level generally enjoyed by the rest of the nation, so far as possible'.

As decisions around public finances are intended to be taken by multiple institutions, the Constitution gives the CRA agenda-setting power, while the final decision is taken by Parliament. The CRA is mandated to make recommendations:

- For the equitable sharing of revenue raised by the national government between national and county governments, and among the county governments – Article 216(1).

- On other matters relating to the financing of, and financial management by, county governments and to encourage fiscal responsibility – Article 216(2).

The CRA recommendations are forwarded to Parliament, which makes the final determination. Even within Parliament, responsibility is divided between the two houses: the Senate has the larger role and can accept/amend the CRA proposal, but the National Assembly has the power to amend if it has a supermajority. Even if the National Assembly does amend it, the proposal has to go back to the Senate for review or mediation. While the decision on the horizontal share is taken every five years (or three at the outset), the Senate can also review it at any time with a supermajority vote. All of this was intended to take financial decisions away from the executive and to make them temporary, reducing the likelihood of permanent losers emerging in financial matters. This intention has been largely realized. The parliamentary process is an important part of policy legitimation, which is a vital step in the public policy process that gives legal force to decisions or authorizes/justifies policy action. It aims to achieve a proper exercise of government authority and its broad acceptability to public and other policy actors (Morse & Struyk 2006).

The process of deciding how to share resources requires a high degree of public participation and concrete mechanisms for accountability. A key innovation in Kenya's ICT sector that has facilitated public participation and accountability is the ubiquity of mobile phones (both web and SMS enabled). Kenya boasts a robust mobile phone market, high mobile penetration, strong uptake of data/internet services, and a large portion of the population that accesses the internet mainly via the mobile phone. The country's rapid ICT development has offered a huge opportunity for social and economic development when combined with political action. Few counties have adapted fast and innovated to use ICT and social media to relay key messages and mobilize participation (NTA 2013; IBP 2019). The update of ICT sector innovations remains a challenge despite the presence of an innovative governance system.

The ability of citizens to communicate through web and SMS-enabled phones, in the context of Kenya's high mobile penetration, is a critical ICT sector innovation that can ensure effective public participation and accountability during the process of determining how resources are shared.

Huduma Centres – optimizing implementation and ICT sector ecosystem linkages

Innovation is crucial to boosting productivity, which is vital for long-term economic growth. Firms innovate usually by combining different products and processes, and a study found that the rate of innovation among formal-sector firms in Kenya was at 63% (Mendi & Mudida 2016). In contrast, Kenya's public service delivery is historically poor and characterized by 'delayed services, long queues and reports of massive corruption' (Wambugu et al. 2016: 4). In response to the demand by citizens for government to deliver services at the same level as the private sector, the Government of Kenya is promoting citizen-centred public service delivery through a variety of channels, including deploying digital technology and putting in place citizen service centres (Huduma Centres) throughout the country (World Bank 2017). *Huduma* is Kiswahili for 'service'.

In November 2013, the Huduma programme was launched with the aim of having at least one centre in each of Kenya's 47 counties. At this centre, people could access public services under one roof, rather than having to go to different buildings to obtain (for example) birth and other certificates, identity cards, passports, business registrations and permits, seasonal parking tickets or drivers' licences (World Bank 2017). A specific intent of the programme was 'to fight and reduce corruption in the public sector' (Wambugu et al. 2016: 4). As of February 2017, the Huduma programme was running in 45 centres, five of which are located in Nairobi. The programme offers a single point of service for many of the government services. The key principles underlying the innovative service delivery offered by the centres include speed, dignity, convenience and value (World Bank 2017). The innovation comes from the ability to implement a policy solution of delivering services aligned with the expectations of citizens based on their experience with the private sector.

An evaluation of the centres found that service delivery had improved at the centres, as a result of the product and service innovations. The positive impacts of these innovations included: 'increasing the number of people served, reducing time of service delivery, increasing accountability and transparency and finally improving public understanding of government activities' (Wambugu et al. 2016: 22).

An important aspect of the Huduma programme is to transform the citizen experience in public service delivery. More recently, the Kenyan government has focused on citizen-centric approaches to service delivery, leading to a dramatic increase in interactions between citizens and government at all levels of the recently devolved political system. The trend towards citizen-centric delivery models (which are more cost-effective from a government perspective) is the result of increasing internet and mobile penetration rates, as well as higher expectations around government service. This has been achieved primarily by innovation in government processes. The e-Government innovation is nested in the much larger vibrant national innovation ecosystem with deep penetration of ICT, private sector innovation and linkages. The private sector has provided the technology used in running Huduma Centres, with the database solutions for running the centres (a backward linkage) from Oracle. Computers at the different counters in the centres are connected to their mother ministries through Safaricom and Telkom Kenya. All Huduma ICT systems are monitored in real time by the Technology Operating Centre of the Huduma Secretariat (World Bank 2017). Despite some challenges, the use of this technology has enabled the Huduma Centres to act as an antithesis to corruption and inefficiency, by reducing the interaction of citizens with the bureaucracy.

Building on the success of Huduma Centres, the 'Huduma Mobile Outreaches dubbed Huduma Mashinani (Kiswahili phrase meaning "service to the grassroots")' was introduced, enabling government services to be taken to reach a wider audience, including 'the marginalized, the old, the poor and the vulnerable'.[4]

In 2015, Kenya's Huduma programme won first prize (out of 398 nominations) in the 'Improving the Delivery of Public Services' category

---

4   Available at https://publicadministration.un.org/en/Research/Case-Studies/
    unpsacases/ctl/NominationProfilev2014/mid/1170/id/5228

of the annual United Nations Public Service Awards. According to the award, the Huduma programme integrates the delivery of public services through five channels: Huduma Centres, Huduma Web Portal, Huduma Mobile Platform, Huduma Call Centre and the Huduma Payment Gateway. 'The programme has enabled customers to access a myriad of Government services. They are currently serving more than 10,000 customers per day. Additionally, over 25 million U.S Dollars have been collected so far from Huduma Centres.'[5]

In 2019, the Government of Kenya began exploring how Huduma Centres can embrace the Fourth Industrial Revolution through a new free government service called Huduma Namba. Biometric data is collected and used to generate a unique number (Huduma Namba) that enables citizens to access government services.[6]

The availability of reliable data connectivity is a critical ICT sector innovation that promotes access to service delivery through digital technology-enabled Huduma Centres.

The National Umushyikirano Council – optimizing institutions and ecosystem linkages

An innovative solution that incorporates participatory governance is Umushyikirano in Rwanda (Mudida 2017). *Umushyikirano* is a Kinyarwanda word that refers to a meeting where participants are able to exchange ideas, share experiences and question one another. Initially called the National Dialogue Council in Article 168 of the Constitution of Rwanda of 26 May 2003 and renamed as the National Umushyikirano Council in Article 140 of the amended Constitution in 2015, the Council was formed in response to the need to reconstruct and nurture a shared national identity. Umushyikirano is an annual event that 'brings together the President of the Republic and citizens representatives', providing Rwandans the opportunity to debate issues of national importance and ask questions directly to their leaders. The first Council took place on 28 June 2003, and has been held annually since then, usually in December. The live televised and radio broadcast event brings together members of the Cabinet, members of Parliament, representatives of councils and local administrative entities, and representatives of Rwandan society (including the Rwandan diaspora and friends of Rwanda) to debate issues relating to the state of the nation, state of the local government and national unity. The strength of Umushykirano comes from the

---

5   UN Public Service Award Winners 2015. Available at http://workspace.un-pan.org/sites/Internet/Documents/UNPAN94633.pdf

6   Nyawira, L., All you need to know about the Huduma Namba. *The Star*, 2 April 2019. Available at https://www.the-star.co.ke/news/2019-04-02-all-you-need-to-know-about-huduma-namba/

direct participation of citizens in holding their leaders to account and fast-tracking government programmes and citizen priorities based on the resolutions tabled each year (Mudida 2017). Each Umushyikirano has a theme. For example, the theme was 'Shaping together the Rwanda we want' in 2016 and 'Rwandans' choices – foundation of national development and dignity' in 2015.

Home-grown solutions enhance governance in developing countries more than externally driven policies to address issues of common concern to a country's citizens. The national dialogues focus on bottom-up implementation of participatory governance based on indigenous values. Much of what is discussed draws on aspects of Rwandan culture and traditional practices that enable development programmes to be enriched and adapted to the country's needs and context. The result is a set of home-grown solutions, which translate culturally owned practices into sustainable development programmes. For example, discussions at the national dialogues improved the implementation of the One Cow Per Family Programme by bringing to light the corruption that had affected the programme, aimed at fighting malnutrition, poverty and vulnerability by building assets for families in rural areas.

Umushyikirano is underpinned by group theory, which argues that power in a state's political system is widely shared among interest groups, each of which seeks access to the policy-making process – power is pluralistic rather than concentrated in the hands of only a few elites (Kraft & Furlong 2015). This balance helps to ensure that no one group dominates the policy process. The Rwanda national dialogues illustrate that innovation in governance can be grounded in indigenous practices and blended with the latest in technological innovation. It is based on inclusive institutions that are better at promoting the common good, which is critical to development (Mudida 2011).

Along with South Africa, Rwanda was an innovator in using national dialogues as a post-conflict resolution mechanism. Participants are selected in a bottom-up process, through local government structures starting from the village to the district levels, as well as through organizational structures of youth, women, associations, cooperatives, non-profits, the private sector, civil society, etc. An election system is used to select opinion leaders vetted by their peers from the village to provincial level, with a pre-determined number of participants being allocated to each level.

To increase local ownership and participation, discussions are conducted in the Kinyarwanda language, and technology is used to reach locations throughout the country. Those unable to attend in person at Rwanda's Parliament building can participate via telephone, SMS, Twitter and Facebook as well as follow the debate live on television and radio. Proceedings are web-streamed and broadcast in real time to other large gatherings taking place simultaneously. Some districts in remote areas are also digitally connected, allowing their populations to follow the proceedings via video conference. All questions during the Umushyikirano are recorded – for example, 127 questions, comments and proposals were received for the 2012 Umushyikirano – and a summary report and recommendations are produced.

Umushyikirano has played an important role in the political and socioeconomic transformation that Rwanda has experienced since the genocide in 1994. Rwanda's GDP quadrupled between 2003 and 2015, from R1.923 billion to R8.278 billion.[7] The rapid growth in GDP was accompanied by outstanding strides in development outcomes:

- Today, 98% of Rwandans are medically insured, which is a remarkable achievement given that the country had just 20 medical doctors in 1994.

- Around 98% of children have access to primary education (Akena et al. 2014).

- In 2018, Rwanda was ranked 29 among 190 economies in the World Bank's Ease of Doing Business, compared to its rank of 41 in 2017.[8]

The national dialogues are part of a broader innovation ecosystem in Rwanda. In June 2018, the Government launched the National Research and Innovation Fund that is supported by a loan of US$30 million from the African Development Bank.

Umushyikirano represents a unique blend of the traditional and the modern methods of participatory governance. In Rwanda, practice at national and community levels is strongly influenced by indigenous institutions (Rwiyereka 2014). The concept of dialogue was initially crafted at village level – in Rwandan society, people used to come together in their villages, to sit around the fire and discuss different issues, and to begin to teach their young ones. Direct conversation with the people has always been important – pre-colonial Rwandan kings would go to a region and ask the local populations what they thought of their leaders and, based on these discussions, decide to promote or remove the local chief. Modernization and technology have enabled these dialogues and conversations to extend beyond the village to the national level. Other practices with cultural roots that are integrated into contemporary Rwandan public policy include: *umuganda* (community work), *muganura* (harvest) and *imihigo* (performance contracts).

---

7   Available at https://data.worldbank.org/country/Rwanda
8   Available at https://www.doingbusiness.org/en/rankings

The use of social media, traditional broadcast channels, SMS, video conferencing and digital recording is a critical ICT sector innovation that facilitates communication between government institutions and citizens.

STRENGTHENING LINKAGES BETWEEN INNOVATIVE
GOVERNANCE SYSTEMS AND OTHER NODES
IN AN INNOVATION ECOSYSTEM

Kenya and Rwanda are innovative continental leaders with growing and dynamic ICT sectors. Innovation in the two countries has an impact on the AfCFTA through their membership in two RECs, the EAC and COMESA, which are key building blocks of the continental effort.

Innovation refers to 'the implementation of a new or significantly improved product (good or service), or process, a new market method or a new organizational method in business practices, workplace organization or external relations' (OECD 2005: 46). For the Kenyan Ministry of Science and Technology (2008), innovation is 'the practical application of creative ideas which often involves introduction of inventions into the marketplace'. It further observes that two fundamental types of innovation exist, namely product and process. Process innovation is described as 'changes that affect the methods of producing outputs' while product innovation is defined as 'changes in actual outputs'. The Rwanda development blueprint, 'Rwanda Vision 2020', underscores the importance of innovation to a country. It notes, 'There is a need to generate, disseminate and acquire scientific skills as well as technological innovations, in addition to integrating them into the social and economic development drive' (Republic of Rwanda 2000: 22).

Innovation ecosystems

The ICT innovation in Kenya and Rwanda represents an ecosystem because of the presence of multiple intermediaries interacting for the successful achievement of an innovation, which is one of the features of ecosystems. Ecosystems are 'characterised by interdependency of and between organisms and resources, and are dynamic rather that static – seeking equilibrium through motion rather than stasis' (Schalkwyk et al. 2012: 3). ICT is one of many sectorial ecosystems within the larger socioeconomic ecosystem that contains dynamically interacting organisms (firms, non-firms, intermediaries and consumers) bound by exchange as well as by the institutions (the repositories of rules, values and norms) in which they are embedded (Fransman 2010). The ICT ecosystem is driven by innovation (i.e. the injection of new knowledge into the ecosystem). The interaction between firms and consumers (i.e. between knowledge creators and knowledge consumers) generates new knowledge, which leads to innovation in the ecosystem. The pursuit of innovation keeps the ICT ecosystem in motion. The interaction between firms and other actors in the ecosystem can also be characterized through the concept of clusters, which are 'critical masses in one place of linked industries and institutions – from suppliers to universities to government agencies – that enjoy unusual competitive success in a particular field' (Porter 1998: 1).

Systems thinking highlights the systemic nature of innovation, best exemplified by Malerba's (2002) sectoral innovation system, which takes into account the users, the knowledge and capabilities, the interactions and the institutional setup. Introducing a systems approach brings to the fore the question of system efficiency, where the emergent behaviour of the system is based on not only the existence of the nodes, but also the interactions between these nodes. The existence of the nodes does not necessarily pre-condition the outcome and may result in varied effects from one country to the next due to collective system efficiency. Therefore, policymakers need to realize that developing a Silicon Valley in Africa goes beyond establishing nodes but also depends on the inter-actions between these nodes.

The ecosystem primarily revolves around a market and industry environment that finds utility in a given innovation. The research and development environment then engenders the ideas and innovations to feed this market. The triple helix concept exemplified by Ranga & Etzkowitz (1993) and Etzkowitz & Leydesdorff (1995) introduces the importance of a third environment, namely governance (Etzkowitz 2008). The definition used borrows from Malerba (2002) and is applied through a stakeholder analysis driven by a causal loop that establishes the systems thinking to the ICT sectors in Kenya and Rwanda (Figure 6.1).

All agents and actors involved in producing, delivering and using ICT tech products set the boundaries and drive the organic and ever-chang-ing (evolutionary) nature of the tech-innovation ecosystem. These agents are the ecosystem stakeholders, which can be 'any organization, group or individual defined as an actor, who can affect or is affected by the outcome' of the delivery of ICT (Freeman 1984: 46). A useful taxonomy can be derived from systems thinking, with the sector stakeholders organized into backward, horizontal and forward linkages of the ICT ecosystem (Hanowsky & Sussman 2009).

- Backward linkages are organizations, groups or individuals that provide inputs (in form of goods, services, finances and knowledge) into the ICT ecosystem.

- Horizontal linkages are those organizations, groups or individuals involved in the process of providing, or

Figure 6.1: Causal Loop Diagram

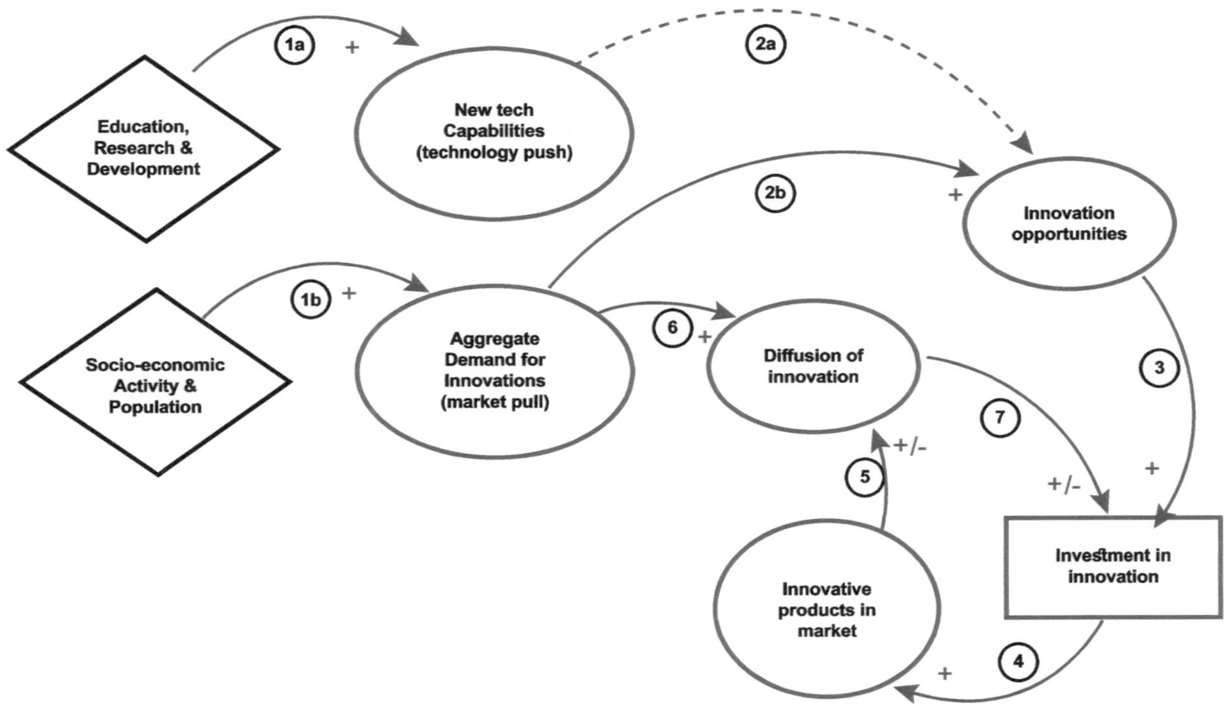

Figure 6.2: Stakeholder analysis representation

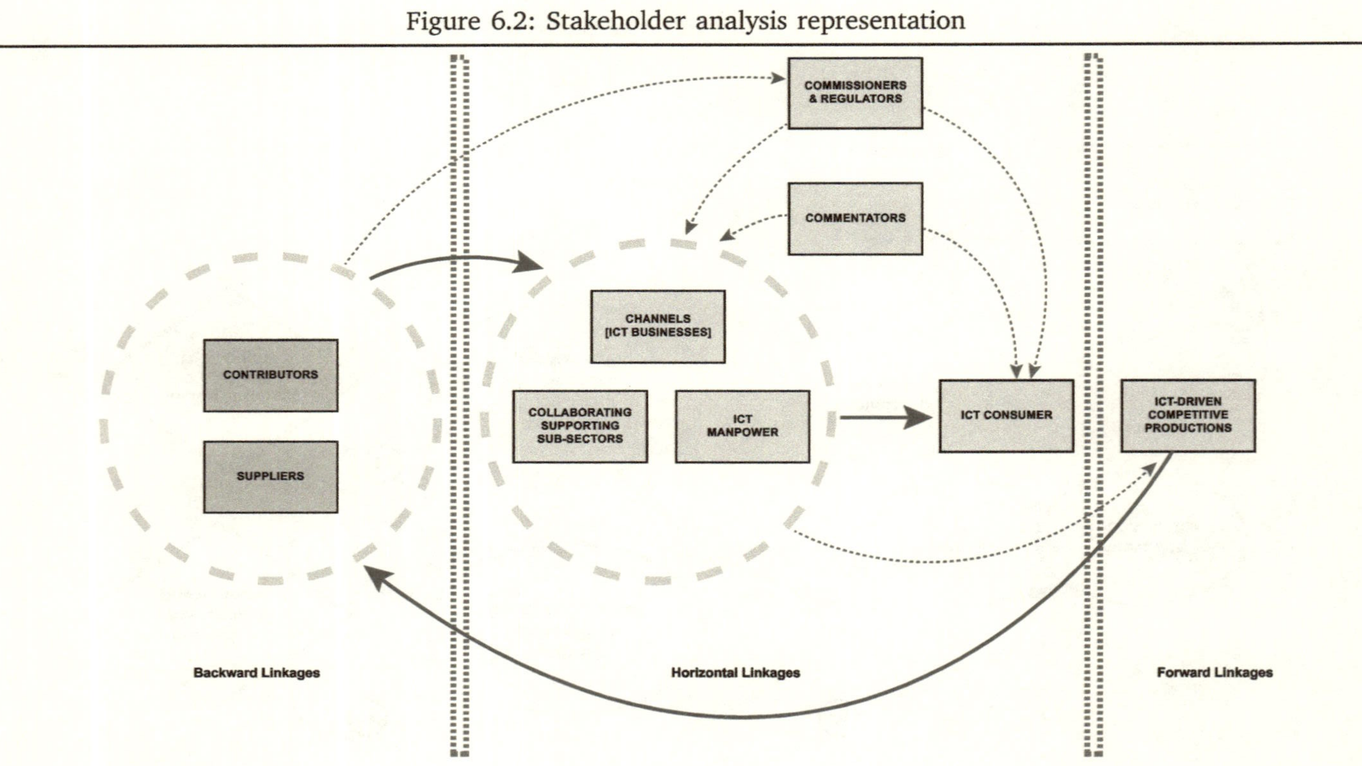

Table 6.1: Linkages for the Rwandan and Kenyan
ICT Innovation Ecosystem

Backward linkages	Horizontal linkages	Forward linkages
• Contributors of knowledge – universities, such as the University of Nairobi and Strathmore University (Kenya); and the Carnegie Mellon University in Kigali and the College of Science and Technology University of Rwanda (Rwanda). • Contributors of finance – banks, international organisations and financial institutions, such as the World Bank. • ICT suppliers or platforms – multinational ICT companies that provide hardware, such as HP, EMC, Cisco, Lenovo and Oracle, and providers of social media platforms such as Facebook, Twitter, etc.	• Commissioners and regulators appointed by government to lead and regulate the sector/ecosystem – State and government agencies, such as the Ministry of Devolution that oversees the Huduma Centres and the Ministry of ICT in Kenya that provides locations for the Huduma centres. • Channels (ICT businesses) – large, medium and small-scale enterprises and start-ups such as certified resellers of software and hardware who supplied and fitted the Huduma centres. • Collaborating/ supporting sub-sectors: transporters, power utility companies. • ICT manpower – trained software engineers, developers, project managers. • ICT consumers – government, communities, households, and individuals of the general public. • Commentators: Associations such as the Bloggers Association of Kenya, and media houses.	• ICT-driven competitive productions – centres of innovation and new product development, hubs, digital economy (ICT as an enabler in other sectors), creation of other sub-sectors (BPO, hardware assembly industry) – In Kenya, Huduma centre service provision, pushed demand for stable internet connectivity all over the country; the success of the programme emboldened the government to undertake the schools' laptop project, as well as the manufacturing/ assembly of these devices in Kenyan universities. • Ripple effect into other sub-sectors and environments, e.g. eGovernment – in Kenya a direct result of the Huduma centres was the eCitizen project that formed the payment gateway through which the government collected money for government services.

ensuring the provision of ICT products and services within the ICT sector.

• Forward linkages are those industries, organizations, groups or individuals that are a resulting output from an established ICT ecosystem (e.g. Digital & Virtual Economies).

An organization may fall into one or more of these conceptual taxonomic groups. Organizations, groups or individuals are a generic grouping of entities ranging from entire sectors or industries to single individuals. This taxonomy therefore establishes a meta-model of stakeholders represented in Figure 6.2.

Examples of linkages for the Rwandan and Kenyan ICT innovative ecosystem are shown in in Table 6.1.

Figure 6.3: Ecosystem pillars and linkages

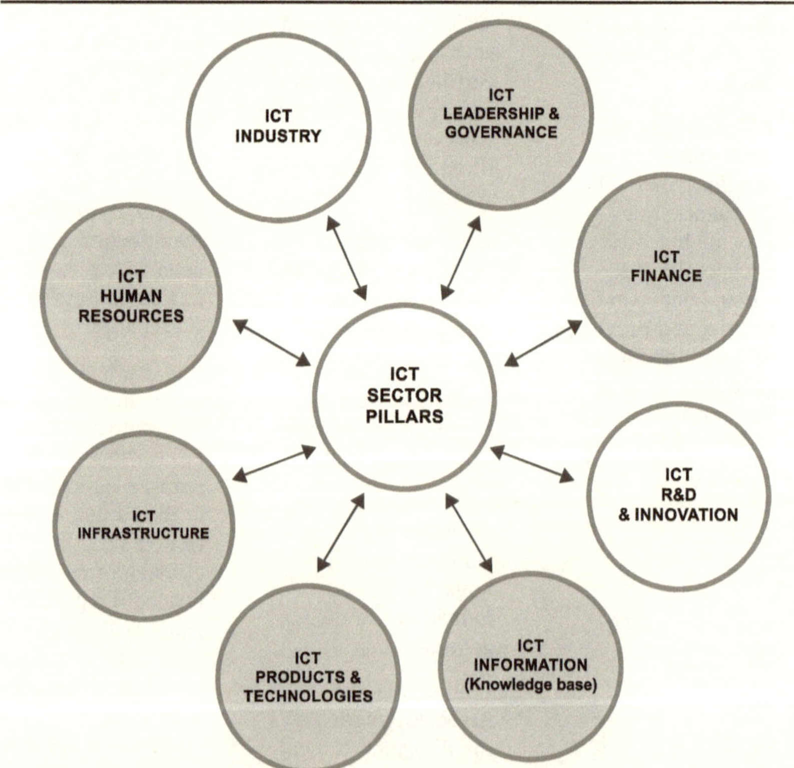

Pillars and linkages in the ecosystem

The above holistic analysis and definition of the ecosystem resulted in the mapping of eight ICT ecosystem pillars, as shown in Figure 6.3. Of specific interest in this chapter is the ICT leadership and governance pillar.

ICT is a key sectoral innovation ecosystem within the continental multi-sectoral innovation ecosystem of the AfCFTA. Replicating the experience of Kenya and Rwanda through the RECs (EAC and COMESA) would advance the integration of Africa's digital economy in line with the AU Vision 2063.

An innovative governance system occupies the intersection of interests, implementation and institutions (Figure 6.4). This 'interests–implementation–institutions' framework enables a seamless analysis of a governance system using a paradigm that spans public policy and innovation. It draws on the three-part framework developed by Cloete and De Coning (2011) that includes contextualisation ('interests'), policy process ('implementation') and capacity building for policy improvement ('institutions'). The relationship between the two frameworks is explained below.

Figure 6.4: Interests–implementation–institutions model of governance systems

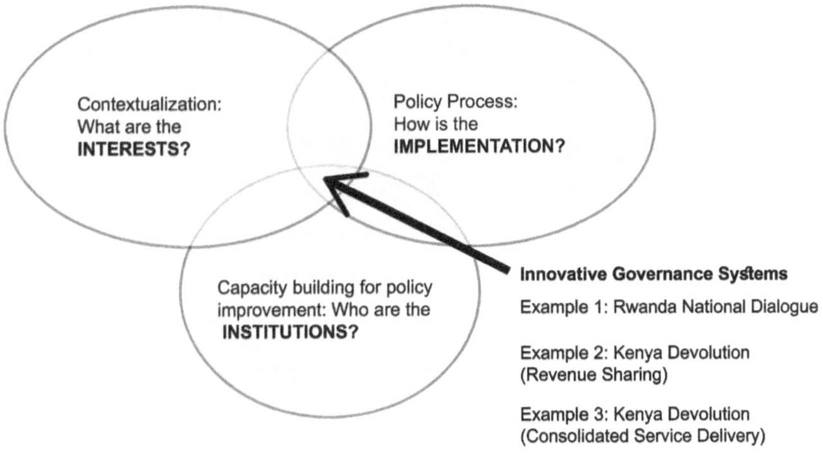

Interests

Contextualisation entails looking at paradigms, theories, models and concepts in relation to public policy, which also helps to define the interests of various actors in a political system. This dimension of public policy is referred to as agenda setting. Therefore, the ICT Governance and Leadership pillar can be analysed[9] by asking the question '*what are the interests?*'

The quotes by President Kenyatta and President Kagame in the introduction of the chapter underscore the need for a partnership spanning multiple helices in the context of an innovation ecosystem that includes government, industry and academia in partnership with civil society. The devolution of revenue sharing in Kenya highlights the optimization of interests, through a systematic process involving all arms of government (executive, legislature and judiciary) that captures and harnesses (through the revenue-sharing formula) the priorities of citizens occasionally representing competing interests, to maximize the public good.

Implementation

The Policy Process Model (Figure 6.5) is anchored in political systems theory and provides a systematic way of moving from a policy problem

Figure 6.5: Policy Process Model

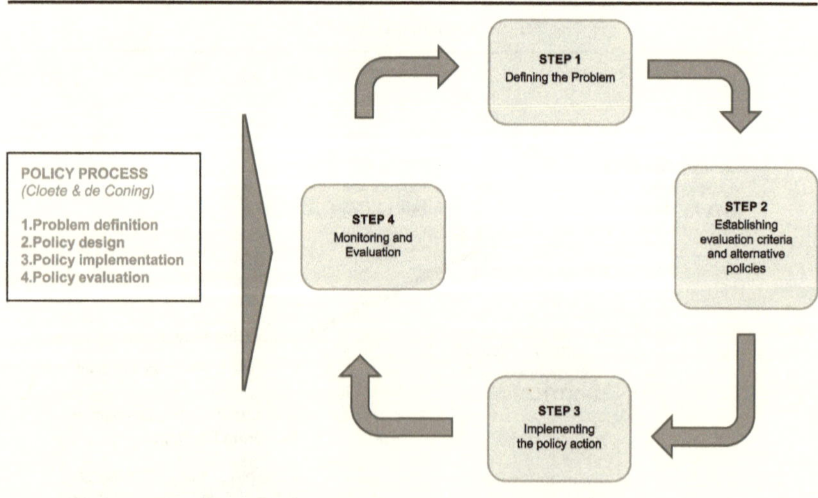

---

9   Political systems theory, the interest group model and the institutional model (classical theory) are useful theories/models for such analysis as discussed by Cloete and de Coning (2011).

to a solution. The ICT leadership and governance pillar can be analysed based on the third step of the policy process model to answer the question *'how is the implementation?'*

Institutions

Capacity building for policy improvement considers institutional arrangements for policy management and the institutionalization of policy capacity in government and beyond. Such capacity building is particularly important in aligning a governance system with an innovation system. Useful frameworks for exploring the link between the two systems are the triple helix innovation (Etzkowitz 2008) and the model of clusters in national competitiveness (Porter 1998). The ICT and Governance pillar combines these two frameworks to explore capacity building for policy improvement and to answer the question *'who are the institutions?'*

Rwanda and Kenya are signatories to various bilateral and multilateral agreements at different levels of government that play a key role in AfCFTA's implementation. They are both members of two RECs: EAC and COMESA. Kenya is also a member of the Intergovernmental Authority on Development, while Rwanda supports the planned merger of three RECs with overlapping membership, i.e. EAC, COMESA and Southern African Development Community (SADC) into the Tripartite Free Trade Area (TFTA). Together, Kenya and Rwanda are part of a network that covers more than half of the African continent. Both countries have played host to multiple high-level multilateral gatherings at a sub-continental, continental and global scale. For instance, in 2018 Kenya hosted UK Prime Minister Theresa May and was hosted by US President Trump (building on a previous 2015 visit to Kenya by US President Barrack Obama), while Rwanda hosted China President Xi Jinping. Kenya and Rwanda have championed triple helix innovation and the establishment of globally competitive clusters within the context of regional integration. In Rwanda, Umushyikirano shows how a country is able to enhance the global competitiveness of specific clusters through a structured set of interactions between citizens and institutions spanning government, industry and academia. Kenya has sought to learn from the experience of Rwanda, with a desire to replicate the concept at a national level.

Ecosystem linkages with the ICT leadership and governance pillar

Rwanda and Kenya provide a useful case study of African countries with strong innovation ecosystems underpinned by strong linkages to the ICT leadership and governance pillar built on the foundation of an action-oriented executive arm. They show how a strong governance system at a national level can be a pillar for establishing linkages with an innovation ecosystem at a continental level, as envisioned by the AfCFTA.[10] What RECs such as EAC, COMESA and SADC need are 'coherent strategies for building regional systems of innovation as nested networks of national systems of innovation with differentiated capabilities and competitiveness' (Mugabe 2011: 28). These strategies should promote shared/regional research and development infrastructure, harmonised technical standards and regulations, collaboration among regional universities, cross-border public–private partnerships, 'regional intellectual property rights protection frameworks' and other measures that would improve 'the climate for regional innovation activities' (Mugabe 2011: 29).

Viewing the experience of Kenya and Rwanda in the context of an innovation ecosystem (pillars and linkages) and a governance system (interests, implementation and institutions) yields a variety of recommendations. One such policy recommendation focuses on the mobility of talent in the context of EAC and is presented in the next section.

RECOMMENDATION: FACILITATE CONTINENTAL AND GLOBAL KNOWLEDGE FLOWS

The policy recommendation, which spans both governance systems and innovation ecosystems, is to facilitate continental and global knowledge flows in order to optimize the linkages among institutions (Saxenian 2006). Practically, this entails mapping out institutions as pillars in an innovation ecosystem and optimizing the linkages among them through increased interactions. For example, a network of university and innovation hubs across the African continent, with anchors in key countries within each REC, would make it easier for other countries to learn from, and replicate within their local context, the experience of Kenya and Rwanda. The AfCFTA would also make it easier for innovation leaders, such as Kenya and Rwanda, to harness new opportunities because their innovative governance systems would enable them to better define their interests and implement policies. A study by Mbaya et al. (2010) proposes a useful framework of global knowledge flows to harness the linkages between governance and innovation systems. It notes:

'Science, technology, and international relations tightly intertwine, with each affecting the other (Weiss 2005). Science yields discoveries subsequently deployed as technologies, with these innovations ultimately having political and economic implications within and across states. In this era of

10 At a continental level, the King Codes on Corporate Governance of South Africa are a useful innovation warranting further study on how to ensure effective leadership, good governance, objectivity, fairness, accountability and transparency. Available at https://home.kpmg/za/en/home/insights/2016/10/king-iv-summary-guide.html

globalization, a dominant aspect of this interplay, particularly in relation to developing countries, is the increased capacities that result from regional integration. This situation also raises new possibilities for diplomatic interactions between developed and developing countries, especially if they are built on a framework of scientific and technological interactions.' (Mbaya et al. 2010: 146)

'An approach for using this African resource pool calls for the circulation of global knowledge flows. Achieving this objective requires a framework that allows scientists and engineers to collaborate on two separate continents with clearly defined goals. The goals also require enabling institutional environments that ensure productive output will yield the desired development outcomes in their respective home countries. This framework requires new forms of diplomacy between developed and developing countries, specifically a strong emphasis on the potential of science and technology. Facilitating these global knowledge flows creates powerful platforms for promoting technological catch-up by developing countries and, ultimately, convergence (Fagerberg 2005).' (Mbaya et al. 2010: 146–7).

The study alludes to the important role of innovative governance systems that harness their diaspora populations towards development priorities.

'Diasporas have sometimes played a critical role in the establishment of entire industries in their home countries. All the instances involved a combination of top-down and bottom-up approaches that were sustained over several years. These examples included Israel and telecommunications, Taiwan and semi-conductor integrated circuit (IC) fabrication, and China: IC fabrication and software development, and India and outsourcing (Saxenian 2006). Proactive actions by governments provide a strong theme around which the Diaspora can rally, for example the Nigeria Diaspora Day held in 2006, the U.S.–based Singapore Philadelphia Innovators Network (SPIN) coordinated through the U.S.–based Singapore community, and the U.S.–based Swiss House of Advanced Research and Education (SHARE) coordinated through the Swiss government.' (Mbaya et al. 2010: 148).

Japan and South Korea are other examples of countries that have excelled in the fields of electronics/ICT-related applications and multi-sectoral innovation ecosystems for alleviating poverty and job creation.

The concept of global knowledge flows can be reimagined as continental knowledge flows, based on a virtual innovation corridor anchored by institutional nodes (pillars) at a national level and cross-border interactions that are aligned with the interests of citizens. The Fourth Industrial Revolution, through technologies such as blockchain and artificial intelligence, can help to address historical challenges in Africa associated with identity and sovereignty. Such challenges can be reconceptualized as opportunities for Africa through continental knowledge flows. For example, Somalian and South Sudanese refugees and their children in Kenya face acute challenges with post-secondary education and employment, due to their immigration status. However, they can be granted virtual citizenship based on innovations in identification underpinned by artificial intelligence and blockchain technology, allowing them to contribute to the economy through knowledge creation and dissemination.[11] Such innovations would allow them to be productive citizens in both their home and adopted countries by enjoying rights equivalent to other citizens. Lessons from such innovations could easily be replicated and scaled for citizens of African countries seeking to pursue economic opportunities beyond their home borders in the context of AfCFTA. The result would be increased global competitiveness of African economies.

The success in achieving continental knowledge flows through AfCFTA would depend on two factors:

- **The ability to harness digital technologies in support of data-driven implementation.** Practically, this entails using data to define, execute and evaluate programmes and projects, which would be defined in the context of innovation ecosystem implementation and aligned with interests of citizens. Two examples of this are the upgrading of micro, small and medium enterprises through digital learning, and the adding of value through manufacturing and processing with a focus on both continental and global markets. The Fourth Industrial Revolution and the First Digital Revolution offer Africa opportunities to leapfrog innovation, especially using digital learning to enhance the skills of Africa's predominantly youthful population.

- **The ability to formalize and deepen existing pillars in the innovation ecosystem.** Practically, this entails identifying all the institutions within each pillar and optimizing the interactions among them, guided by citizen interests, for example, the establishment of a technology savings and credit cooperative (SACCO), as a way of addressing the diverse needs of citizens. This approach can collectively address challenges of capital, finance, community intellectual property and the personal welfare of innovators. It takes the form of the successful co-operative model that has been tested in the agricultural commodities sector on the continent. Such a cooperative model in the ICT sector would yield a strengthened innovation ecosystem by involving the community in the innovation production

---

11 Onyango Obbo, "Fasten your seatbelt, folks, the East African century is already upon us" *The East African,* March 4, 2019. Available at https://www.theeastafrican.co.ke/news/ea/The-East-African-Century-is-already-upon-us/4552908-5008138-aqdg9vz/index.html

process. As innovations scale and span across national borders, challenges associated with governance may be experienced. In spite of these challenges, such cross-border involvement is an example of how eCommerce can help to achieve the ambitious AfCFTA goals.

CONCLUSION

Africa's ambitious Agenda 2063 is achievable through an agreement such as the AfCFTA. It requires an innovative governance system (based on interests, implementation and institutions) with optimal linkages to other pillars within an innovation ecosystem. The success story of Kenya and Rwanda in the ICT sector and their experience with innovative governance systems can offer models for the rest of the African continent. Such governance systems are innovative, inclusive, integrated and supportive of the Fourth Industrial Revolution. They are structured to maximize the provision of public goods underpinned by a social contract and embracing the SDGs.

BIBLIOGRAPHY

Akena, J., Blair, T., Kagame, P., Mwenda, A.M. & Rwanda Development Board (2014) *Rwanda: A remarkable turnaround of a nation,* Kampala: Independent Publications Limited.

Cloete, F. and de Coning, C. (2011) *Improving Public Policy: Theory, practice and results,* Cape Town: Van Schaik Publishers.

Etzkowitz, H. and Leydesdorff, L. (1995) The Triple Helix: University–Industry–Government Relations: A laboratory for knowledge-based economic development *Glycoconjugate Journal 14(1):14–19*

Etzkowitz, H. (2008) *The Triple Helix: University–Industry–Government Innovation in Action,* New York: Routledge.

Fransman, M. (2010) The new ICT ecosystem: Implications for policy and regulation. *The New ICT Ecosystem: Implications for Policy and Regulation.* 1–251.

Freeman, E. (1984) *Strategic Management: A stakeholder approach,* Boston: Pitman.

Hanowsky, M. & Sussman, J. (2009) Design of ground delay programs considering the stakeholder perspective. *Transportation Research Record* 2016: 109–117.

IBP (International Budget Partnership) (2019) Are Kenya counties making budget documents available to the public? A review of county websites.

Ismael, F. (2016) Advancing the continental free trade area (CFTA) and Agenda 2063 in the context of the changing architecture of global trade.

Juma, C. (2011) *The New Harvest: Agricultural Innovation in Africa,* Oxford: Oxford University Press.

Juma, C. & Mangeni, F. (2018) African regional economic integration: The emergence, evolution, and impact of institutional innovation. *Faculty Research Working Paper Series,* Harvard Kennedy School.

Kraft, M.E. & Furlong, S.R. (2015) *Public Policy: Politics, analysis, and alternatives* (Fifth Edition), London: Sage.

Lakin, J. (2015) The values of money. In Y.P. Ghai & J.C. Ghai (eds.) *National Values and Principles of the Constitution,* Nairobi: Katiba Institute.

Lakin, J. & Mudida, R. (2015) Sharing resources fairly: The evolution of Kenya's revenue-sharing formula, 2012–2015, International Budget Partnership and Strathmore Business School Case Study.

Malerba, F. (2002) Sectoral systems of innovation and production. *Research Policy* 31: 247–264.

Mangeni, F. (2018) The African continental free trade area – A beacon of free trade? *ATDF Journal-AfCFTA* Vol. 9(2).

Mangeni, F. & Juma, C. (2019) African regional economic integration: The emergence, evolution and impact of institutional innovation. Discussion Paper 2018-1, Belfer Centre for Science and International Affairs, Harvard Kennedy School.

Mbaya, M., Mrina, P. & Levin, M.J. (2010) What the 2000 U.S. census tells us about the Kenyan diaspora. *Journal of Global Initiatives: Policy, Pedagogy, Perspective* Vol. 2(2). Available at: https://digitalcommons.kennesaw.edu/jgi/vol2/iss2/3

Mendi, P. & Mudida, R. (2016) Complementarity in firm-level innovation strategies: A comparative study of Kenya and Nigeria. *Innovation and Development* 6(1): 87–101.

Morse, K. & Struyk, R.J. (2006) *Policy Analysis for Effective Development: Strengthening transition economies,* Boulder, CO: Lynne Rienner Publishers.

Mudida, R. (2011) Effective institutions as the foundation of development: A conceptual and empirical discourse. In D. Lutz, P.M. Shimiyu & G. Osengo (eds.) *Rethinking Integral Development in Africa,* Nairobi: Consolata Institute of Philosophy Press.

Mudida, R. (2015) *Structural Sources of Constitutional Conflicts in Kenya,* Riga, Latvia: Scholar's Press.

Mudida, R. (2017) The Rwanda National Dialogue Council (Umushyikirano): A study in African participatory governance, Strathmore Business School Case Study.

Mugabe, J. (2011) Science, technology and innovation in Africa's regional integration: from rhetoric to practice. *ACODE Policy Research Series* No.44.

NTA (National Taxpayers Association) (2013) Budget transparency and citizen participation in counties in Kenya.

OECD (2005) *Oslo Manual: Guidelines for collecting and interpreting innovation data,* Paris: OECD.

Porter, M. (1998) Clusters and new economics of competition. *Harvard Business Review* November–December. Available at https://hbr.org/1998/11/clusters-and-the-new-economics-of-competition

Porter, M., Miller, K., McCreless, M., Carlsson, K., Hudson, J. & Sheldahl-Thomason, H. (2013) Rwanda: National economic transformation. Harvard Business School Case 706491.

Ranga, M. and Etzkowitz, H. (1993) Triple helix systems: An analytical framework for innovation policy and practice in the knowledge society. *Industry and Higher Education* 27(4): 237–262.

Republic of Kenya Ministry of Science and Technology (2008) Science technology and innovation policy and strategy.

Republic of Rwanda (2000) Ministry of Finance and Economic Planning, Rwanda Vision 2020, Kigali.

Republic of Rwanda (2013) Economic Development and Poverty Reduction Strategy II, 2013–2018.

Rwiyereka, A.K. (2014) Using Rwandan traditions to strengthen programme and policy implementation. *Development in Practice* Vol. 24: 686–692.

Saxenian, A. (2006) *The New Argonauts: Regional advantage in a global economy.* Harvard University Press.

Schalkwyk, F., Willmers, M. & McNaughton, M. (2016) Viscous open data: The roles of intermediaries in an open data ecosystem. *Information Technology for Development* 22(1): 68–83.

United Nations (2015) Public Service Forum, Day and Awards Ceremony 23–26 June 2015 Medellin, Columbia.

Wambugu, D., Wachira, M. & Mwamba, D. (2016) The effect of innovation on service delivery in the public sector in Kenya. *International Journal of Business Strategies* 2(2): 1–21.

World Bank (2017) Citizen service centers in Kenya: The role of Huduma centers in advancing citizen-centred service delivery in the context of devolution and digitization.

7.

COLLABORATIVE INNOVATION AND NETWORKED ENTREPRENEURSHIP IN AFRICA

*Erika Kraemer-Mbula, Jeremy de Beer, Caroline Ncube,
Chidi Oguamanam, Nagla Rizk, Isaac Rutenberg
& Tobias Schonwetter*

Innovation and entrepreneurship are known to drive economic growth, especially in African countries where the formal job market offers limited opportunities, and where persistent social challenges demand new creative approaches. Today, Africa is the most entrepreneurial region in the world, with higher rates of business start-ups than any other region, and overall positive perceptions of opportunities to start a business – particularly among the youth (Kew et al. 2013). Mauritius, Rwanda, Kenya and South Africa are among the highest ranked countries in Africa in the *Doing Business* report (World Bank 2018). Although innovation is rampant in Africa, recent studies have also highlighted that existing innovation indicators do not adequately recognize the continent's contributions to the global knowledge economy (de Beer et al. 2014; Kraemer-Mbula & Wunsch-Vincent 2016; Rizk et al. 2018). African countries achieve low scores in standard innovation measures, such as the Global Innovation Index, where 75% of the featured African countries fall within the lowest scored quarter (Cornell University et al. 2018). This is because conventional approaches to capturing innovation still rely largely on activities by formal firms and their connections to formal knowledge institutions, such as universities and formal training providers (Kraemer-Mbula et al. 2019). In addition, the outputs of innovation are almost exclusively assessed through the lens of what is happening on the 'technology frontier' in mature economies. As a result, innovation activities by African entrepreneurs remain largely misconstrued, underestimated and often overlooked. This knowledge gap has many implications, especially that it hampers the ability of policymakers to adequately support innovation in Africa (Adesida et al. 2016; Kraemer-Mbula & Konte 2016).

The understanding of innovation within an institutional and socio-economic context has led to a growing interest in innovation ecosystems. In this regard, innovation ecosystems in Africa are often described as fragmented because they do not have, or have only limited, institutions that provide education and skills, financial resources, infrastructure and other key ingredients for innovation. Institutions play an important role in the diffusion of knowledge and innovations, as they shape networking activities among various stakeholders. This chapter argues that the institutional framework generally used to assess innovation systems in Africa remains narrowly limited to formal institutions and formally organized knowledge systems, and largely ignores the informal economy and traditional knowledge systems that are rooted in local communities and are important assets to African innovation ecosystems.

In Africa, the informal economy provides livelihoods to a substantial (and growing) share of the population. Many of these activities offer valuable examples of entrepreneurship, resilience, cooperation and social integration, despite operating in very constrained circumstances (Kraemer-Mbula & Wunchs-Vincent 2016). Yet the informal economy hardly features in the literature of innovation systems. The informal economy is very diverse and includes activities that range from waste-picking to manufacturing and film-making. The one common feature among informal actors is the intensity of networking and social interactions, which are central to the concept of an innovation ecosystem (Lundvall 2010). Moreover, networking is important for innovation and offers other benefits, including risk-sharing, access to new markets and technologies, the pooling of complementary skills and obtaining external knowledge (Pittaway et al. 2004). The literature suggests that firms that do not cooperate or exchange knowledge (either formally or informally) not only limit their knowledge base and learning opportunities, but also reduce their long-term ability to enter into fruitful relationships that are conducive to innovation. Therefore, the networking abilities in the informal economy could provide a means of identifying ways to strengthen innovation systems in Africa.

The coexistence of traditional systems with scientific or 'modern' knowledge systems is also a typical feature of the African continent. Traditional knowledge systems play an important role in the livelihoods of most populations in Africa and are generally transmitted verbally, within a specific cultural context and from generation to generation. The links between modern and traditional knowledge systems tend to be weak, but these links are changing in the applied context of the informal economy. This chapter illustrates some of these changes and discusses possibilities for strengthening the interactions that promote knowledge flows between traditional and modern knowledge systems.

OPEN AFRICAN INNOVATION RESEARCH NETWORK

The African continent does not lack innovative ideas or innovative actors, it lacks effective innovation ecosystems. What is required is systematic evidence of interventions that can improve the relevance of innovations for the context in which they emerge.

For more than a decade, the Open African Innovation Research network (Open AIR) has built a reputable Afrocentric community of researchers and institutions that collects new evidence of the multiple dimensions of African innovation in a range of settings across the continent. Open AIR's primary research goal has been to reconcile tensions between appropriation and access, owning and sharing, competing and collaborating in order to scale up innovation. These dynamics have been explored in three distinct but closely interconnected contexts.

- **High-tech hubs.** Open AIR research has explored the proliferation of high-tech hubs on the continent over the last decade, describing their key role in African innovation ecosystems as enablers for the emergence of innovative start-ups. Earlier classifications of innovation hubs (Comins & Kraemer-Mbula 2016) have been complemented and expanded by insights from more recent studies (de Beer et al. 2017; Kraemer-Mbula & Rutenberg 2018). African innovation hubs provide a range of services and opportunities for aspiring and actual entrepreneurs. In addition, high-tech hubs constitute a point-of-entry to the continent for new technologies, with 3D printing being a prime example (Schonwetter & van Wiele 2018). Newer varieties include hubs based on co-creation principles, such as makerspaces, that emphasize the importance of access to peer learning and networking for innovative entrepreneurship.

- **Informality.** In economic environments characterized by high and persistent formal unemployment, particularly among the youth, the informal economy continues to provide income opportunities to a substantial segment of the population. It offers a seedbed for the lower-risk experimentation and entrepreneurship that are the foundations for innovation. Yet people engaged in informal activities are commonly perceived as survivalists, with little to offer in terms of entrepreneurship, let alone innovation. However, recent studies show that informal entrepreneurs generate frequent innovations, which can have sizeable social and economic impacts (de Beer et al. 2014; Adesida et al. 2016; Kraemer-Mbula & Wunsch-Vincent 2016). Several Open AIR case studies have substantiated these initial findings, providing detailed evidence of different economic activities and geographical locations.

- **Indigenous peoples and local communities** (IPLCs). Open AIR has examined entrepreneurial activities by IPLCs in Africa and their evolving relationship with traditional knowledge and the digital revolution. Recent research has been able to reframe 'traditional' knowledge as a valuable driver of innovation and entrepreneurship, while demonstrating how the uptake of new technologies is a source of economic empowerment with the potential to make IPLCs active participants in the digital economy.

This chapter is based on 12 case studies conducted by Open AIR in seven African countries (Botswana, Egypt, Ethiopia, Ghana, Kenya, Nigeria, and South Africa) between 2016 and 2018. It distils some of the central features of African innovative entrepreneurship, focusing on three aspects: the integration of formal and informal modalities of skills development and training, the rise of collaborative communities, and the combination of traditional knowledge with new and emerging technologies.

INTEGRATING FORMAL AND INFORMAL SKILLS DEVELOPMENT AND TRAINING

Apprenticeships and informal modalities of skills development are conventionally seen as a last resort, i.e. a way of transmitting technical skills to those who cannot afford formal training. However, learning relies on two types of knowledge: one based on codified scientific and technical knowledge, or the Science, Technology and Innovation mode; and the other based on practical and experience-based knowledge, or Doing, Using and Interacting mode (Jensen et al. 2007) – the latter is essential in an African context (Kraemer-Mbula et al. 2019).

Informal modalities of skills development and learning are complementary to formal training modalities and are key ingredients of innovation, particularly the 'soft' components of innovation at the firm level. Batten et al. (2000) distinguish between the 'hard' and 'soft' components of innovation – between the 'hard' investments in research and development and in material components, such as machinery and equipment, and the 'soft' assets such as organizational and relational capabilities, including interactions, networking, interpersonal contacts and the like.

The case study by Adu-Gyamfi and Adjei (2018) explored the integration of formal and informal modes of skills development in Suame Magazine in Kumasi, Ghana. With origins that can be traced back to the 1950s and 1960s, Suame Magazine has evolved from an informal cluster into a hub for skills development and knowledge sharing for artisans. Today, more than 210,000 people work and live in what is Ghana's largest informal cluster. Informal firms in the cluster initially specialized in metalworking and then expanded, developing production capabilities in car repairs and manufacturing of vehicle spare parts, and later in food processing and agricultural equipment. The expansion of diverse capabilities was intimately connected to regulatory shifts, such as the restrictions of vehicle importations in the 1970s and trade liberalization in the 1980s. The Intermediate Technology Transfer Unit (ITTU) linked to Kumasi's Kwame Nkrumah University of Science and Technology played an important role, by boosting the technical skills of artisans and introducing physical technologies to Suame Magazine, which led to the establishment of new firms that used new technologies.

The majority of the 59 informal artisans studied rely on apprenticeship training from their masters and friends. However, relying exclusively on the apprenticeship system has its limits, due to the undocumented nature of apprenticeships and the lack of modern technological content, such as knowledge about ICTs, which restricts access to new knowledge. Those artisans who manage to combine knowledge from a variety of sources, especially combining formal and informal apprenticeship training, have an advantage. In this respect, Suame Magazine can be seen as an industrial cluster for skills acquisition, where informal vocational training and practical hands-on training thrive and coexist with a high potential for impact. Nevertheless, questions are raised about the suitability of the current mechanisms for knowledge sharing and training, especially given the rapid technological changes. Despite artisans' continual innovations in vehicle repair and manufacturing, their incremental improvements appear to be insufficient for the innovative leap that is required in Ghana's technical development (Waldman-Brown et al. 2013).

On the other side of the spectrum, a study by Nzomo et al. (2018) delved into the emerging mobile technology ecosystem in Nairobi, Kenya, where the proliferation of tech-hubs is providing a dynamic and fertile ground for mobile tech start-ups to move from the idea stage through to the minimum viable prototype, and ultimately to enter the appropriate market. The study explored the activities of 25 mobile tech start-ups and found that skills and knowledge for businesses are often acquired informally, through apprenticeships, learning-by-doing, and on-the-job training. A growing trend is the reliance on online training resources, with courses through Coursera and EdX, as well as YouTube videos, becoming common resources used to develop skills at mobile tech start-ups. In addition, and in the face of budgetary constraints, firms are increasingly using their own employees to train other employees, which leads to the development of highly customized internal training programmes with practical applications grounded in the firm's activities.

On-the-job training and peer-to-peer training offer customized, hands-on learning opportunities that contribute to developing other 'soft' components of the innovation process, such as the creation of a learning and sharing culture within the firm and improved communication and cohesion among employees. These forms of learning translate into a higher incidence of innovation, by providing start-up members with access to new skills, the development of decision-making capabilities and practical knowledge leading to innovative solutions (Nzomo et al. 2018). A study of 200 informal ICT firms in Nigeria's Otigba ICT informal cluster also found that in-house training efforts are highly correlated with a firm's innovation activities (Jegede & Jegede 2018).

A study by Belete (2018) sought to understand the innovation patterns in Ethiopian informal enterprises, focusing on two informal clusters: the Shiro Meda handloom-weaving cluster and the Merkato leather footwear-manufacturing cluster, both located in the Ethiopian capital, Addis Ababa. The study of 35 informal weavers and shoemakers describes the tensions between informal apprenticeships and formal education. Weaving skills are passed on from parents to offsprings through apprenticeships at an early age and are 'tailored to the needs of the particularly student, who is taught the skill in a personalized way' (Belete 2018: 18). However, currently, experienced weavers prefer their children to pursue formal education and work, rather than learn weaving skills. Despite this apparent conflict between formal and informal education, the study also highlights the recent trend of Ethiopian graduates with university, technical and vocational training choosing to establish micro and small enterprises. The study found that weavers with formal higher education display more innovative and entrepreneurial tendencies, for instance, introducing improvements in their production processes, and experimenting with non-cotton (traditional) yarns such as rayon and acrylic. They also introduce new designs to target new consumers more frequently than those without formal education. This shows some valuable complementarities between vocational education and training and informal apprenticeships.

These case studies raise important questions about the need to integrate formal academic knowledge and more informal modalities of knowledge and skills development, through the recognition of practical skills. A case study in Ghana (Beem & Adomza *forthcoming*) explored the implications of integrating practical hands-on Science, Technology, Engineering and Mathematics (STEM) education in a school environment, examining how a 'micro-franchizing' model incorporating hands-on learning can help sustain and scale-up STEM education in Ghanaian schools. Kenya provides multiple examples of training and educational institutions providing practical training applications, such as Moringa School and Gebeya (Nzomo et al. 2018). These forms of education and training offer great potential to the growing base of African innovative start-ups and established entrepreneurs. Practical hands-on learning in schools allows young people readier access to the more engaging aspects of the STEM fields. It is this type of innovative approach that Africa's education and training systems need to ensure that they remain relevant and current.

THE RISE OF COLLABORATIVE COMMUNITIES

African clusters have received considerable attention in the literature (Oyelaran-Oyeyinka 2005; Meagher 2007; Oyelaran-Oyeyinka & McCormick 2007; Zeng 2008). Clusters are 'open innovation' environments, displaying several features that are known to be beneficial for innovation. For firms, spatial proximity contributes to higher productivity and economies of scale. Agglomeration reduces transportation costs, enables collaboration, provides space for interaction and often facilitates access to specialized skills. Firms tend to rely largely on the open exchange of ideas, collaboration and networking (Kraemer-Mbula & Wunsch-Vincent 2016), particularly in environments shaped by conditions of scarcity (Srinivas & Sutz 2008).

Collaboration and networked entrepreneurship are important for African innovation. Collaborations are positively associated with the implementation of innovation in the Otigba ICT informal cluster (Jegede & Jegede 2018), while open collaboration and knowledge sharing are commonplace among artisans in Suame Magazine (Adu-Gyamfi & Adjei 2018). In Suame Magazine, intermediaries are the key drivers of knowledge sharing and diffusion of innovations. They include artisans' associations within the cluster, as well as collaborations among entrepreneurs through sub-contracting.

African firms have different reasons for engaging in the collaborative arrangements that drive the spread of knowledge relevant for innovation among micro and small enterprises. Several factors determine the propensity of firms to collaborate with others, and cultural proximity emerges as a relevant factor in some clusters but not in others (Belete 2018). For instance, in Ethiopia, the Shiro Meda weaving cluster has a strong ethnic origin in a particular group of people (the Dorze), which shapes their preferences for collaborations and location – entrepreneurs choose to locate their business in clusters primarily to interact with relatives and be part of a community with shared cultural values. Yet this is not the case in all clusters. For instance, in the Merkato footwear cluster, proximity to input suppliers and customers seems to be of more importance than the cultural component. A study of 206 micro, small and medium enterprises in Botswana (Ama & Okurut 2017) identified the main obstacles and benefits for firms to engage in open collaborative innovation, which include financing, marketing and networking.

Over and above traditional clusters in Africa, an emerging literature has started to explore the activities and innovation-related impacts of co-creation spaces (Comins & Kraemer-Mbula, 2016) or makerspaces. These collaborative communities are a relatively new phenomenon but are growing exponentially across countries, attracting the interest of innovative start-ups. Tapping into collaborative communities, such as those in the maker movement, holds great potential for informal entrepreneurs to upscale, access larger markets and develop technological innovations. The maker movement is a global technology-enabled extension of the DIY culture, and refers to a new generation of hackers, artisans, designers, artists and entrepreneurs. It emphasizes hands-on, informal, networked, peer-led and shared learning. Open AIR's ground-breaking research provides new insights about the potential of Africa's maker movement (de Beer & Baarbé 2017), and other studies have looked at the emergence of new collaborative communities (Nzomo et al. 2018; Kraemer-Mbula & Armstrong 2016; El Houssamy & Rizk 2018).

The maker movement in South Africa is a new and emergent phenomenon, with the first maker-focused collectives dating back to around 2010. A study explored eight collectives in South Africa's Gauteng province with a variety of institutional set-ups in terms of governance, management, staffing and funding. It categorized them as community-based, university-based, government-based, and hybrid (Kraemer-Mbula & Armstrong 2016). This study was later expanded to all of South Africa, iteratively developing a set of 13 spatial-, activity- and management-related variables that can be used to characterize different kinds of maker 'communities of practice' (de Beer et al. 2017) and complemented with further insights into the 'institutionalization' of South Africa's maker communities (Armstrong et al. 2018). A distinct finding of these studies is the centrality of collaboration through learning and knowledge sharing, and the adherence to the principle of openness, which is core to the maker movement.

User innovation in maker communities can provide significant employment opportunities (El Houssamy & Rizk 2018). Case studies in North African countries, such has Egypt, Tunisia and Morocco, found substantial evidence that tech-entrepreneurs determine their location based on the location of other like-minded start-ups. This could be either at co-working spaces or at other localities that contain a large population of start-up businesses. Co-working spaces or incubators offer start-ups not only affordable serviced offices but also numerous opportunities for networking and developing business ideas. Start-ups rely on open and interactive spaces to meet new techies and investors, access mentorship opportunities, remain aware of tech trends, and exhaust business and networking opportunities with other start-ups. Indeed, the networking opportunities offered by co-working spaces are so crucial to business development that some start-ups would consider moving from one space to another once they have exhausted the opportunities at the first space (Nzomo et al. 2018).

The case studies also hint at the role that makerspaces can play in inclusion, although further research is needed to flesh out how to realize their full potential. Several maker collectives in South Africa (in Pretoria, Johannesburg, Knysna and Cape Town) have an explicit focus on skills building and enterprise development for marginalized individuals and groups (Kraemer-Mbula & Armstrong 2016). In particular, the 'I Make' maker collective fosters linkages to rural craftspeople and, since August 2015, has been conducting rural outreach through their 'I Make Mobile Lab', which is headquartered at the non-profit Makers Village in Irene, Pretoria. For example, 'I Make' entered into an agreement with a group of roughly 80 crafters in the remote St Lucia region of KwaZulu-Natal, through which 'I Make' and the Makers Village would work for three years with the crafters to develop a new product, using a combination of local traditional crafting practices and other practices made possible by equipment in the Mobile Lab, such as 3D printers, laser cutters, and embroidery machines (Kraemer-Mbula & Armstrong 2016). Other makerspaces provide opportunities to start-ups located on the margins, to enable them to scale up and access markets that they could not have reached otherwise. In this respect, several of South Africa's maker communities prioritize links and bringing informal artisans into contact with formalized market opportunities (Armstrong et al. 2018).

These collaborative communities provide important avenues for net-working, collaboration and knowledge sharing but also face challenges to increase their impact and reach. Common to most of them is the pressing challenge of financial sustainability and their ability to establish solid connections to the broader innovation ecosystem, which affects their ability not only to scale-up but also to survive. In this respect, maker collectives in Africa strive to establish and strengthen partnerships with government and other formal entities, which offer the potential to function as part of multi-stakeholder innovation ecosystems that can contribute to alleviating shortfalls in areas such as STEM/STEAM [STEM (Science, Technology, Engineering and Mathematics) with the addition of Art] education, youth employment and enterprise development (Armstrong et al. 2018).

Support has been forthcoming from development partners who believe that open collaboration is the key to the success of start-ups in Africa, and that hubs can enable sustainable entrepreneurship. Hubs create spaces where innovators can meet new people, find resources and investors, and test their business models. While starting a business has many obstacles, the prevailing view is that no one can do it alone and that entrepreneurs can counter some of the challenges of entrepreneurship through collaboration.

COMBINING TRADITIONAL KNOWLEDGE WITH NEW AND EMERGING TECHNOLOGIES

Traditional knowledge is a distinct feature of Africa's entrepreneurship and is intrinsically linked to essential cultural dimensions particular to the continent. However, the role of traditional knowledge in African innovation ecosystems is still insufficiently studied. In this respect, Open AIR's studies on cultural industries, handicraft production, and environmental activism have shed valuable light on innovation driven by traditional knowledge, and especially its impact on empowering women and girls.

An emerging area of interest is digitalization and its coexistence with prevailing traditional knowledge-based practices in the African context. Digital technologies have conventionally been regarded as a tool for preserving traditional knowledge, by enabling the record-keeping of indigenous knowledge and history. However, in the current innovation ecosystem, the interactions between digital technologies and traditional knowledge are morphing and leading to fascinating dynamics in specific industries. For example, Nigeria's movie industry (Nollywood) is a critical repertoire of African entertainment, a socio-cultural force for many Africans, and a massive driver of employment and innovation. Oguamanam (2017) explores the Nollywood phenomenon, through the lens of innovation, openness and technological opportunism. Using cutting-edge digital technologies, such as 4K filming and technology-intensive production techniques, Nollywood seems to be scaling down – the focus is shifting from high-volume/low-margin local storytelling to low-volume/high-margin blockbusters (Oguamanam 2017). Openness has broken down industrial barriers to entry via a permissive and democratic process of open recruitment, mentorship, and intermediate training and curating of talents outside conventional frameworks. However, it remains to be seen whether this will continue to be the case, as globalization and transnational content acquisitions threaten to deprive the industry of full control. Nollywood also shows that deliberately and pragmatically including outliers in intellectual property systems, such as informal movie marketers (usually alienated as pirates), as meaningful partners and stakeholders reflects a novel knowledge management or governance framework, which seeks an inclusive understanding of stakeholders whose value-added and interests need to be recognized.

Studies by Open AIR researchers are uncovering the complexities of entrepreneurship as practised by Indigenous and local communities (ILCs). In Uganda, a study of traditional knowledge (TK)-based agricultural production has identified the role that information and communication technologies (ICTs) can play in support of scaling up collaborative innovation and marketing (Dagne & Oguamanam 2018). A study in Tanzania of a Maasai women's collective producing and selling traditional handicrafts has revealed the ways in which the enterprise is contributing to the alleviation of gender imbalances (Laltaika 2019). In South Africa, Open AIR researchers have identified strong social entrepreneurship dimensions in the work of two rural traditional healer organizations, thus challenging narrow conceptions of entrepreneurial behaviour as being driven purely by economic motivations (Rutert & Traynor 2019).

The role of traditional knowledge in the African Fourth Industrial Revolution deserves further attention, especially in connection to the proliferation of networked and collaborative forms of entrepreneurship and the new modalities of skills development described above.

CONCLUSION

This chapter summarizes the findings from a rich repertoire of studies conducted by researchers in the Open AIR network between 2016 and 2017. The evidence collected through these case studies shows the importance of taking into account the various modalities of skills development and training, the rise of collaborative communities, and the new dynamics whereby traditional knowledge is combined with new and emerging technologies.

The majority of African innovators still operate in the informal economy and remain at the margins of the broader innovation ecosystem. Such marginalization hinders their ability to scale up and expand. At the policy level, it is essential to accommodate the knowledge-sharing dynamics that exist in the informal economy, especially at the product and service development stage, and their networking assets, while ensuring that they can reap the benefits of their innovations at the commercialization stage. Openness and collaboration improve the ability of informal entrepreneurs to acquire new skills, and access improved technology and knowledge to enhance products and services. The case studies described in this chapter illustrate the varieties of clustering and collaborating communities that are emerging in response to new technologies and the willingness of African start-ups to learn and access new knowledge. Some of these communities relate to the maker movement, or maker collectives, which still operate at a small scale but could scale up if adequately linked to the broader innovation ecosystem.

This chapter also raises important questions about considering different forms of knowledge and learning. Currently, African innovation ecosystems place high value on formal academic knowledge and give little social status or recognition to the value of practical skills. It has been argued that such a system reproduces the uneven spread of skills and competences, and may lead to more unequal societies (Lorenz et al. 2016). However, in the context of Africa, knowledge acquired in the workplace, learning acquired through daily work experience and problem-solving, must be recognized further as foundations for expertise. They are generated largely through interaction and experimentation, which are commonplace in the majority of African innovative productive environments, such as informal clusters, maker collectives and traditional communities.

ACKNOWLEDGEMENTS

This work was carried out by the Open AIR network, in partnership with the University of Cape Town (South Africa), the University of Ottawa (Canada), the American University in Cairo (Egypt), Strathmore University (Kenya), the Nigerian Institute of Advanced Legal Studies (Nigeria), and the University of Johannesburg (South Africa). Financial support came from the International Development Research Centre, Canada, and the Social Sciences and Humanities Research Council of Canada. Prof. Kraemer-Mbula is supported by the NRF Grant No. 118873. The views expressed in this work are those of the creators and do not necessarily represent those of the research funders.

BIBLIOGRAPHY

Adesida, O., Karuri-Sebina, G. & Resende-Santos, J. (eds.) (2016) *Innovation Africa: Emerging hubs of excellence,* Bingley: Emerald.

Adu-Gyamfi, Y. & Adeji, F. (2018) Skills development, knowledge and innovation at Suami Magazine, Kumasi. Open AIR Working Paper.

Ama, N. O. & Okurut, F. N. (2017) Challenges MSMEs face and benefits in the adoption of open collaborative innovation: A principal component approach. *Archives of Business Research* 5(7): 85–103.

Armstrong, C., de Beer, J., Kraemer-Mbula, E. & Ellis, M. (2018) Institutionalization and informal innovation in South African maker communities. *Journal of Peer Production* 1(12): 14–42.

Batten, D.F., Bertuglia, C.S., Martellato, D. & Occelli, S. (eds.) (2000) *Learning, Innovation and Urban Evolution,* Norwell: Kluwer Academic Publishers.

Beem, H. & Adomza, G. (forthcoming). Modeling the dissemination of local STEM innovation in Ghana: Can teachers be grassroots innovators and entrepreneurs? Open AIR.

Belete, W. (2018) Determinants of innovative performance by Ethiopian informal-sector micro and small enterprises (MSES). Open AIR.

Comins, N.R. & Kraemer-Mbula, E. (2016) Innovation hubs in Southern Africa. In O. Adesida, G. Karuri-Sebina & J. Resende-Santos (eds.) *Innovation Africa: Emerging hubs of excellence,* Bingley: Emerald.

Cornell University, INSEAD, and WIPO (2018) *The Global Innovation Index 2018: Energizing the world with innovation,* Ithaca, Fontainebleau, and Geneva.

Dagne, T.W. & Oguamanam, C. (2018) ICTs in agricultural production and potential deployment in operationalising geographical indications in Uganda. Open AIR Working Paper No. 14. University of Cape Town and University of Ottawa: Open African Innovation Research (Open AIR).

de Beer, J., Armstrong, C., Ellis, M. & Kraemer-Mbula, E. (2017) A scan of South Africa's maker movement. Open AIR. Retrieved from http://www. openair.org.za/

de Beer, J., Armstrong, C., Oguamanam, C. & Schonwetter, T (2014) *Innovation and Intellectual Property: Collaborative Dynamics in Africa,* Cape Town: University of Cape Town Press.

de Beer, J. & Baarbé, J. (2017). Africa's maker movement: An overview of ongoing research. (October) Open AIR. Retrieved from http://www.openair. org.za/africas-makermovement- an-overview-of-ongoing-research/

de Beer, J., Millar, P., Mwangi, J., Nzomo, V. & Rutenberg, I. (2017) A framework for assessing technology hubs in Africa. *Journal of Intellectual Property and Entertainment Law* 6(2): 237–277. Retrieved from https://jipel.law.nyu. edu/a-framework-for-assessing-technology-hubs-in-africa/

Elahi, S. & de Beer, J. (2013) Knowledge and innovation in Africa: Scenarios for the future. Open AIR.

El Houssamy, N. & Rizk, N. (2018). The maker movement across North Africa. *Open AIR Working Paper No. 17*. University of Cape Town and University of Ottawa: Open African Innovation Research (Open AIR).

Glaser, B.G. & Strauss, A.L. (1967) *The Discovery of Grounded Theory,* Chicago: Aldine.

Jegede, O.O. & Jegede, O.E. (2018) Determinants of innovation capability in informal settings: The case of Nigeria's clustered ICT microenterprises. Open AIR Working Paper 12.

Jensen, M.B., Johnson, B., Lorenz, E. & Lundvall BÅ (2007) Forms of knowledge and modes of innovation. *Research Policy,* 36(5): 680–693.

Kew, J., Herrington, M., Litovsky, Y. & Gale, H. (2013) Generation entrepreneur? The state of global youth entrepreneurship. *Youth Business International and Global Entrepreneurship Monitor,* Newcastle, UK.

Kraemer-Mbula, E., Lorenz, E., Takala-Greenish, L., Jegede, O.O., Garba, T., Mutambala, M. & Esemu, T. (2019) Are African micro- and small enterprises misunderstood? Unpacking the relationship between work organisation, capability development and innovation. *International Journal of Technological Learning, Innovation and Development*, 11(1): 1–30.

Kraemer-Mbula, E. & Armstrong, C. (2017) The maker movement in Gauteng Province, South Africa. Open AIR.

Kraemer-Mbula, E. & Konte, A. (2016) Innovation policy and the informal economy: toward a new policy framework. In E. Kraemer-Mbula & S. Wunsch-Vincent (eds.) *The Informal Economy in Developing Nations: Hidden engine of innovation?*, Cambridge: Cambridge University Press.

Kraemer-Mbula, E. & Wunsch-Vincent, S. (2016) *The Informal Economy in Developing Nations: Hidden engines of innovation?*, Cambridge: Cambridge University Press.

Kraemer-Mbula, E. & Rutenberg, I. (2018) Innovation and technology hubs in Africa, paper presented at AERC biannual research workshop, Mauritius.

Laltaika, EI (2019) Innovation, collaboration and entrepreneurship by the Maasai Women Development Organization (MWEDO), Arusha. Unpublished research report. University of Cape Town and University of Ottawa: Open African Innovation Research (Open AIR).

Lorenz, E., Lundvall, B.Å., Kraemer-Mbula, E. & Rasmussen, P. (2016) Work organisation, forms of employee learning and national systems of education and training. *European Journal of Education*, 51(2): 154–175.

Lundvall, B.Å. (ed.) (2010) *National Systems of Innovation: Toward a theory of innovation and interactive learning* (Vol. 2). Anthem Press.

Maselwanyane, O. (2018). Making at AfricaOSH Summit 2018. Open AIR. Retrieved from http://www.openair.org.za/making-at-africaosh-summit-2018/

Meagher, K. (2007) Manufacturing disorder: Liberalization, informal enterprise and economic 'ungovernance' in African small firm clusters. *Development and Change* 38(3): 473–503.

Nzomo, V., Mwangi, J., Matu-Mureithi, L. & Rutenberg, I. (2018) Open collaborative models of mobile technology innovation in Kenya. Open AIR.

Oguamanam, C. (2017) The Nollywood phenomenon: Innovation, openness and technological opportunism in the modeling of successful African entrepreneurship. Open AIR.

Oyelaran-Oyeyinka, B. (2005) Inter-firm collaboration and competitive pressures: SME footwear clusters in Nigeria. *International Journal of Technology and Globalisation* 1(3–4): 343–360.

Oyelaran-Oyeyinka, B. & McCormick, D. (2007). *Industrial Clusters and Innovation Systems in Africa*. Papers from an author's workshop funded by UNU-INTECH (now UNU-MERIT) and held in Maastricht, the Netherlands at the end of July 2004. United Nations University Press.

Pittaway, L., Robertson, M., Munir, K., Denyer, D. & Neely, A. (2004) Networking and innovation: a systematic review of the evidence. *International Journal of Management Reviews* 5(3–4): 137–168.

Rizk, N., El Said, A., Weheba, N. & de Beer, J. (2018) Towards an alternative assessment of innovation in Africa. Open AIR.

Rutert, B. & Traynor, C. (2019). Complexities of entrepreneurship as practised by two Indigenous organisations in rural South Africa. Open AIR Working Paper No. 20. University of Cape Town and University of Ottawa: Open African Innovation Research (Open AIR). Available at https://openair.africa/complexities-of-social-innovation-and-social-entrepreneurship-by-two-indigenous-organisations-in-rural-south-africa/

Schonwetter, T. & Van Wiele, B. (2018) 3D printing: Enabler of social entre-preneurship in Africa? The role of low-cost 3D printers and fab labs. Open AIR Working Paper No. 18. Available at https://openair.africa/3d-printing-enabler-of-social-entrepreneurship-in-africa-the-roles-of-fablabs-and-low-cost-3d-printers/

Srinivas, S., & Sutz, J. (2008). Developing countries and innovation: Searching for a new analytical approach. Technology in society, 30(2), 129-140.

Waldman-Brown, A., Yaw Obeng, G. & Adu-Gyamfi, Y. (2013) Innovation and stagnation among Ghana's technical artisans. Paper presented at the 22nd Conference for the International Association of Management of Technology (IAMOT). Science, Technology and Innovations in the Emerging Markets, April 14–18, 2013, at Porto Alegre, Brazil.

World Bank (2018) *Doing Business 2019 – Training for reform*. Washington: World Bank.

Zeng, Z.D. (2008) *Knowledge, Technology, and Cluster-based Growth: Africa*. Washington, DC: World Bank.

8.

UNDERSTANDING COGNITIVE BEHAVIOURS OF INNOPRENEURS

Jeff Yu-Jen Chen & Davlin Richardson

Innovation and entrepreneurship are two important driving forces that influence the competitiveness and future preparedness of a nation (Ferreira et al. 2017). They both continue to attract keen interest from scholars and the general public (Acs et al. 2017b; Cornell University et al. 2018; Ferreira et al. 2017) but are often studied in isolation. Two helpful indices for assessing the underlying factors that drive innovation and entrepreneurship are the Global Innovation Index (GII) (Dutta et al. 2018) and the Cornell University Global Entrepreneurship Index (GEI) (Acs et al. 2017b). The GII provides a detailed annual analysis that reflects various countries' capacity for, and success in, innovation. In 2018, the GII ranked 126 countries according to their ability to catalyze innovative activities based on their institutions, human capital and research, infrastructure, market and business sophistication, as well as the actual evidence of knowledge and technology outputs and creative outputs (Cornell University et al. 2018). Similarly, the GEI assesses the vibrancy of the entrepreneurship ecosystems of various countries annually. In 2018, 137 countries were ranked according to 14 measuring pillars: opportunity perception, start-up skills, risk acceptance, networking, cultural support, opportunity start-up, technology absorption, human capital, competition, product innovation, process innovation, high growth (businesses percentage), internationalization and risk capital (Acs et al. 2017b).

Figure 8.1 shows the correlation between a country's innovativeness and the vibrancy of its entrepreneurship ecosystems, which was done by plotting the respective ranking of the countries featured in both GEI 2018 and GII 2018.

The direct and significant correlation shown in Figure 8.1 suggests the importance of studying in conjunction how individuals can be more

Figure 8.1: Correlation between GEI and GII 2018

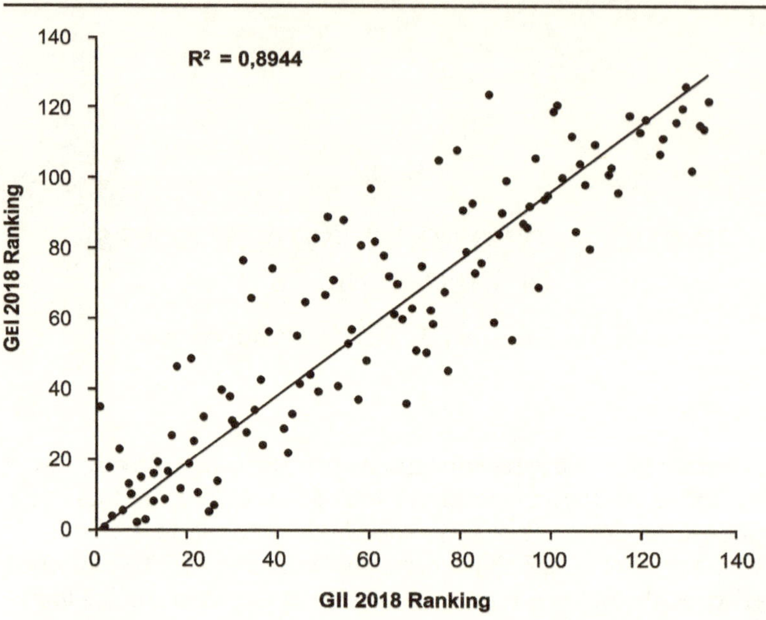

innovative and entrepreneurial, or 'innopreneurship', which is the term used to describe the innovative undertakings that lead to successful entrepreneurship. Innopreneurship has attracted increasing attention in recent years (Baruah & Ward 2015; Gündoğdu 2012; Lynn & Lynn 1992). However, few nations are looking at how to make individuals more innopreneurial and subsequently establishing a holistic plan to promote innopreneurs. Much research gravitates around the types of national infrastructure that policymakers should invest in to enhance innovation activities and entrepreneurial endeavours in a country (Acs et al. 2017b; Alvedalen & Boschma 2017; Audretsch & Belitski 2017; Cornell University et al. 2018; Engel 2015). Yet without understanding how individuals can foster innovative ideas more effectively and complement their ideas by viable entrepreneurship, any investment in infrastructure may prove to be fruitless and wasteful expenditure. In addition, given the exponential rate at which disruption is occurring in most sectors today, private sector entities are encouraging their leaders and employees to become more innopreneurial in response to the fierce business landscape (Hill & Rothermael 2003). By grasping the key underlying innopreneurial cognitive-behavioural components, policymakers and leaders in all sectors will be able to establish enablers that harness higher degrees of innopreneurial output. However, the constructs of innovation and entrepreneurship are often studied in isolation rather than within a consolidated innopreneurial cognitive-behavioural framework based on empirical research. After describing the importance of innopreneurship, this chapter proposes an innopreneurial cognitive-behavioural framework based on input from 57 co-founders of innovative businesses within South Africa and elsewhere on the continent. These findings inform the recommendations for policymakers seeking to foster innopreneurship.

INNOPRENEURIAL THINKING AND BEHAVIOURS

A commonly held view is that an innovative idea must be transformed into a commercially viable offering before it can be considered as an innovation that may disrupt an industry. However, there are few comprehensive models based on empirical research that connect innovation and entrepreneurship (Afuah 2003; Vogel 2016). Discovering new disruptive ideas is difficult and can often be hampered by an individual's cognition ability (Christensen et al. 2015; Slater et al. 2014), as there is a 'significant direct relationship between balanced thinking style and innovative intention and behavioural measures' (Ettlie 2014: 311; Schlaegel & Koenig 2014). The richness of entrepreneurship may lie within the entrepreneur's mental response that developed during the winding path of venture creation, as entrepreneurship is a largely unscripted, unpredictable and uncontrollable temporal journey (Morris et al. 2012). When chasing the next innovative idea, irrespectively of whether the ideas are incremental or disruptive, aspirant innopreneurs must be disciplined in selecting and prioritizing promising concepts (Gündoğdu 2012; Kock et al. 2014). Given the scarcity of research into innopreneurship and the fact that the current theories of disruptive innovation are predominantly based on *a posteriori* views (Christensen et al. 2015; King & Baatartogtokh 2015; Yu & Hang 2010), a framework capable of assisting individuals to come up with innopreneurial concepts would be highly valuable (Politis 2008; Shepherd et al. 2000).

The proposed cognitive-behavioural framework, which may guide the thinking style of aspirant innopreneurs, is based on a two-year long research project initiated in late 2015 and was derived from interviews with 57 co-founders of successful large business ventures, start-ups and/ or disruptive interventions within South Africa and elsewhere on the continent. In total, South African (45), African (9), European (2) and American (1) innopreneurs were interviewed and allowed to freely express their thinking styles and behaviours as they had developed throughout the journey of their innopreneurial ventures (Richardson 2017). The study did not monitor the ongoing success of these innopreneurs nor take into account collective ideation. The possibility of hindsight bias cannot be excluded, as the research was qualitative and, therefore, requires further empirical investigation. Although the research found that interviewees use several dominant cognitive behaviours (see Figure 8.2), the direct validation of actual innovative behaviours in their specific environments, including at the firm level, requires further investigation (Ettlie et al. 2014a). The majority of these innopreneurs are considered disruptors in their respective region, industry and organization by credible media, award committees or their executives. They operate across different industries and sectors, targeting a wide range of customers segments.

Disruption is defined in various ways, with the most prominent definition being that of Christensen (1997), but many other definitions exist and can be found in Kilkki et al. (2018). In addition, the theory of disruptive innovation requires further refinement (Christensen et al. 2018; King & Baatartogtokh 2015). As this research is not about improving definitions, existing definitions were adapted (Christensen et al. 2018; Kilkki et al. 2018; King & Baatartogtokh 2015). It is proposed that a disruption generates significant impact through discontinuous change that requires users and adopters to change their behaviours, or the organization to reposition its modus operandi or business model. Therefore, a disruptor is an agent that disrupts the behaviours or the key stakeholders, the way in which an organization does business, or the dominant logic within an industry.

The research found that five complementary cognitive-behavioural dimensions contribute to the overall innopreneurial endeavours, as illustrated in Figure 8.2. They are: audacious identity and credulous curiosity; intuition, scanning and envisioning; moments of significant and value–construct associations; fragmentation, borrowing and tailoring; and strategic bricolage and enriched navigation.

Quotes from selected interviewees are used to illustrate the findings of this research, in particular the insights from one of the interviewees, Dr. Aisha Pandor, the co-founder of SweepSouth, a start-up venture that has disrupted the domestic services sector in South Africa by offering a platform that connects cleaners with people in need of home or office cleaning services. It provides customers and cleaners with convenience, using an on-demand business model.

Audacious identity and credulous curiosity

Innovators and entrepreneurs need courage to discover and create alternative ways of offering higher values to their customers and stakeholders (Gündoğdu 2012; Kock et al. 2014; Renko et al. 2015). This courage,

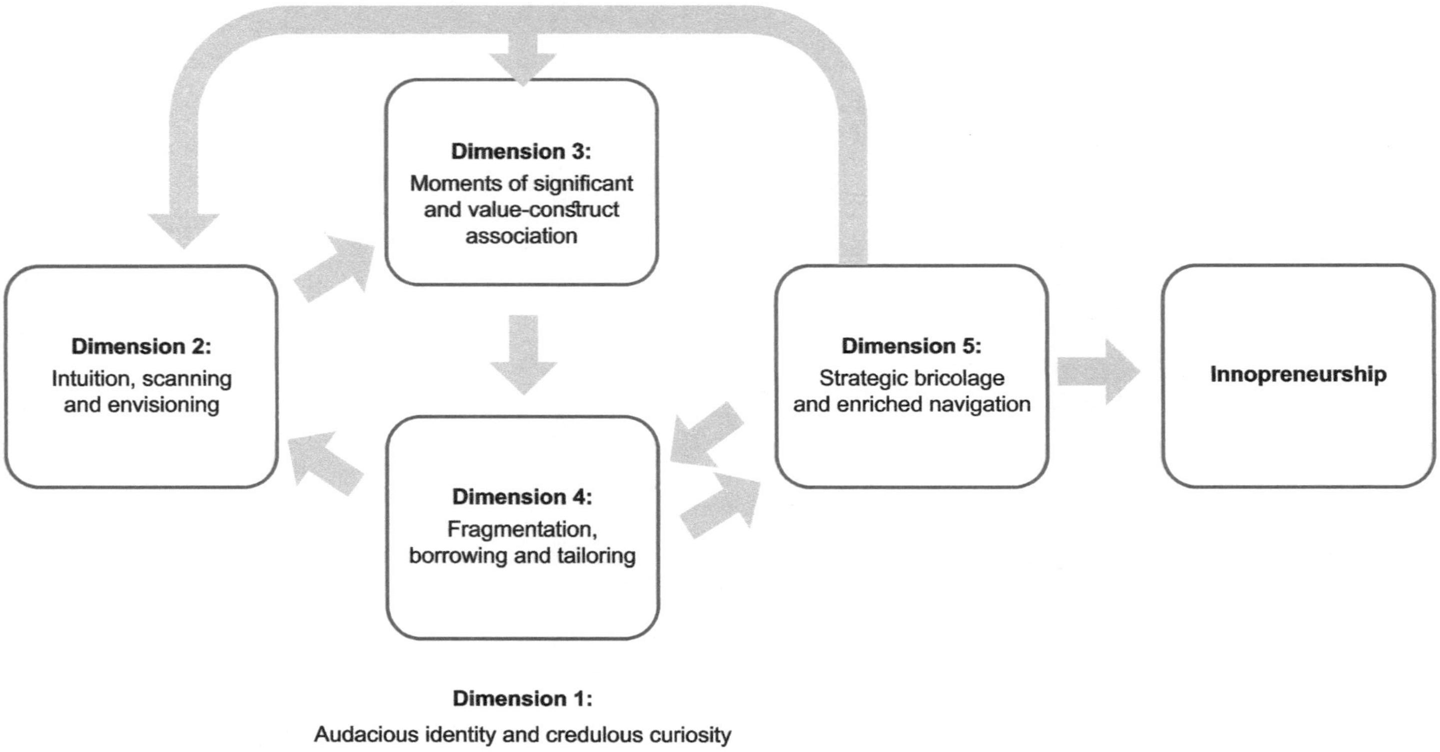

Figure 8.2: The five integrative cognitive-behavioural dimensions of innopreneurship

which is rooted in the audacity to challenge the dominant logic (the common way of thinking across different businesses and/or society) is needed to avoid staying trapped within the confines of established belief systems (Prahalad & Bettis 1986). At some point along their innopreneurial journey, all interviewees began to see themselves differently. Although the root causes that led to the emergence of a new identity varied from one interviewee to another, they were all driven by a strong desire to contribute to the stakeholders. A few interviewees had a score to settle, but their visions and conviction were influenced profoundly by the audacity with which they envisioned their future identities. This emergence and affirmation of an **audacious identity** also contributed towards their entrepreneurial intention (Sweida & Reichard 2013; Schlaegel & Koenig 2014), entrepreneurial orientation (Covin & Lumpkin 2011) and entrepreneurial self-efficacy (Sweida & Reichard 2013). When deeply connected with an entrepreneur's identity, passion and resilience, audacity may greatly influence opportunity recognition, venture creation and venture growth (Arora et al. 2013; Cardon & Kirk 2015; Mooradian et al. 2016; Nordstrom et al. 2016; Vaghely & Julien 2010). As Themba Baloyi, Founder and Executive Director of Discovery Insure Ltd, an innovative motor insurance company under the Discovery Group, states, 'People build a business to make the world a better place, not about the money.' For Neo Hutiri, Founder of Technovera, technology company and the Winner of the Hack.Jozi Awards 2016, his business is his calling: 'I feel that I have to get it done. I have to do it. If nothing else ever came of it, at least when I look back at it, I know I have tried.'

However, courage and purpose do not lead to discovering and creating opportunity. What is required is the ability to be curious about the current status quo and to empathize with the stakeholders. An essential behaviour for innovators is the ability to come up with powerful questions (Dyer et al. 2008; Schoemaker & Krupp 2015), and curiosity is integral to new discoveries resulting from asking these powerful questions (Grant et al. 2012). **Credulous curiosity** is a cognitive-behavioural style that requires continuously asking relevant questions while temporarily suspending all personal assumptions. For the interviewees, many of the milestones in their innopreneurial pursuits resulted from various profound and well-timed questions. These questions appeared to become more profound, seeking a higher order of overarching purpose in support of the questioning, as the audacious identity of the interviewees evolved. For example, when Peter Alkema gathered a few like-minded colleagues to question how the First National Bank (FNB) could accelerate its innovation output despite already being a highly innovation company, the outcome was the birth of codeFest – an internal hackathon that empowered more FNB employees who were kindred spirits to work collectively to foster innovation output (Chen & Scheepers 2019).

Audacious identity and credulous curiosity embolden innopreneurs to challenge the status quo, and to question, observe, network, experiment and take risks. This results in noticeable improvements in their innopreneurial endeavours. The development of identity has been posited as a dynamic transitioning rather than a sequential process (Van Knippenberg et al. 2004; Watson 2009). By being credulously curious, innopreneurs allow new experiences to shape their identity. Therefore, the two sub-components of audacious identity and credulous curiosity hold mutual reinforcing relations and must be developed together.

All of the interviewees strongly exhibited the cognitive behaviours of audacious identity and credulous curiosity. Pandor sees herself as one of South Africa's agents of change who can contribute towards job creation. Her sense of audacious identity influenced the innovativeness of the risks she took and the solutions that she formulated. Pandor and her co-founder constantly ask themselves if the company is still providing value, and constantly adapt their business operations, while maintaining their belief that they will be able to turn SweepSouth into a successful shared value-driven organization.

Intuition, scanning and envisioning

Innovative ideas are often sparked by intuitive hunches rather than by an informed understanding of the business environment (Cohnn et al. 2013; Prahalad 2010). **Intuition** is considered an important trigger of entrepreneurial and innovation-related phenomena (Matzler et al. 2014; Mitchell et al. 2005; Verganti 2016). During the intuiting phase, innovators and entrepreneurs frequently use creative counter-factual thinking to **envision** alterative ways to offer value (Arora et al. 2013). To envision a very different future, innopreneurs often compare actual events to alternatives that were constructed through imagination and dissatisfaction with the current situation, rather than based on past experience (Arora et al. 2013). The interviewees confirmed these cognitive-behavioural components. Furthermore, when supported by an audacious identity, innopreneurs are able take their intuition, scanning and envisioning to a more ambitious level. In the context of innopreneurship, where a future-focused opportunity orientation pervades, a key ingredient for success is envisioning through counterfactual thinking that determines 'what may yet be'.

Successful innopreneurs do not merely base their pursuits on intuiting and envisioning, but also scan locally and globally for past and emerging trends. **Scanning** refers to the continuous assessment of the business environment in search of opportunity and to affirm or shape their intuition and vision (Oyson & Whittaker 2015; Short et al. 2010; Vaghely & Julien 2010). Through such evidence-based approaches, aspiring innopreneurs are also able to create the foresight necessary to predict the feasibility and plausibility of an opportunity (Sarpong & O'Regan 2014), and consequently refine their envisioning process. All the interviewees actively scan the business environment, and many of them immerse themselves in the environment of their key stakeholders in order to personally understand their perspectives. Exercising a healthy level of credulous curiosity also empowers them to tease out the under-lying thoughts and emotions of their key stakeholders. For example, Sharaan Amod, the founder of RecoMed, intuitively sensed that there must be a better way for patients to find and book appointments with all kind of medical practitioners. This intuition prompted him to scan through the relevant technology and business models that formed the developing concept of the disruptive offerings to date.

The interviewees displayed a high tendency to intuit, scan and envi-sion. These three complementary cognitive-behavioural dimensions were observed particularly, but not necessarily exclusively, when intuitive hunches were being transformed into plausible opportunities. Moreover, many interviewees frequently carry out their intuiting, scanning and envisioning activities in partnership with stakeholders, friends, mentors or trusted advisors. Having diverse views and understanding the needs of the customers were seen as pivotal to their innopreneurial endeav-ours. As Jannie Mouton, the Founder and Chairman of the PSG Group, explained: 'We just want to build something that makes sense and adds value to people. Sometimes one doesn't have to complicate things. If you feel where you can make a difference, and look for the areas where others failed, there could be a gap' (Richardson 2017).

Pandor used intuition, scanning and envisioning when she founded her company, SweepSouth, which offers products that had not existed previously in South Africa or elsewhere in Africa – potential customers had never before booked cleaning services online. As far as possible, the SweepSouth founding team tried to use intuition to anticipate obstacles before launching the venture. As Pandor points out, 'As an entrepre-neur and as a disruptor you are entering into a field that is completely new and where you don't have the necessary data available to make decisions, and so intuition becomes quite important.' Pandor used her intuition to envision how the cleaners would be received in terms of both their physical appearance (uniform) and their manner (whether or not they would make the customer feel at ease). This small detail proved to be important when Pandor later interacted with her cleaners and customers. Pandor also frequently referred to 'solving a problem for the customer', which required envisioning an alternative reality. Her vision was initially on a local scale but, once she had learnt more about the state of unemployment among the large numbers of domestic cleaners in South Africa, she envisioned working towards bettering the entire industry, an industry that was 'broken'. Scanning across the business environment permitted her to lay firm foundations for SweepSouth and to pursue new partnerships.

Moments of significance and value–construct associations

Aspirant innopreneurs frequently exercise the appropriate level of empathy to dig deeper into the root causes of the unmet needs of customers and stakeholders, and then to use the insight gained as the springboard of their ideation process (Liedtka 2015). Recent theoretical conceptualizations of value focus on the context of customers' experiences, goals, and desired gratification (Epp & Price 2011; Grönroos & Helle 2010; Grönroos & Voima 2013). In this research, **'moments of significance'** (MoS) are defined as those opportune moments when customers interact, could have interacted and should be thinking of interacting with the innopreneur's offerings. The starting point of a successful innopreneurial venture is a detailed and in-depth understanding of how to create value for the targeted customers (Prahalad 2010). The developing concepts derived from the previous cognitive-behavioural dimensions can only be validated when aspiring innopreneurs are able to tease out the moments that are significant to customers – and, in those moments, how customers assign a certain degree of 'value' to the offering they intend purchasing. To extract meaning from the uncovered MoS, innopreneurs must be skilled in probing the **'value–construct associations'** (VCAs) of their customers. VCAs involve an analytical approach rooted in the theoretical underpinnings of 'job-to-be-done' (Christensen et al. 2016), **'value-percept disparity theory'** (Locke 1967; Wirtz 1993), and personal construct psychology (Karnaze 2013; Kelly 1970).

Job-to-be-done is one of the most pertinent theories in innovation knowledge and is about grasping the higher purpose for which customers buy products, services and solutions – the 'jobs' that they need to be done (Christensen et al. 2016). The value-percept disparity theory highlights that an individual's satisfaction or dissatisfaction is an emotive response generated from an ongoing mental evaluative process. The level of response is highly dependent on an individual's personal perceptions of a particular object, action or condition, as compared to other alternative options and personal values (Locke 1967). However, each individual holds multiple constructs (perceptions, beliefs, thoughts and mental models) that are often not congruent with one another (Kelly 1970). Innopreneurs can use a VCA analysis to gain a better understanding of how a customer assigns value to a product, service or experience received despite the presence of multiple, and possibly conflicting, inner constructs. VCA involves the methodical process of unpacking the underlying rationales of customers based on their relevant behaviours and not merely on what they said. By being credulously curious about how and why customers construe the degrees of value associated with an existing offering, innopreneurs are better able to explore new ways of achieving better results than those currently offered by the market (Brown & Martin 2015; Christensen et al. 2015; Mickahail 2015; Oestreicher 2009). These cognitive-behavioural qualities were highly apparent during interviews with innopreneurs such as Akinola Jones (Aella Credit), Richard Leftley (MicroEnsure) and Chris Czerwonka (Mosabi, then InvestED).

With innovation, especially disruptive innovation, customers have no existing solution or prototype to which they can relate (Gustafsson et al. 2012; Verganti 2009). Therefore, customers do not have the *a priori* knowledge necessary to accurately articulate the value of innovation until they test that innovation. In the case of disruptive innovation, applying the job-to-be-done approach in its simplest form, such as using ethnographical techniques coupled with empathy-driven design thinking, has its limitations (Gebauer et al. 2013; Liedtka 2015; Yu & Hang 2010). Collecting customers' feedback without examining their behaviours and underlying rationales can lead to erroneous assumptions. Individuals are constantly rationalizing their interactions with their surroundings, by construing and reorienting their personal realities and conflicting thoughts to create meaning based on their own narrow views (Karnaze 2013; Kelly 1970). To gain a better understanding of their customers' thoughts and behavioural patterns, innopreneurs may make a concerted effort to deeply sense what customers do, how they attempt to accomplish their goals, what they avoid, how they internalize meaning under different circumstances, and what their cognitive dissonances permit (Epting & Paris 2006). This leads to superior clues for a particular business context. Susie Lonie, Co-Founder and Commercial Head of M-PESA in Kenya, underscores the importance of these construct, 'I have the experience as a customer. I knew what is needed to make things work. I even went to Kenya to experience what customers are experiencing.'

More than 90% of the interviewees analyze the MoS and VCA of both their customers and their customers' customers. Many of them even immerse themselves within the environments of their customers' customers to gain deeper insights, so that they can tailor their offers to enable their customers to satisfy their own customers. Prior to cementing their business concepts, Pandor and her co-founder researched thoroughly MoS and VCA. By diligently interacting with and observing their potential customers, which include both those who provide the cleaning services and those that need the services, they were able to finetune many of their initial ideas. This practice, of analyzing MoS and VCA, continues despite the significant growth of the SweepSouth team over the years. For Pandor, innopreneurs can solve a problem or improve business efficiency when they understand their customers intimately. Practically, this means learning what customers were doing before they used SweepSouth, studying their habits on the website and personally phoning every customer and cleaner for feedback after each interaction, paying special attention to how existing offerings influence a customer's behaviour. Customers' perceptions are often clouded because they have nothing to compare a product to and so it is important to note their behaviour. Pandor describes her approach as 'customer obsessive', and often personally visits customers to gain a better understanding of the customer's job-to-be-done, so that she can help her customers develop a higher level of appreciation for SweepSouth's operations.

Fragmenting, borrowing and tailoring

Having gained an in-depth understanding of customer expectations through MoS and VCA, innopreneurs need to produce a superior offering that is delivered in a simple manner and results in maximum benefits with reduced effort, cost and risks. Many existing plausible ideas and products, including from sectors/industries other than those in which an innopreneur is operating, provide the potential to assist innopreneurs in addressing opportunities at hand (Poetz et al. 2014). However, ideas and products that are highly successful elsewhere may not be perfectly suited to an innopreneur's particular context (Gündoğdu 2012). Conversely, certain core business concepts of failed ventures could offer great commercial value, having simply failed because of the poor execution of other components of business operations. By fragmenting the operations or offerings of relevant entrepreneurial pursuits, innopreneurs are able to 'borrow' certain previously unleveraged innovative concepts and 'tailor' them to suit their own context. This dimension of the cognitive-behavioural approaches is called 'fragmentation, borrowing and tailoring', and its components coincide with Corbett's views (2007). Corbett suggests that entrepreneurs' excellent recognition of opportunity and performance of other key tasks are the result of having the right information and knowledge (i.e. fragment) and the underlying capacity to use this knowledge effectively (i.e. borrow and tailor).

The interviewees concurred that fragmenting, borrowing and tailoring provided them with more strategic options to match and deliver beyond customers' expectations. For example, Barry Swarzberg, the Co-Founder of Discovery Limited, shared how Discovery made use of fragmenting, borrowing and tailoring to assist in the creation of a shared-value based business model that subsequently disrupted the health insurance industry. As he explains,

> No solution is entirely brand new, it's a confluence of ideas. One borrows concepts from someone else. When we read that book from John Goodman, we know we were on the right track. We borrowed the loyalty product concept from the Edgar's club [...] then when Health and Racquet club asked us how can they sell more memberships through Vitality, we borrowed some ideas and incorporated them into our business (Richardson 2017).

For Pandor, the SweepSouth team combined its own creativity and innovation with various existing ideas from other businesses to create better value. The company's aim was not to change completely the way in which the home and office cleaning industry in South Africa functions, but rather to make the current processes more convenient. SweepSouth is an 'improved re-application' of what already existed. SweepSouth connects two sides of the business model, like Uber, and offers a service that involves people's homes and so requires a trust-building ethos, like Airbnb. Pandor uses her intuition and empathy to detect objections or potential objections that her customer base may have to using a service, and borrows from existing business practices to lessen or circumvent such objections. For example, SweepSouth borrowed from Uber's on-demand functionality and Airbnb's ethos of building trust and bringing a community together to create a new and innovative product.

Strategic bricolage and enriched navigation

Central to the pursuit of innovation is actively challenging existing commercialization strategies to transform an innovative idea into a viable venture (Chesbrough 2010). Innovators and entrepreneurs acknowledge that 'bricolage' is a helpful technique and refers to 'something constructed or created from a diverse range of things' (Baker & Nelson 2005; Fisher 2012; Linna 2013). Popular methods, such as the business model canvas (Osterwalder & Yves 2010), the ten types of innovation (TToI) framework (Keeley et al. 2013) and a variety of combinations thereof, are in fact based on the principle of strategic bricolage. **Strategic bricolage** enables innopreneurs to formulate a holistic strategy to maximize profitability, with reduced effort and lowered risk, even during times when bootstrapping is required (Read et al. 2016). Strategic bricolage also encompasses how founders can assemble a team of talents with diverse worldviews and competencies that complement one another (Jin et al. 2017).

The majority of practitioners treat the business model canvas or TToI frameworks as static decision-making tools, but business models need to be adaptive to changes happening within the marketplace

(Wrigley & Straker 2016). Visualizing business models as a road map can provide inspiration for critically strategizing on the interrelation, evolution, potential timing and envisaged impact of the business model's operational actions (De Reuver et al. 2013; Mark et al. 2013). Such approaches allow innopreneurs to improve their businesses through dynamic experimentation, continually improving the value proposition by modifying various business dimensions (Andries et al. 2013; Nicholls-Nixon et al. 2000). Iterations between different structural modes and varying combinations have proved important in enabling a company's transformation to an improved business model (Khanagha et al. 2014). Innovators and entrepreneurs need to continuously learn from the environment and from others in order to be adaptive (Baruah et al. 2015; Blank 2013; Gündoğdu 2012; Lynn & Lynn 1992; Minniti & Bygrave 2001; Ries 2011).

As customers' preferences can change rapidly, innovators, entrepreneurs and innopreneurs have to increase their agility and adaptiveness (Gündoğdu 2012; Ries 2011; Sarasvathy 2001). This calls for rapid learning, subsequent iterations and experimentation. Supported by audacious identity and credulous curiosity, such insights further prompt innopreneurs to look beyond their business models to how they intuit, scan, envision, fragment, borrow and tailor. This effort at adaptive learning in support of a range of interlinked cognitive-behavioural approaches is described as **enriched navigation.** After examining the behaviours of serial entrepreneurs, Saravathy (2001) coined the concept of effectuation – parts of effectuation theory describe the dynamic process of strategic bricolage and enriched navigation. Entrepreneurs constantly attempt to gather more resources and knowledge through personal networks and committed partners. These new resources and knowledge often generate the new means and/or new goals, which enable entrepreneurs to increase the efficiency of their current modus operandi or pivot for new business models and offerings (Saravathy 2001).

The interviewees strongly agreed that the development of their business models is not a static, once-off exercise, but rather their business models resemble roadmaps that evolve dynamically. They consistently show purposeful learning and intellectual experimentation in their approaches to innopreneurial ventures. The interviewees also extensively discussed adopting strategic bricolage and enriched navigation in developing business insights gained from previous thinking steps. They constantly question how they could best translate nascent ideas into even more profitable business ventures based on their lessons learned and that, at times, these lessons lead them to audaciously abandon some of their existing rationalities. Adewale Yusuf, Co-Founder of Techpoint

Nigeria attributes the success of the company to the effective interplay between strategic bricolage and enriched navigation:

> Part of our success is that we continuously try to differentiate. Continuously innovate. [...] Offer more services after we understood the customers and anticipate customers' need. We are constantly changing. [...] When experiencing turmoil, how to adapt and keep going become important. Must know how to adapt. And if needed, change the offerings. Your customers keep on changing. Your industry keeps on changing. One cannot just stay on the same spot even if the first product disrupts the industry (Richardson 2017).

At SouthSweep, Pandor relies on the clues derived from the first three cognitive-behavioural dimensions to detect objections or potential objections that her customer base may have when exercising strategic bricolage. Given that innopreneurs have aggressive goals, any network or recourse needs to be used in multiple ways to gain leverage. One of SweepSouth's determinants for success is giving preference to resources, networks and talents more apposite to a task through iterative improvement. Frequent iteration may lead to transformative ways of solving a situation – 'iteration is to entrepreneurs what compound interest is to bankers'. Pandor notes that some iterations may not be significant, but they tend to be compounded, resulting in a polished end product.

Pandor regards herself as an avid learner. The holistic approach of combining knowledge, resources and talents supported by perpetually learning from the environment, stakeholders and outcomes of their strategies has enabled SweepSouth to grow from strength to strength. In addition, timing and intuition need to accompany bricolage, for example when to call on a particular resource or who to use. What is important is continuous learning and an ability to set aside one's ego while simultaneously 'aggressively pursuing goals'. For Pandor, innopreneurs need to be able to review critically their resources and assumptions, including who would be the best person to undertake a particular task (themselves or bring in someone more suited), and whether or not to pivot some of the business operations, as they steer their ventures into uncharted territories.

RECOMMENDATIONS AND APPLICATION OF FINDINGS

Across the different regions of Africa, economic growth and the improvement of living standards remain inconsistent (Grey 2017; OECD 2018). Many emerging economies continue to experience low economic growth, in part owing to the rapid pace of the Fourth Industrial Revolution, and become vulnerable to global economic turbulence (OECD 2018).

Therefore, they need to develop sound strategies to promote innopreneurship and prioritize innopreneurial activities that can strengthen productivity, narrow inequality and catalyze inclusive growth. Policymakers must be able to identify, develop and encourage innopreneurs who have technical competency, leadership skills and a risk-taking attitude (Camacho 2012; Pistol et al. 2016).

Africa's greatest economic growth opportunity is to foster innopreneurship and increase trade and partnership among its members (Makhubela 2018). The innopreneurship journey differs from individual to individual, and depends on the industry, business model, region, historical context and capabilities of founders. Leaders who aim to design holistic strategies to support African innopreneurs must take these unique challenges into consideration. Beyond simply instituting funding mechanisms to foster high-growth businesses and launching incentives to encourage aspirant innopreneurs to take risks, many African governments may need to revise their policies to reduce the lack of expertise, complex regulation, high compliance costs and negative implications of insolvency (Mazur et al. 2016). Having the right combination of factors and policies can advance the progress of innopreneurship within a region and consequently increase the economic vitality, social upliftment and competitiveness of communities (Engel 2015). Policymakers can establish an effective strategy that cultivates and supports the innopreneurial cognitive-behavioural dimensions uncovered in this research.

Policymakers should adopt an innopreneurial-centred view and formulate a holistic 'clusters of innopreneurship' (CoI) strategy to promote innopreneurial businesses. Drawing from the key concepts of systems of innovation (Acs et al. 2017a; Chen et al. 2018; Cornell University et al. 2018), entrepreneurship ecosystems (Alvedalen & Boschma 2017; Audretsch & Belitski 2017), helical models of innovation (Carayannis et al. 2018) and clusters of innovation (Engel 2015; Mazur et al. 2016), a CoI can be defined as a critical mass of relevant actors who generate an interconnected, vibrant ecosystem of synergistic activities that are conducive for innopreneurial undertakings. Educators and incubators within a CoI are skilled with the tactics that can encourage innopreneurial thinking (Engel 2015) and cultivate effective multi-stakeholder partnerships across the business value-chain (Acs et al. 2017a; Alvedalen & Boschma 2017; Audretsch & Belitski 2017; Carayannis et al. 2018; Chen et al. 2018; Cornell University et al. 2018; Engel 2015; Mazur et al. 2016). As high-growth innopreneurial endeavours typically face a range of challenges, such as accessing finance, workforce skills, networks and technology, an effective CoI embraces the ethos of being strategic, total, open and collaborative (Chen et al. 2018). The relentless pursuit of synergistic partnerships with other CoIs by key stakeholders brings about new business opportunities, more enabling mechanisms, the consolidation of value-chain and staged financing, while reducing the risk of being disrupted by the rapid revolution of business models.

Innopreneurship must be nurtured, spread and encouraged. Considering that the cognitive-behavioural dimensions and CoI share a complementary relationship, policymakers cannot blindly create CoI without understanding how disruptive ideas and innovative businesses are best conceived. Similarly, individuals possessing these innopreneurial cognitive-behavioural dimensions may struggle unless a holistic CoI can be created. Therefore, informed by the findings of this research and combining the insights of influential publications (Cornell University et al. 2018; Engel 2018; Acs et al. 2017b), eight CoI key components are proposed that policymakers should emphasize:

1. Refine the necessary regulation, administration processes and tax benefits to encourage the creation of new businesses. This would not only reduce the frustration of aspirant individuals to create innopreneurship, but also increase their tendency to exercise Dimensions 1 and 5 of this framework.

2. Democratize innopreneurship education and mentorship to elevate the depth of innopreneurial thinking capability within the CoI. Human capital development schemes should be anchored on these five dimensions. Moreover, the interventions must emphasize how to generate practically tangible outputs instead of narrowly focusing on the input only. The cost of training and mentorship should ideally be subsidized through public sector grants and private sector corporate social investment grants. Training and knowledge exchange activities for mentors should also be implemented. Most importantly, all aspirant innopreneurs who benefit from these activities must be contracted upfront to contribute back to the CoI, so that a self-enriching, vibrant ecosystem can be established.

3. Create policies to attract investment from venture capitalists and large corporates into the CoI. The lack of funding can be a key factor that determines the success of innopreneurship. A balance between aggressive and conservative working capitals ensures that different types of the innopreneurship can be nurtured contextually. Moreover, from the strategic bricolage perspective, partnerships with these key stakeholders may bring about new business opportunities within the existing ecosystems and business value-chains.

4. Institute incentives to entice service providers and professional management to do business with aspirant innopreneurs, or to bridge the skill gaps during the emerging stage of the ventures. Not all innopreneurs possess all the competencies in the five dimensions required to launch and sustain a successful innopreneurship.

5. Implement policies that can motivate research centres and universities to collaborate with aspirant innopreneurs. The national research governing body must motivate research that will spur the technological advancements or generate business insights. In so doing, it will close the gaps between academic research and emerging business needs.

6. Harness vibrant innopreneurial communities by promoting open innovation. Crucial to the overall success of CoIs is networking with other stakeholders and establishing an informal community for the purpose of exchanging valuable resources and support. Policymakers should implement comprehensive and open innovation mechanisms, such as online databases and portals, to match multiple stakeholders who share common goals.

7. Enhance living conditions by introducing basic infrastructure, including safety and security, access to the internet and other living conditions to attract all key stakeholders. Unless their primary needs are addressed, individuals will have to spend considerable energy on mitigating daily challenges, which takes a significant portion of time away from advancing their pursuits.

8. Invest in large, frequent public advocacy and marketing campaigns to increase the awareness, culture and philosophy that may lead to more innopreneurship. After all, the national culture is one of the biggest contributors towards innovation and entrepreneurship.

CONCLUSION

With high unemployment rates and yet a strong entrepreneurial ecosystem foundation, Africa will benefit significantly by increasing support for its ambitious innopreneurs. A new breed of entrepreneurs and innopreneurs will emerge if the cognitive-behavioural process model (as extracted from the research presented in this study) is included in the curriculums of educational institutions and policy making, and aspirant innopreneurs are exposed to the practice of innovation. These innopreneurs will have the intuition, audacity, credulity, and the resources and training to discover and create new or re-applied innovations capable of disrupting the African economy while increasing employment, living standards, socio-political advancements and an inclusive socio-economic order.

Limitations

These research findings are based on the contributions of successful innopreneurs, the majority of whom are seen as disruptors by their peers and credible sources. Future research should incorporate unsuccessful cases and possibly use quantitative research to validate the impact of these dimensions. Studies to validate the underlying factors within these dimensions can make use of factor analyses and structural modelling equation methodologies. Despite this being a challenging task, the findings may bring about additional insight into the correlations between the cognitive-behavioural factors and dimensions.

BIBLIOGRAPHY

Acs, Z.J., Audretsch, D.B., Lehmann, E.E. & Licht, G. (2017a) National systems of innovation. *The Journal of Technology Transfer* 42(5): 997–1008.

Acs, Z.J, Szerb, L. & Lloyd, A. (2017b) The global entrepreneurship and development index 2018. *SpringerBriefs in Economics*.

Afuah, A. (2003) *Innovation Management* (Second Ed.). New York: Oxford University Press.

Alvedalen, J. & Boschma, R. (2017) A critical review of entrepreneurial ecosystems research: Towards a future research agenda. *European Planning Studies* 25(6): 887–903.

Andries, P., Debackere, K. & Looy, B. (2013) Simultaneous experimentation as a learning strategy: Business model development under uncertainty. *Strategic Entrepreneurship Journal* 7: 288–310.

Arora, P., Haynie, J.M. & Laurence, G.A. (2013) Counterfactual thinking and entrepreneurial self-efficacy: The moderating role of self-esteem and dispositional affect. *Entrepreneurship: Theory & Practice* 37(2): 359–385.

Audretsch, D.B. & Belitski, M. (2017) Entrepreneurial ecosystems in cities: Establishing the framework conditions. *The Journal of Technology Transfer* 42(5): 1030–1051.

Baker, T. & Nelson, R.E. (2005) Creating something from nothing: Resource construction through entrepreneurial bricolage. *Administrative Science Quarterly* 50: 329–366.

Baruah, B. & Ward, A. (2015) Metamorphosis of intrapreneurship as an effective organizational strategy. *International Entrepreneurship and Management Journal* 11(4): 811–822.

Blank, S. (2013) Why the lean start-up changes everything. *Harvard Business Review* 91: 63–72.

Brown, T. & Martin, R. (2015) Design for action. *Harvard Business Review* (September): 3–10.

Camacho, R. (2012) How to build science capacity. Nature (October 18): 490.

Carayannis, E.G., Grigoroudis, E., Campbell, D.F., Meissner, D. & Stamati, D. (2018) The ecosystem as helix: an exploratory theory-building study of regional co-opetitive entrepreneurial ecosystems as quadruple/quintuple helix innovation models. *R&D Management* 48(1): 148–162.

Cardon, M.S. & Kirk, C.P. (2015) Entrepreneurial passion as mediator of the self-efficacy to persistence relationship. *Entrepreneurship: Theory & Practice* 39(5): 1027–1050.

Chen, J., Yin, X. & Mei, L. (2018) Holistic innovation: An emerging innovation paradigm. *International Journal of Innovation Studies* 2(1): 1–13.

Chen, J.Y.J. & Scheepers, C. (2019) *FNB codeFest: Fostering corporate innovation through in-house hackathons.* Ontario: Ivey Publishing.

Chesbrough, H. (2010) Business model innovation: opportunities and barriers. *Long Range Planning* 43(2–3): 354–363.

Christensen, C.M. (1997) *The innovator's dilemma: When new technologies cause great firms to fail.* Brighton, MA: Harvard Business Review Press.

Christensen, C.M., Raynor, M. & McDonald, R. (2015) The big idea: what is disruptive innovation? *Harvard Business Review* (December): 44–56.

Christensen, C.M., Hall, T., Dillon, K. & Duncan, D.S. (2016) Know your customers' 'jobs to be done'. *Harvard Business Review* 94(9): 54–62.

Christensen, C.M., McDonald, R., Altman, E.J. & Palmer, J.E. (2018) Disruptive innovation: An intellectual history and directions for future research. *Journal of Management Studies* 55(7): 1043–1078.

Cohnn, J., Squire, P., Estabrooke, I. & O'Neill, E. (2013) Enhancing intuitive decision making through implicit learning. *Foundations of Augmented Cognition:* 401-409

Corbett, A.C. (2007) Learning asymmetries & the discovery of entrepreneurial opportunities. *Journal of Business Venturing* 22: 97–118.

Cornell University, INSEAD, and WIPO (2018) *The Global Innovation Index 2018: Energizing the world with innovation.* Ithaca, Fontainebleau, and Geneva

Covin, J.G. & Lumpkin, G.T. (2011) Entrepreneurial orientation theory and research: Reflections on a needed construct. *Entrepreneurship: Theory & Practice* 35(5): 855–872.

De Reuver, M., Bouwman, H. & Haaker, T. (2013) Business model roadmapping: a practica lapproach to come from an existing to a desired business model. *International Journal of Innovation Management* 17.

Dutta, S., Lanvin, B., & Wunsch-Vincent, S. (Eds.). (2018). *The global innovation index 2018: Energizing the world with innovation.* WIPO.

Dyer, J.H., Gregersen, H.B. & Christensen, C. (2008) Entrepreneur behaviors, opportunity recognition, and the origins of innovative ventures. *Strategic Entrepreneurship Journal* 2(4): 317–338.

Engel, J.S. (2015) Global clusters of innovation: Lessons from Silicon Valley. *California Management Review* 57(2): 36–65.

Epp, A.M. & Price, L.L. (2011) Designing solutions around customer network identity goals. *Journal of Marketing* 75 (March): 36–54.

Epting, F.R. & Paris, M.E. (2006) A constructive understanding of the person: George Kelly and humanistic psychology. *The Humanistic Psychologist* 34(1): 21–37.

Ettlie, J.E., Groves, K.S., Vance, C.M. & Hess G L (2014) Cognitive style and innovation in organizations. *European Journal of Innovation Management* 17(3): 311–326.

Ferreira, J.J., Fernandes, C.I. & Ratten, V. (2017) Entrepreneurship, innovation and competitiveness: what is the connection? *International Journal of Business & Globalisation* 18(1): 73–95.

Fisher, G. (2012) Effectuation, causation, & bricolage: A behavioural comparison of emerging theories in entrepreneurship research. *Entrepreneurship Theory & Practice* 1019–1051.

Gebauer, J., Füller, J. & Pezzei, R. (2013) The dark and the bright side of co-creation: Triggers of member behavior in online innovation communities. *Journal of Business Research* 66(9): 1516–1527.

Grant, A., Grant, G. & Gallate, J. (2012) *Who killed creativity?* Melbourne: Jossey-Bass. A Wiley imprint.

Grey, A. (2017) These are the world's fastest-growing economies in 2017. *World Economic Forum*.

Grönroos, C. & Helle, P. (2010) Adopting a service logic in manufacturing. Conceptual foundation and metrics for mutual value creation. *Journal of Service Management* 21(5): 564–590.

Grönroos, C. & Voima, P. (2013) Critical service logic: Making sense of value creation and co-creation. *Journal of the Academic of Marketing Science* 41: 133–150.

Gündoğdu M C (2012) Re-thinking entrepreneurship, intrapreneurship, and innovation: A multi-concept perspective. *Procedia-Social and Behavioral Sciences* 41: 296–303.

Gustafsson, A, Kristensson P & Witell L (2012) Customer co-creation in service innovation: A matter of communication? *Journal of Service Management* 23(3): 311–327.

Hill, C.W.T.N. & Rothermael, F.T. (2003) The performance of incumbent firms in the face of radical technological innovation. *Academy of Management Review* 28(2): 257–274.

Ismael, F. (2016) Advancing the continental free trade area (CFTA) and Agenda 2063 in the context of the changing architecture of global trade. *TIPS Working Paper* December 2016.

Jin, L., Madison, K., Kraiczy, N D, Kellermanns F.W., Crook, T.R & Xi, J. (2017) Entrepreneurial team composition characteristics and new venture performance: A meta-analysis. *Entrepreneurship Theory & Practice* 41(5): 743–771.

Juma, C. (2011) *The New Harvest – Agricultural innovation in Africa,* Oxford: Oxford University Press.

Juma, C. (2018) *A new culture of innovation: Technology, entrepreneurship and prosperity*;

Juma, C. & Mangeni, F. (2018) African regional economic integration: The emergence, evolution, and impact of institutional innovation. *Faculty Research Working Paper Series*, Harvard Kennedy School

Karnaze, M.M. (2013) A constructivist approach to defining human emotion: from George Kelly to Rue Cromwell. *Journal of Constructivist Psychology* 26(3): 194–201.

Keeley, L., Ryan, P., Brian, Q. & Helen, W. (2013) *Ten Types of Innovation: The discipline of building breakthroughs,* Hoebeken, NJ: John Wiley & Sons.

Kelly, G.A. (1970) A brief introduction to personal construct theory. In D Bannister (ed.) (1970) *Perspectives in Personal Construct Theory,* London: Academic Press, 1–29.

Khanagha, S., Volberda, H. & Oshri, I. (2014) Business model renewal and ambidexterity: structural alteration and strategy formation process during transition to a Cloud business model. *R and D Management* 44(3): 322–340.

Kilkki, K., Mäntylä, M., Karhu, K., Hämmäinen, H. & Ailisto, H. (2018) A disruption framework. *Technological Forecasting and Social Change* 129: 275–284.

King, A.A. & Baatartogtokh, B. (2015) How useful is the theory of disruptive innovation? *MIT Sloan Management Review* 57(1): 77–90.

Kock, A., Heising, W. & Gemünden, H.G. (2014) How ideation portfolio management influences front-end success. *Journal of Product Innovation Management* 32(4): 539–555.

Kraft, M.E. & Furlong, S.R. (2015) *Public Policy: Politics, analysis, and alternatives,* California: CQPress.

Lakin, J. & Mudida, R. (2015) Sharing resources fairly: The evolution of Kenya's revenue sharing formula, 2012–2015. International Budget Partnership and Strathmore Business School Case Study.

Liedtka, J. (2015) Perspective: Linking design thinking with innovation outcomes through cognitive bias reduction. *Journal of Product Innovation Management* 32(6): 925–938.

Linna, P. (2013) Bricolage as a means of innovating in a resource-scarce environment: a study of innovator-entrepreneurs at the BOP. *Journal of Developmental Entrepreneurship* 18(3): 1–24.

Locke, E.A. (1967) Relationship of success and expectation to affect on goal seeking tasks. *Journal of Personality & Social Psychology* 7(2): 125-134.

Lynn, G.S. & Lynn, N.M. (1992) *Innopreneurship: Turning bright ideas into breakthrough business for your company,* Chicago: Probus Publishing Company.

Makhubela, K. (2018) Africa's greatest economic opportunity: trading with itself. *World Economic Forum Annual Meeting.*

Mangeni, F. (2018) The African continental free trade area – A beacon of free trade? *ATDF Journal-AfCFTA* 9(2).

Mark, D.R., Bouwman, H. & Kaaker, T. (2013) Business model roadmapping: a practical approach to come from an existing to a desired business model. *International Journal of Innovation Management* 17(1).

Matzler, K., Uzelac, B. & Bauer, F. (2014) Intuition's value for organizational innovativeness and why managers still refrain from using it. *Management Decision* 52(3): 526–539.

Mazur, V.V., Barmuta, K.A., Demin, S.S., Tikhomirov, E.A. & Bykovskiy, M.A. (2016) Innovation clusters: Advantages and disadvantages. *International Journal of Economics & Financial Issues* 6(1S): 270–274.

Mickahail B (2015) Corporate implementation of design thinking for innovation and economic growth. *Journal of Strategic Innovation & Sustainability* 10(2): 67–79.

Minniti, M and Bygrave, W (2001) A dynamic model of entrepreneurial learning. *Entrepreneurship theory and practice 25*(3), 5–16.

Mitchell, J.R., Friga, P.N. & Mitchell, R.K. (2005) Untangling the intuition mess: Intuition as a construct in entrepreneurship research. *Entrepreneurship: Theory & Practice* 29(6): 653–679.

Mooradian, T., Matzler, K., Uzelac, B. & Bauer, F. (2016) Perspiration and inspiration: Grit and innovativeness as antecedents of entrepreneurial success. *Journal of Economic Psychology* 56: 232–243.

Morris, M.H., Kuratko, D.F., Schindehutte, M. & Spivack, A.J. (2012) Framing the entrepreneurial experience. *Entrepreneurship: Theory & Practice* 36(1): 11–40.

Mudida, R. (2015) *Structural Sources of Constitutional Conflicts in Kenya: A conflict analysis of constitution-making in Kenya, 1997–2005,* Germany: Scholar's Press.

Mugabe, J. (2011) Science, technology and innovation in Africa's regional integration – from rhetoric to practice. *ACODE Policy Research Series No.44.*

Nicholls-Nixon, C.L., Cooper A.C., & Woo, C.Y. (2000) Strategic experimentation: understanding change and performance in new ventures. *Journal of Business Venturing* 15(5): 493–521.

Nordstrom, C., Siren, C.A., Thorgren, S. & Wincent, J. (2016) Passion in hybrid entrepreneurship: the impact of entrepreneurial teams and tenure. *Baltic Journal of Management* 11(2): 167–186.

OECD (2018) In Africa, government action is key to overcoming challenges related to growth, jobs and inequalities, according to the new joint report by the African Union Commission and the OECD Development Centre, July 11. Available at https://www.oecd.org/dev/africa-government-action-key-to-overcoming-challenges-related-to-growth-jobs-inequalities-according-to-new-joint-report-by-african-union-commission-and-the-oecd-development-centre.htm

Oestreicher, K. (2009) Segmentation and the jobs-to-be-done theory: A conceptual approach to explaining product failure. *Journal of Marketing* 5(2): 103–122.

Osterwalder, A. & Yves, P. (2010) *Business model generation: A handbook for visionaries, game changers, and challengers*. Chichester: John Wiley & Sons Ltd.

Oyson M J & Whittaker H (2015) Entrepreneurial cognition and behavior in the discovery and creation of international opportunities. *Journal of International Entrepreneurship* 13(3): 303–336.

Pistol L, Epure M & Bucea-Manea-Toniş R (2016) WEB-Marketing Strategy for SMEs. *Procedia of Economics and Business Administration* 1: 128–137.

Poetz, M., Franke, N., & Schreier, M. (2014) Sometimes the Best Ideas Come from Outside Your Industry. *Harvard Business Review* (November), 1–8.

Politis, D. (2008) Does prior start-up experience matter for entrepreneurs' learning? A comparison between novice and habitual entrepreneurs. *Journal of Small Business & Enterprise Development* 15(3): 472–489.

Prahalad, C.K. (2010) Innovation's holy grail. *Harvard Business Review* 88(7/8): 132–141.

Prahalad, C.K. & Bettis R.A. (1986) The dominant logic: A new linkage between diversity and performance. *Strategic Management Journal* 7(6): 485–501.

Read, S., Sarasvathy, S., Dew, N. & Wiltbank, R. (2016) *Effectual Entrepreneurship*, New York: Routledge.

Renko, M, El Tarabishy A., Carsrud, A.L. & Brännback, M. (2015) Understanding and measuring entrepreneurial leadership style. *Journal of Small Business Management* 53(1): 54–74.

Ries, E. (2011) *The Lean Startup: How today's entrepreneurs use continuous innovation to create radically successful businesses*, New York: Crown Business.

Richardson, D. (2017) A preliminary cognitive framework towards effective ideation for disruptive innovation. (Masters dissertation). Gordon Institute of Business Science, University of Pretoria. Available at https://repository.up.ac.za/bitstream/handle/2263/59759/Richardson_Preliminary_2017.pdf?sequence=1&isAllowed=y

Sarasvathy, S. (2001). Causation and effectuation: Toward a theoretical shift from economic inevitability to entrepreneurial contingency. *Academy of Management Review,* 26(2), 243–263.

Sarpong, D. & O'Regan, N. (2014) The Organizing Dimensions of Strategic Foresight in High Velocity Environments. *Strategic Change,* 23(3-4), 125-132.

Schlaegel, C. & Koenig, M. (2014) Determinants of entrepreneurial intent: A meta-analytic test and integration of competing models. *Entrepreneurship: Theory & Practice* 38(2): 291–332.

Schoemaker, P.J.H. & Krupp, S. (2015) The power of asking pivotal questions. *MIT Sloan Management Review* 56(2): 39–47.

Shepherd, D.A., Douglas, E.J. & Shanley, M. (2000) New venture survival: ignorance, external shocks, and risk reduction strategies. *Journal of Business Venturing* 15: 393–410.

Short, J.C., Ketchen, D.J., Shook, C.L. & Ireland, R.D. (2010) The concept of "opportunity" in entrepreneurship research: Past accomplishments and future challenges. *Journal of Management* 36: 40–65.

Slater, S.F., Mohr, J.J. & Sengupta, S. (2014) Radical product innovation capability: Literature review, synthesis, and illustrative research propositions. *Journal of Product Innovation Management* 31(3): 552–566.

Sweida, G.L. & Reichard, R.J. (2013) Gender stereotyping effects on entrepreneurial self efficacy and highgrowth entrepreneurial intention. *Journal of Small Business & Enterprise Development* 20(2): 296–313.

Vaghely, I.P & Julien, P.A. (2010) Are opportunities recognized or constructed? An information perspective on entrepreneurial opportunity identification. *Journal of Business Venturing* 25(1): 73–86.

Van Knippenberg, D., van Knippenberg, B., De Cremer, D. & Hogg, M.A. (2004) Leadership, self and identity: A review and research agenda. *The Leadership Quarterly* 15: 825–856.

Verganti, R. (2009) *Design Driven Innovation: Changing the rules of competition by radically innovating what things mean,* Boston, Massachusetts, USA: Harvard Business Press.

Verganti, R. (2016) The innovative power of criticism. *Harvard Business Review* (February): 88–95.

Vogel, P. (2016) From venture idea to venture opportunity. *Entrepreneurship Theory & Practice* (June): 1–29.

Watson, T.J. (2009) Entrepreneurial action, identity work and the use of multiple discursive resources: The case of a rapidly changing family business. *International Small Business Journal* 27(3): 251–274.

Wirtz, J. (1993) A critical review of models in consumer satisfaction. *Asian Journal of Marketing* 2(1): 7–22.

Wrigley, C. & Straker, K. (2016) Designing innovative business models with a framework that promotes experimentation. *Strategy & Leadership* 44(1): 11–19.

Yu, D. & Hang, C.C. (2010) A reflective review of disruptive innovation theory. *International Journal of Management Reviews* 12(4): 435–452.

9.

LEVERAGING NEURO-PHENOMENOLOGY INSIGHTS TOWARDS PARADIGM-SHIFTING FOR SUSTAINABLE CITY TRANSITIONING

Daniel Irurah, Heinrich Kammeyer,
Sechaba Maape & Vipua Rukambe

We cannot solve our problems with the same thinking we used when we created them (commonly attributed to Albert Einstein, but without date or traceable original source)

Today, humanity is facing escalating challenges, as gains from our socio-technical innovations are not translating fast enough into changes that would enable us to avert global crises, such as climate change, loss of biodiversity or even socio-economic inequalities. At the same time, insights from neuroscience and consciousness studies (especially in the field of neuro-phenomenology, with its emphasis on the understanding of mind as the coupling of brain, body and environment) are enhancing our capacity to tackle this inertia, and thus allow for expedited transitioning. These insights are also dislodging the prevailing model of a fixed reality that pre-exists independently of the human observer, in favour of a worldview (paradigm) based on *perpetual flux* and *interdependency* (a co-emerging of our existence) as the foundation of our newly emerging sense of reality.

This chapter presents multi-disciplinary scholarship anchored in architecture that leverages the above insights to tackle the prevailing inertia in paradigm shifting with specific focus on sustainable city transitioning. This is substantiated along the three key themes of: innovative multi-disciplinary research; innovative multi-disciplinary postgraduate curriculum; and prototyping of trans-disciplinary guided leadership skills for transitioning. In addition, a brief outline is presented of a newly launched prototyping of the convergence towards smart- and sustainable-city transitioning for Mombasa, Kenya. A perspective is then offered into how these insights could not only help expedite sustainable city transitioning in general, but also contribute to embedding futures-literacy across all levels of the education system. The human mind's creative capacity (as a coupling of brain, body and environment) is also highly inspiring, especially for innovation towards sustainable city transitioning. The chapter closes with some key insights and recommendations, in particular on the critical need for the establishment of context-responsive, neuroscience research labs in Africa, where no meaningful or systematic research is currently happening in these multi-disciplinary domains of neuroscience and neuro-phenomenology.

PLANETARY CHALLENGES AND CRISES
OF THE ANTHROPOCENE ERA

Our contemporary planetary crises have now gained geological recognition through their categorization as the Anthropocene period (see Davies 2016; Lewis & Maslin 2018). Africa's rapid urbanization at the peak of the Anthropocene strongly manifests the dystopias of modernism and globalization among other myths of the overarching utopia of *human development* and *progress* (Bello-Schünemann 2018; UN-Habitat 2014; Irurah et al. 2004) Some of the popular readings on the ramifications of these myths include Fleming (2017), de Rivero (2010) and Orrell (2012). The materialistic translation of the once noble goals (human development and progress) into consumerism and individualism has not only undermined most of the other values once held dear but is also contributing to a heightened sense of scarcity and anxiety over insufficiency of resources for everyone's well-being and survival (Wuellner 2011).

Our dystopia is therefore characterized by this incapacity to grasp the opportunity from humanity's integration into the western model of development and progress, while abandoning other models of alternative futures. With WCED (1987) as the primary example of our re-visioning efforts, we hope to pursue our common future guided by sustainability as our new vision and utopia. For Africa specifically, the pursuit of development and progress has marginalized African worldviews and values, such as *botho/ubuntu,* which is commonly popularized as 'I am because we are'. Although such African worldviews have been systematically studied, and multiple sources are now available (see for example Ramose 1999 and Eze 2010), complementary scholarship guided by the emerging science-based methods of neuro-phenomenology has not yet taken root. As narrated later in this chapter, the study team participated in the *botho/ubuntu* dialogue in Botswana 2017, which was aimed at kick-starting such multi-disciplinary scholarship, with neuro-phenomenology as a critical component. This would thus complement the prevailing *ubuntu* scholarship as commonly framed within philosophy, psychology, sociology or anthropology.

Contrary to the principles of worldviews such as *ubuntu*, humanity has relentlessly pursued development within the utopia of a modernizing progress, anchored in a fixed-reality paradigm (or *essentialism*) and positivistic scientism mainly informed by an extremely narrow cause – effect mental model of the world. Therefore, progress continues to be understood as – and pursued through – accelerating incremental growth in economic wealth (with forecasting as the primary steering tool) for improving our well-being. In urban development, this translates into techno-spatial master planning aimed at underpinning (rather than questioning or disrupting) a consumerism-driven vision of well-being and improved quality of life in the city (see Markard et al. 2012; Wuellner 2011).

As a result, despite almost 50 years of scientific evidence of the crises now facing humanity (e.g. Meadows et al. 1972), inertia (at both the collective and individual scale) is increasingly evident and constraining our capacity to transition. To have a better understanding of this inertia, related human behaviour and its key drivers were studied using a neuro-phenomenological approach and starting from architecture as an academic and practice discipline. This approach to studying related human behaviour and its key drivers provides better insights to the resultant inertia, as well as possible paradigm-shifting tools and methods for tackling the inertia, especially through the more empowering paradigm of *constructivism* (Gichia 2013; Maape 2016).

Commenting on the need for paradigm shifting, Kuhn (1962) differentiated between normal science and scientific revolutions, arguing that the practice of normal science inevitably takes place within an established paradigm, until increasing anomalous findings (scientific observations that are contrary to the paradigmatic assumptions of the time) necessitate the birth of a new paradigm that can accommodate the growing range of anomalies. Shifting her reference from scientific revolutions to systems thinking, Meadows (1999: 17–18) defines paradigms as:

> The shared idea in the minds of society, the great big unstated assumptions – unstated because unnecessary to state; everyone already knows them – constitute that society's paradigm, or deepest set of beliefs about how the world works. There is a difference between nouns and verbs. Money measures something real and has real meaning (therefore people who are paid less are literally worth less). Growth is good. Nature is a stock of resources to be converted to human purposes. Evolution stopped with the emergence of Homo sapiens. One can "own" land. Those are just a few of the paradigmatic assumptions of our current culture, all of which have utterly dumbfounded other cultures, who thought them not

the least bit obvious. Paradigms are the sources of systems. From them, from shared social agreements about the nature of reality, come system goals and information flows, feedbacks, stocks, flows and everything else about systems.

This updated understanding of paradigm and paradigm shifting within systems thinking constitutes the foundation of this chapter. The study team has investigated various paradigm-shifting approaches in the form of studies and prototyping under action research.

PARADIGM-SHIFTING IMPERATIVE: FROM *ESSENTIALISM* TO A CO-CREATED REALITY UNDER *CONSTRUCTIVISM*

The term *constructivism* was developed and applied in diverse fields long before neuroscientists adopted the terms into their disciplines (e.g. Gergen 1997; 1999; 2000; 2001). It espouses a worldview of an indeterminate reality, which is more malleable to co-creation and interdependency between the observer and actor-agent, and the observed outer phenomena. Studies in neuro-phenomenology (especially over the last 50 years) and in quantum science (especially over the last 100 years) are now converging towards a paradigm of a co-created and co-emerging reality, where the observing agent is a key ingredient of what manifests as the experienced reality. This is commonly contrasted with *essentialism* (as the prevailing worldview), whereby a fixed reality is deemed to exist independently of the experiencing observer or actor. The study team prioritized the neuro-phenomenology perspective of constructivism because of its balance between verifiable positivistic science approach anchored in brain anatomy and physiology, complemented by subjective experience and phenomenology as a disciplinary tradition in philosophy.

A constructivist worldview thus treats reality as indeterminate, co-emerging and interdependent (e.g. Barrett 2017; Newen et al. 2018), such that we perpetually co-create our reality through inferred *meaning* and *re-meaning* of our experiences and observations of our external and internal (psycho-physiological) phenomena. Once a prior experience and observation is *re-meaned*, it yields a new reality that is inevitably different from what emerged on the basis of the initial meaning inferred from the same experience. This cognitive ability for meaning and re-meaning of our experiences is emerging as one of the most fundamental tools of reality making (and in particular for futures thinking) in support of shifting paradigms towards sustainable city transitioning.

Complementary studies within psychology also provide evidence of the two systems of cognition that manifest through different thinking speeds. Kahneman (2011) calls them *slow* and *fast* thinking systems, where slow thinking takes place at a conscious level and exhibits most of the qualities commonly attributed to rational choice- and decision-making. In contrast, fast thinking takes place at a subconscious level and outside the control of conscious reasoning. Under the field of *prospect theory*, the conflicting attributes of the two systems can therefore be viewed as the key driver of the commonly observed biases in human behaviour, which significantly deviates from the idealized behaviour expected on the basis of the rational-agent model commonly advocated in mainstream economics (Kahneman & Thaler 1979). The two imperatives of expediting sustainable city transitioning and the rethinking of the rational-agent model of human behaviour constitute the core motivation of our scholarship as synthesized in this chapter.

MULTI-DISCIPLINARY GUIDED RESEARCH INTO TRANSITIONING INERTIA AND PARADIGM SHIFTING

Historically, the approach taken in this chapter is primarily anchored in a process of re-meaning, which refers to a retrospective re-discovery of fresh meaning that allowed the authors to synthesize and integrate previously disparate and disjointed experiences along personal, professional and scholarly development pathways. This approach resonates with the more contemporary re-assessment of methods in history (see Carr 1961; Guldi & Armitage 2014; Lowenthal 2015).

The chapter focuses on scholarship aimed at adapting and applying principles from neuro-phenomenology (mainly neuroscience and consciousness studies combined with phenomenology) into sustainable city transitioning studies. It is rooted in the fertile ground of the study team's prior piecemeal tasks and knowledge development that were not initially conceptualized within the overarching frame now being used to present them. Instead, most of the tasks and their outcomes were archived without the benefit of explicit *carry-forward* insights or lessons into long-term scholarship, as now narrated in the chapter. This resonates with the view that life can only be understood backwards *[retrospectively]*; but it must be lived forward *[prospectively]* (Kierkegaard 1843, words in italics our own). With such a carry-forward experience, the study team was able to sense the close resonance between phenomenology and neuroscience studies, which made research and publications in neuro-phenomenology accessible to the team.

In the teaching of architecture, phenomenology, as a sub-field in philosophy, is commonly introduced under *theory of architecture* with an emphasis on understanding the nuances of place or project-site. Such an understanding ensures that the overall spirit of the context – the *genius loci;* see for example Norberg-Schulz (1979) – can *imbue* the site and the project as a whole through the design process of the architect. Therefore, the ultimate objective of the resultant knowledge is to develop expertise in integrative skills and competencies that would enable the project architect, as leader of the larger project team, to provide a holistic design response.

Most of the *genius-loci* inspiration in design has to be innately sensed and tacitly applied (rather than rationally or objectively measured with standardized methods or instruments). Therefore, to be able to experience directly the place and site of a project, the architect's process of perception and feeling has to be fine-tuned. This calls for a significant role of the body as a sensing and feeling tool, as opposed to merely engaging a rational mind with the body factored out of the knowing process. The phenomenological understanding is aimed at awakening and heightening embodied and embedded cognition, even though the course is normally based on a highly objectivistic and rational-agent syllabus that over-emphasizes rote-learning (as opposed to experiential bodily-knowing).

In the pursuit of holistic design, the engagement of the human body and integral mind happens in three other sub-fields in architecture training and practice: *anthropometrics, ergonomics* and *bioclimatic analysis* of site and building (aimed at ensuring thermal, visual and audio-comfort, especially through passive cooling and heating). Once again, even in these sub-fields in architecture, the presentation of content and the assessment of learning outcomes are primarily objectivist-guided with minimal engagement of bodily-knowing.

The core significance of phenomenology in architecture has been most elaborated through the scholarship of the Finnish architect, Juhani Pallasmaa, who also recently started applying neuroscience principles to his studies. While his earlier publications were primarily anchored in phenomenology-in-architecture, or knowing through tacit and direct or subjective bodily experience (Pallasmaa 2005; 2009; 2011), he has recently co-edited a book entitled *Mind in Architecture* (Robinson & Pallasmaa 2017). The book includes chapters titled 'Towards a neuroscience of the design process', 'Neuroscience for architecture' and 'Architecture and neuroscience'. A few other publications have attempted to hypothesize similar linkages between architecture and neuroscience, although not explicitly through phenomenology or neuro-phenomenology. These include Eberhard (2009), Goldhagen (2017) and Mallgrave (2011).

Outside of these few and very recent cases, objectivist-guided understanding remains the mainstream approach, mainly because of ongoing rigidity in disciplinary boundaries. As a result, the highly relevant insights from neuroscience and consciousness studies are still not applied in the teaching and practice of architecture. However, the insights that have emerged from the team's studies so far demonstrate realistically and systematically the process and opportunities of leveraging neuro-phenomenology principles into architecture and sustainable city transitioning. This could significantly enhance the teaching, learning and practice of architecture (as well as urban planning and design), especially given its unwavering commitment to holistic design.

MULTI-DISCIPLINARY EXPLORATIONS AND INSIGHTS FROM NEUROSCIENCE STUDIES

Around 2010, in an *aha!* or *eureka!* moment, the team's pathways to multi-disciplinary scholarship crossed into prospect theory (psychology and behavioural economics) and neuro-phenomenology (neuroscience, mind and consciousness studies), as indicated in Figure 9.1. It was triggered by intractable challenges in the PhD studies undertaken by two of the team members. The Kammeyer (2010) study was in mainstream architecture and focused on the process-of-making in traditional Sotho architecture (in South Africa and Lesotho in particular) in relation to a woman's gendered role, and how her social role is influenced by the everyday practice of making and maintaining the house and home. Based on a phenomenological approach coupled with ethnographic methods of direct observations, the study findings affirmed the *reciprocity hypothesis,* where the making of artefacts (the vernacular architecture and home) within the Sotho culture co-evolves in a reciprocal relation to the *making* of the woman-maker.

Although phenomenology was one of the theoretical fields of the study, neither the candidate nor the supervisors had the slightest hunch of the neuroscience significance of what was accomplished over the eight years it took to complete the study. This demonstrates once again how disciplinary boundaries remain so rigidly in place such that neither the candidate nor the supervisors chanced into an encounter with the expanding neuro-phenomenology literature within that period. It was only three years after completing the study that both the graduate and supervisor realized how close they had come to a neuro-phenomenology perspective of the study. This insight emerged from the process of the third doctoral study (Maape 2016), again in mainstream architecture, where neuro-phenomenology was explicitly adopted as one of the theoretical fields.

The third doctoral study greatly leveraged insights from a second one (Gichia 2013) that, unlike the other two, focused primarily on sustainability, with climate-change mitigation (within the built environment) as the main sub-field. Instead of restricting itself to techno-policy and related institutional mechanisms, Gichia (2013) was drawn more towards the commonly experienced inertia in responsive human behaviour even when faced with the prospect of a dire crisis. In particular, the study sought to substantiate whether or not human beings can qualify as truly rational agents, as commonly argued in economics and other disciplines, given their inertia in face of the gloomy prospects posed by climate change. It sought to explain the contradiction of market biasing (supposedly guided by objective cost-benefit evaluation) towards conservative (or status-quo reinforcing) choices and decisions until a crisis manifests; and the sudden choice-flipping, once a crisis manifests, to a willingness to try out whatever solution is available *out there*. Having started off with theoretical fields in philosophy and psychology (in particular the principle of moral values, with care, morals and ethics as the key elements), the study failed to gain traction for almost three years.

This changed suddenly when the candidate and supervisor stumbled upon the emerging fields of *prospect theory* and *behavioural economics* that bridge mainstream psychology and economics disciplines.

Close to four decades of studies in psychology and behavioural economics (especially by the psychologist, Daniel Kahneman, and behavioural economist, Richard Thaler) have demonstrated beyond any doubt that a 'normal' human agent is overly conservative (*risk averse*) when faced with the possibility (*prospect*) of gain, and overly risk-driven (*risk seeking*) when confronted with the prospect of loss. This finding strongly resonates with the common saying that, for the normal/average human being 'losses loom larger than gains' when making choices and decisions under uncertainty. Kahneman (2011) popularized the scientific findings in his book *Thinking fast and slow,* while Thaler popularized the economic aspects and their application (especially in policy-making), through *Nudge Theory* (Thaler & Sunstein 2008). Others who have followed up on these themes include Ariely (2008) and Schiller (2013; 2016).

Gichia (2013) focused on the contradictory experience of the adoption of solar water-heating technology as characterized by market inertia prior to the 2008 electricity-supply crisis in South Africa, followed by rapid adoption of the technology during the crisis in 2008/09. The study findings strongly corroborated Kahneman and Thaler's prospect theory findings and also closely corroborated the *bounded-rationality* model argued in Simon (1979). The study findings thus strongly contradicted the rational-agent model most favoured in mainstream economics and often applied in cost-benefit analysis and evaluation for policy-making, even in sustainability studies. Besides *prospect theory* and *behavioural economics*, Gichia (2013) gained traction through another chance encounter with Antonio Damasio's neuroscience studies (Damasio 1994;

Figure 9.1: Multi-disciplinary scholarship pathways into transitioning inertia and paradigm shifting

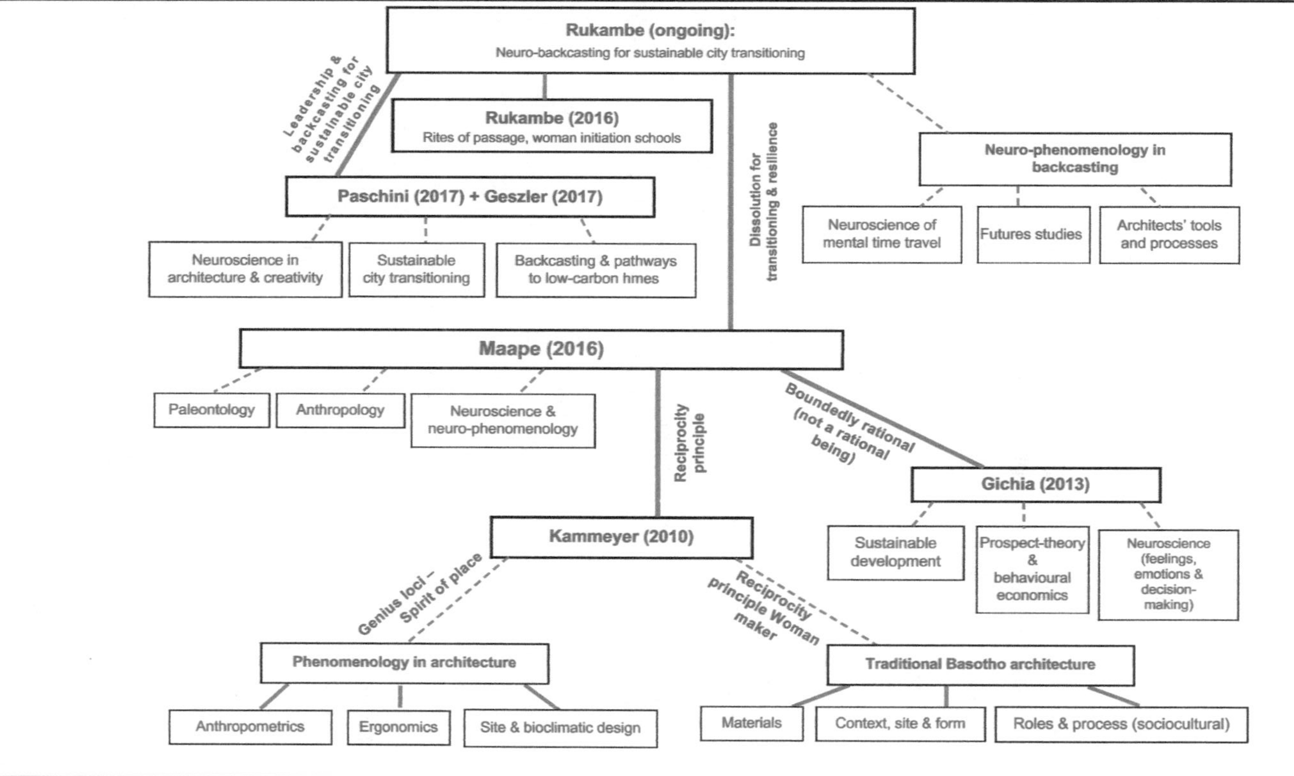

2000; 2003; 2010). Through Damasio's publications, the team's *aha!* moment emerged regarding the close relationship between *phenomenology* and *ergonomics* (as knowledge fields in embodied-knowing in architecture) and the emerging insights from neuroscience, mind and consciousness studies.

Gichia (2013) was, therefore, eventually located within the following three core theoretical fields:

- Sustainable development (as a sub-field in futures studies and with its three key components of environmental, social and economic concerns).

- Prospect theory and behavioural economics (choice- and decision-making in face of uncertainty).

- Neuroscience and consciousness studies (applied principles of bodily and brain processes that underpin mind, consciousness and decision-making).

While working on Gichia (2013), neither the candidate nor the supervisor realized that neuroscience scholars had already forged a crucial bridging between phenomenology (as a sub-field in philosophy) and neuroscience, such that a new multi-disciplinary field of neuro-phenomenology had emerged as far back as the 1980s, primarily under the pioneering scholarship of the late Francisco Varela. It was through our search for theoretical traction for Maape (2016) that another chance encounter with neuro-phenomenology catapulted the study team into previously unimagined frontiers.

Located in mainstream architecture, Maape (2016) was primarily concerned with the possibility of gaining sustainability-transitioning insights about *resilience* (survival and continuity across multiple cycles of transitioning) from extant indigenous African communities, especially those who had inhabited their current ecosystem niches over the longest periods. Under the main title of *Architecture for resilience*, the study explored the area around the Kuruman Caves (in the Northern Cape Province of South Africa) that had been inhabited for over 10,000 years (based on data from paleontological and rock-art studies).

Guided by the rich data-pool and key findings, Maape (2016) concluded that the enactment of rituals were intentional-dissolution mechanisms of mental schemas and served as effective mind-body (mental) tools for enabling sustained transitioning across both slow and rapid environmental and socioculturally induced changes. The most inspiring finding was that these communities were practising intentional brain and consciousness-altering practices as early as 10,000 years ago. These practices enhanced their fitness for survival, especially in transitioning through rapidly changing socio-ecological contexts. The findings inspired the study's sub-title: *Dialogues with place in indigenous communities of Kuruman during the Holocene period.*

In addition to the mainstream paleontological studies, Maape (2016) leveraged findings from neuro-phenomenology studies on the evolution of mind and cognition that are based on ancient rock art of similar communities in southern Africa (Lewis-Williams 2002, among others). One of the findings was the deliberate (although only innately understood) practice of altering states of mind or consciousness (through rituals such as the trance dance and other shamanistic practices). When cross-referenced to contemporary neuro-phenomenology studies, Lewis-Williams' work yielded a highly inspiring theoretical base for the research question that Maape (2016) had set out to substantiate. It also allowed the study team's research to move confidently into the neuro-phenomenology domain, thus creating a firm base that subsequent studies could systematically build on.

Above all else, Maape (2016) provided an indisputable base for the relevance of indigenous belief and knowledge systems, as well as the related practices, especially in relation to resilience through successful sustainability transitioning. This newly broadened corroboration of the *reciprocity principle*, through interactions between a people's culture, belief systems, mind and environmental milieu, reinforced the team's full appreciation of the immense role of the body in mind-and-consciousness processes and strongly corroborated findings by Damasio (2003; 2010), Freeman (2001), Varela (1999) and Varela et al. (1991).

These insights on the critical role of emotions and feelings as a crucial bodily-process in making choices and decisions strongly contradict the enlightenment-era paradigm of pure mind or reason being independent of the body, and the body being essentially viewed as detraction and potentially a compromising burden to reason. Subsequently, this shift to a more diverse theoretical home for the team's studies guided several prototyping initiatives, especially the Botswana *botho/ubuntu* dialogue with the Dalai Lama in August 2017, in collaboration with Mind & Life Institute in USA, as described later in the chapter.

One of the additional theoretical threads in sustainability studies relates to the temporal dimension with the future (rather than the past) as the primary focus. This locates the field in futures studies, especially based on comparison of forecasting and backcasting approaches. In leveraging futures studies into sustainable city transitioning, our primary theoretical home has been the cognitive competencies of the human species for mental time-travel. Studies completed by the team under the futures-studies theme are at a Master's level. The two key examples are Paschini (2017), which focused on creativity and leadership for sustainable city transitioning, and Geszler (2017), which focused on backcasting versus forecasting for pathways to low-carbon homes in South Africa by 2050.

Insights from the two studies are now anchoring a doctoral study; Rukambe (ongoing), which is on envisioning and pursuing alternative futures for sustainable city transitioning, especially guided by insights on our species' competence of mental time-travel, as substantiated in several neuroscience studies. The study proposes that the neuro-phenomenologically rigorous tools of training and practice in architecture could be adaptable to a more systematic dissemination and application in backcasting for sustainable city transitioning in Africa. To gain traction for the study required a re-engaging with a re-conception of the *nature of reality*, and especially questioning our currently flawed *everyday experience* of reality as pre-determined in a manner where we (as observers of that reality) are merely passive participants in otherwise independently existing phenomena that would continue to exist even in absence of the observer. This has been historically reinforced by a flawed science practice and culture that remain fixated on an unwavering goal of *discovering the laws of nature*, based on the unwarranted assumption that the act of observing and analyzing constitutes a neutral process, which has no material effect on the *lawful* behaviour of the parts or sub-systems of the phenomenon being observed. In addition, the fixed-reality worldview assumes an unchanging *self* – the *I* that does the observing. As noted earlier in the chapter, this is underpinned by the *essentialist* paradigm which denotes the expectation or belief that any phenomenon can be reduced to its basic or unchanging *essence*, which in turn allows us (the observing subjects) to differentiate, unambiguously categorize and group observed phenomena in a manner that can *objectively* guide the strategy of our responsive actions within our world.

Until the end of the nineteenth century, essentialism had served humanity at varying levels of success, but in the early twentieth century its key shortfalls started to manifest, when relativity and quantum science paradigms emerged as both initial instigators and contenders for alternative ways of understanding and engaging with our world(s). While the study team is aware of the linkage currently being forged between quantum theory and neuroscience (with *neuroquantology* as a new multi-disciplinary field – see the journal *NeuroQuantology*), it has not yet pursued this direction because of an inadequate understanding of the quantum science component at this stage. Instead, the team is using the neuroscience principles on the malleability of reality, especially depending on states of mind, consciousness and worldview. As our initial gateway into quantum science, the team is using the lay-reader books by Rovelli (2015; 2016; 2018), among others.

Under this emerging constructivism paradigm as underpinned by neuroplasticity, and complemented by an understanding of the *I* or *self* as constituted of a *perpetual becoming* (an emergence out of the dynamic interactions between body, brain, mind and environment), reality is also better understood as a *perpetual becoming*, which is as malleable as the *I* or *self* – see for example Barrett (2017) and Newen et al. (2018). In principle, this surmises that our mentally held belief systems (especially at a subconscious level) in interaction with the stimuli from our environment (both natural and sociocultural) significantly influence the meaning we attribute to the perception, as well as how we respond to what has been perceived. It is this dynamic interplay between our meaning-making system (belief system or worldview), stimuli and response or action, that helps us construct the reality we experience or perceive on an everyday basis.

The nature and perception of the experienced reality would thus change if the internal components (i.e. the beliefs and meaning-making, mind-body processes) of this dynamic system change. In the short term (within a single life cycle), ongoing neuroplasticity (changes in neural connectivity in the brain that in turn entails changes in patterns of interactions across neural networks) has been demonstrated to be the key mechanism by which internal brain changes can alter the perception of reality through a change in the meaning-making processes. Multiple neuroscience studies have now demonstrated that the efficacy of neuroplasticity persists across the full life cycle. This contradicts our earlier understanding, which assumed that capacity for such radical changes in our neuro-network dramatically diminishes once we reach adulthood.

Based on neuroplasticity and constructivist insights, the future can no longer be viewed as an absolute unknown over which the *I* or *self* totally lacks a meaningful basis for agency. Instead, it is now evident that the *self* influences which futures are eventually co-created and thus experienced through both mental time travel (as a common human cognitive competence) as well as the most sophisticated and creative strategies for envisioning and pursuing alternative futures. This radical understanding inspired the prioritizing of *constructivism* as the more effective paradigm within which to tackle our contemporary crises, especially when grounded in neuroplasticity and the commonly known range of altered states of consciousness accessible to any human being.

Rukambe (ongoing) hypothesises that the use of the word *architect*, which commonly translates to *chief builder* as inferred from its Greek roots (Tait 2018), metaphorically signifies a *master minder* of radical social transformations across diverse spheres. This could actually be more than a mere mechanistic technique of language. Furthermore, there are strong commonalities between the processes of architecture (when viewed as a backcasting practice focused on the process-of-becoming for buildings) and of radical social-technical transformations that are now being sought under sustainable city transitioning.

Rukambe (ongoing) further hypothesizes that backcasting (as an overarching futures-practice tool) can be adapted to embrace prevailing architectural tools and practices, thereby enhancing the pursuit of sustainable city transitioning with African cities in mind. The study plans to run a parallel investigation into indigenous communities' rituals as a tool for altered states of consciousness for facilitating transitioning, as per the *rites of passage* explored in Rukambe (2016). The study will also explore a sub-hypothesis that the *ritual master* (or *mistress*) in such practices serves a role similar to that of the architect (master minder) of self and community, with an innate knowing of backcasting as a possible common mental point of reference. If the sub-hypothesis is substantiated, the study team could infer an implicit element of backcasting know-how in the practice of such transitioning rituals, although they are primarily targeted at an individual scale, unlike the more collective sustainable-city transitioning scale being pursued by the study team.

TRANS-DISCIPLINARY APPLICATION OF INSIGHTS
FROM THE MULTI-DISCIPLINARY SCHOLARSHIP

The rapid adoption of creativity as an essential cognitive competence in innovation across numerous domains emboldened the commitment of the study team. One example is that conventional business schools globally are embracing design thinking. This illustrates the increasing imperative of multi- and trans-disciplinarity and the need for a better balance between analytical and integrative competencies.

Neumeier (2013) has made a credible attempt to map out the key skills and competencies required for a synthesis-oriented, solution-seeking (integrative) process, as opposed to the prevailing analytical skills mode (breaking apart) followed by most tertiary education disciplines. Neumeier highlights five overarching crucial competencies: *feeling (empathy and intuition), seeing (systems thinking), dreaming (applied imagination), making (design and testing)* and *learning (auto-didactics)*. Within this framework of meta-skills, the study team pursues the primary objective of developing fundamental principles that could allow such skills to be mainstreamed and thus become basic integrative competencies for all, rather than for the select few who enter the so-called creative disciplines such as architecture.

Within this design-thinking and synthesis-skills paradigm, the study team engaged in multiple trans-disciplinary initiatives that were used as prototypes for tackling real-world challenges. The following three initiatives benefited from the insights achieved by the team, especially in the last ten years (see Figure 9.2).

- Master's in Architecture in the field of Sustainable and Energy Efficient Cities – MArch(SEEC)

- Climate Leadership Programme (CLP) and Climate Leadership Plus (CLP+)

- Mind & Life Institute (USA) Dialogue with His Holiness the Dalai Lama in Botswana

In addition to describing these three initiatives, a recently-launched prototyping initiative (under the City-Futures Lab framework) on the convergence of smart- and sustainable-city transitioning for Mombasa, Kenya, is presented. However, the key insights from this prototyping will only emerge over the next three years as the project implementation process unfolds.

Figure 9.2: Interactions across the three key elements
of the study-team's scholarship journey

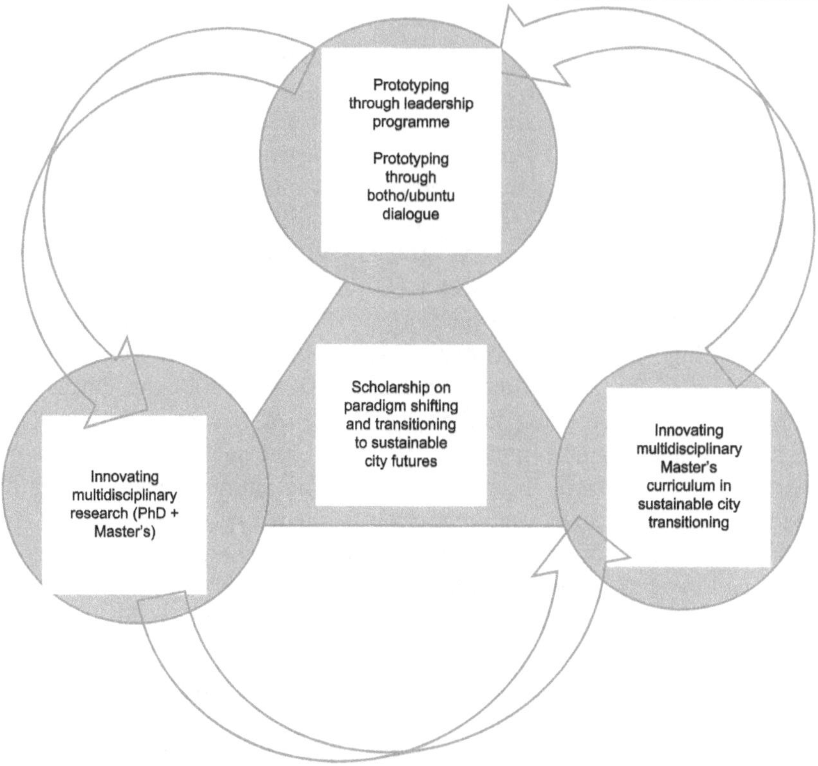

Innovative multi-disciplinary postgraduate Master's curriculum: MArch (SEEC)

Policymakers, city government actors and property developers lack the knowledge to lead and guide cities in sustainable-city transitions. This is in part because of the inertia and slow adoption of sustainability imperatives into the mainstream curriculum of the built-environment professions globally and in Africa. Similarly, engineering, planning and urban-design graduates may enter the profession with basic sustainability competencies, but they are not given satisfactory opportunities to deepen their practice skills beyond the theoretical competence achieved through their academic qualification. As a result, the School of Architecture & Planning at the University of Witwatersrand (Wits) motivated for a multi-disciplinary Master's programme that could draw applicants from diverse disciplines, including humanities, engineering, basic sciences and the built environment professions. The programme would take students through a transformative programme that allows them to mediate in the built environment-skills market to catalyze expedited transformation. Such a programme needed to emphasize integrative direct-experience as the main mode of teaching and learning, with futures studies as the primary theoretical orientation. The programme structure is shown in Figure 9.3 – it is set at 180 credits and aligned to the 50:50 framework for Master's qualification in South Africa (i.e. 50% of the credits from coursework and examination and the other 50% from research report or mini-dissertation). The coursework is structured into four compulsory courses and one elective from a choice of two options. The compulsory courses are: understanding cities of the South, energy for sustainable cities, energy efficiency and renewable energy for buildings, and research methods. The two electives are: social and technical sustainability for housing, and environmental planning and sustainable development

Following a stakeholder consultative process and subsequent conceptualization of the curriculum between 2006 and 2009, the initial call for applications was launched in 2010 (for admission in 2011). The minimum entry requirement is an honours-level qualification and two-years' work experience in any field. The programme started with only three students in 2011 but, following a major curriculum revision in 2013, now has around ten fresh registrations per year, with an output of 6–8 graduates per year as of 2017/2018. Close to 80% of the admitted students already hold positions with employers in the public, private and non-governmental sectors, and so they register to study part-time over two years – the full-time students have to complete the programme in one year. From 2019, the programme title changed to Master's in Urban Studies (Sustainable and Energy Efficient Cities) or MUS(SEEC),

Figure 9.3: Framing the multi-disciplinary Master's programme in MArch (SEEC)

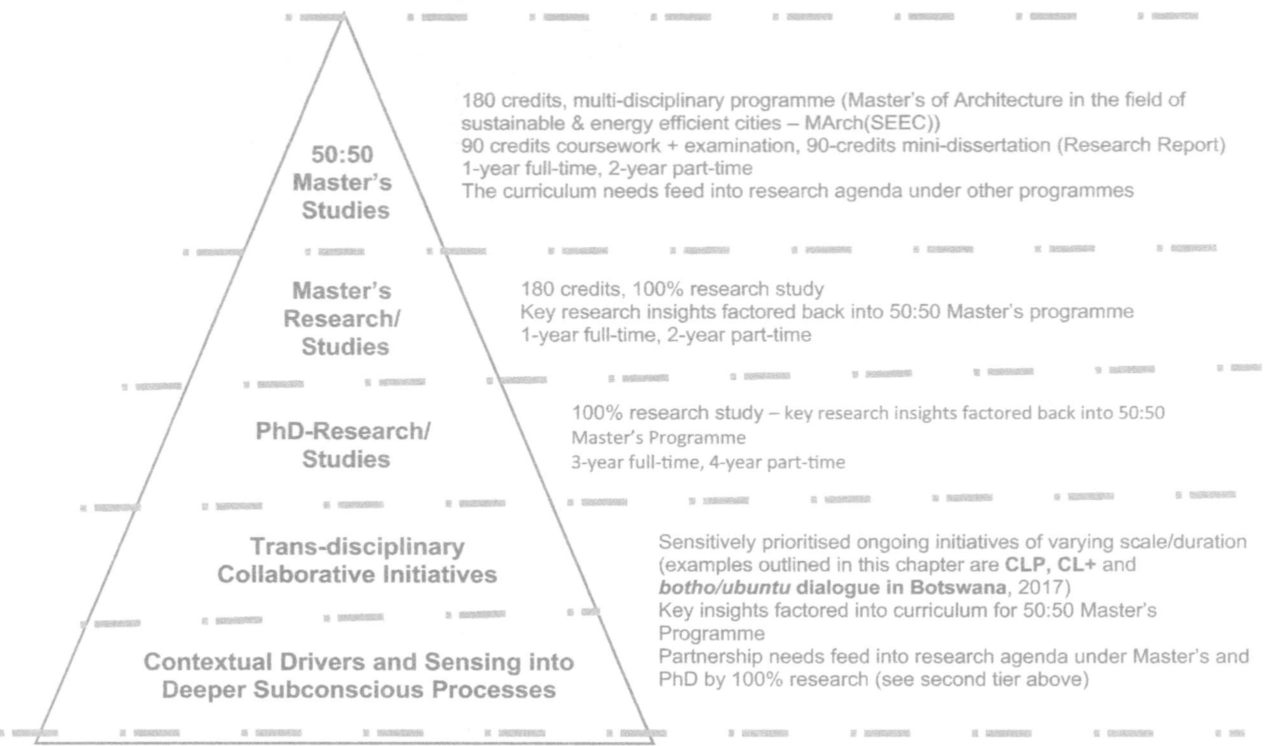

following the streamlining of postgraduate qualifications in the School, but its overall purpose and course offerings remain unchanged.

An encouraging feature of the programme is the participation of students from other African countries including from Uganda (2), Tanzania (1), Nigeria (3), Zambia (1) and Malawi (1), as well as Jordan/Palestine (1) and India (1). Most of the students from other Africa countries are from built-environment professions (especially architecture), while the South African students are mainly from other disciplines, including psychology (1), geology (2), engineering (several) and environmental sciences (several). This diversity – different countries, disciplines, work experience and roles played in their positions of employment or business – is the programme's unique value. In particular, students are encouraged to base their research reports within a theoretical field closely aligned to their home/prior discipline and also apply case studies from their respective home-country.

TRANS-DISCIPLINARY-GUIDED PROTOTYPING OF LEADERSHIP SKILLS FOR TRANSITIONING: CLP AND CL+

In collaboration with GIZ (Deutsche Gesellschaft fur Internationale Zusammenarbeit) of Germany, Wits conceptualized and implemented the Climate Leadership Programme, CLP (2010/11 and 2011/12), followed by the CL+ that focused on sustainable energy transitions (2012/13 and 2013/14). In both cases, the primary objective of the trans-disciplinary initiative was to initiate a peer-to-peer learning process of self-development, as opposed to conventional studies towards a formal academic qualification. The approach was to gain skills and competencies that would allow 'graduates' to take leadership roles in guiding collective energy-related responses in mitigation of climate change at multiple scales (individual behaviour, organizational transformation and city/national policies and programmes).

Participants were drawn from mid-level personnel in public, private and non-governmental sectors, with around 20 participants in each cycle. Learning tasks included:

- Interactive workshops – about 6 x 3-day block sessions distributed across 8–10 months;

- Presentation dialogues, with subject-matter experts;

- Leadership journey, with related journal record;

- A prototype project executed over the ten months, with clearly articulated stages and feedback from peer participants and programme convenors (mainly a dedicated Wits professor with several assistants).

Theory U (Sharmer 2016) was the key academic-reference text applied in the first and second cycles of the programme. In 2010/2011, one of the study-team members successfully completed the first cycle of CLP and then took over as the Wits academic convenor for the two cycles in 2012/13 and in 2013/14. In the process, he shifted the primary reference from *Theory U* to a more neuro-phenomenology-oriented trajectory, especially based on neuroscience and contemplative practices. This shift was primarily guided by insights emerging from Gichia (2013) and Maape (2016). At the same time, a wider group of expert-subject presenters for dialogue sessions included well-known custodians of indigenous-knowledge systems in South Africa, such as Professor Wally Serote, who is a highly established academic, poet and traditional healer, and Ms Helen Sebidi (a well-established artist).

During the second cycle (2013/14), under the convenorship of two of the study-team members, the programme included an additional feature of contemplative practice (meditation and mindfulness in particular), based on the increasing scientific evidence that such practices enhance the potential for unlearning deeply embedded but undesirable or obsolete habits, thereby facilitating learning of the more desirable knowing and practices. However, the highly experiential aspects of the initial programme (in particular the leadership journey, journal and prototype project) were retained and deeply enriched.

TRANS-DISCIPLINARY PROTOTYPING: BOTSWANA MIND & LIFE
DIALOGUE WITH THE DALAI LAMA

One of the study team's primary gateways into neuroscience, mind and consciousness publications was through studies by Francisco Varela, the founding scholar of neuro-phenomenology. The field of neuro-phenomenology had evolved quite extensively by the time the study team adopted this theoretical positioning in around 2014/15. By the time of his passing, in 2001, Varela had not only prioritized contemplative practices in his neuroscience studies under neuro-phenomenology, but had also (since the 1980s) established a dynamic scientific and multi-disciplinary collaboration with the Dalai Lama and his Buddhist monks in researching neuroscience, including the mind, consciousness and contemplative practices. While most of the initial collaboration entailed dialogues that took place in Dharamsala, India (the home-in-exile of the Dalai Lama), subsequent dialogues were also held in several North American universities, convened by various neuroscientists, thereby expanding scientific concerns beyond Varela's initial curiosity.

Varela had also incubated the Mind & Life Institute (USA), to convene and disseminate the findings of the dialogues through diverse channels, with the annual Summer Research Institute (SRI) conferences being the primary platform. The Mind & Life Institute promotes research into neuroscience and contemplative practices, especially mindfulness, empathy and compassion towards human flourishing. It had started evaluating the possibility of holding a similar dialogue oriented to African mind and worldviews, focusing on *botho/ubuntu,* for the purpose of enhancing human flourishing. In June 2016, this interest was consolidated during the SRI in New York, which one of the study team members attended. After the 2016 SRI event, planning for an Africa-hosted dialogue intensified and, after confirming the availability of the Dalai Lama, the dialogue was set for 17–19 August 2017 in Gaborone, with the following four objectives (Mind & Life Institute 2017: 2):

- To explore the indigenous African ethic of *Botho/Ubuntu* as it relates to Buddhist ideas of interdependence and compassion

- To examine the current scientific understanding of how our socio-interconnectedness impacts one another for good or ill

- To understand how *Botho/Ubuntu* can be distorted to maintain cultural norms and systems of power that lead to oppression of, and violence against, women, children and other marginalized groups

- To envision how our connectedness can heal division, forgive profound transgression and point toward a richer understanding of what it means to be human.

Guided by the dialogue title of: *Botho/Ubuntu: A dialogue on spirituality, science and humanity*, discussants were drawn from diverse fields including the *neuroscience basis of human-social relations* (Rebecca Shansky, Uri Hasson and Carsten de Dreu), *social breakdown, violence, trauma and related healing* (Graça Machel, Pumla Gobondo-Madikizela), *African philosophy and ubuntu* (Michael Eze), *indigenous knowledge and healing practices* (Mandaza Kandemwa). A youth session was factored into the final day of the programme, with Donald Molosi of Botswana as the anchor person, accompanied by other youth participants drawn from South Africa, Kenya and Namibia. Botho University in Gaborone served as the venue, and video-recording of the event is available on the Mind & Life Institute website (see www.mindandlife.org/mind-and-life-dialogues). The participation of the study-team members across all stages of the dialogue (planning, hosting and dissemination) still stands as the pinnacle of our scholarship experience to date.

PROTOTYPING CONVERGENCE OF SMART- AND SUSTAINABLE-CITY TRANSITIONING FOR MOMBASA, KENYA

An opportunity arose for on-the-ground prototyping of the convergence of smart- and sustainable-city transitioning, for Mombasa in Kenya in partnership with the Mombasa County Government, following the study team's response to a call for proposals by WIOMSA (West Indian Ocean Marine Science Association). The call was for action/trans-disciplinary research addressing the challenges of coastal cities and towns along the western sphere of the Indian Ocean (primarily the eastern coastal towns and cities of Africa and adjacent island states). Based on an ongoing collaboration with key actors in Mombasa, the study team submitted a proposal entitled Miji Bora Mombasa (Better Cities Mombasa), which was approved for implementation in 2019–2021. The core of the proto-typing is the City Futures Labs as well as four sub-components (Figure 9.4).

Figure 9.4: Key smart- and sustainable-city transitioning components for Miji Bora Mombasa, Kenya

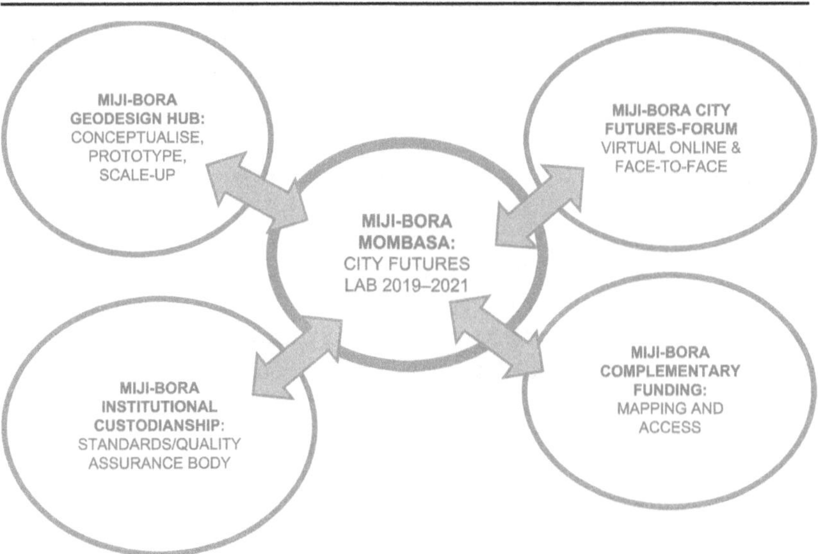

- Miji Bora Geo-Design Hub: the digitalization and smart-city data strategy, with Geo-Design Hub as the starting point based on a bottom-up approach;

- Miji Bora City Futures Forum: the consultative venue or platform within which interactions across stakeholders will be hosted;

- Miji Bora Institutional Custodianship: a data-trust body to steer the development and application of data standards and quality assurance, as a critical component of smart cities;

- Miji Bora Complementary Funding: complementary funding will be needed both within the three-year project cycle and afterwards, in order for Mombasa County to fully exploit and leverage the opportunity opened up by WIOMSA and grow into a mature smart city.

The value of the study team's contribution will be in assisting other partners to factor in the futures-thinking insights and embodied cognition for the capacity- and skills-development components of the project.

OVERALL INSIGHTS

Kammeyer (2010) and Gichia (2013) helped the study team substantiate the dynamics of the transitioning inertia within sociocultural systems and, especially, how such inertia ultimately manifests through the biasing of individual and collective choice- and decision-making in favour of the status quo. Through the reciprocity principle, Kammeyer (2010) found that cultural systems and values in meaning-making (at collective and individual level) become embedded in mind and body, which in turn guides purpose and process of choice, action and behaviour. Once embedded, the cultural values and meaning-making systems recede to the subconscious state and so become innate, such that their influence on day-to-day behaviours remains hidden and normally inaccessible to the conscious *self* when considering choices for decision-making. This corroborates Kahneman's (2011) finding that fast and slow thinking systems influence (and often bias) our choice- and decision-making when confronted with current choice options that entail future prospects of gain or loss. Gichia (2013) systematically explored this biasing with regard to the formal and day-to-day application of cost-benefit evaluation in the adoption of solar water heating technologies prior to and since the 2008/09 electricity supply crisis in South Africa.

Maape (2016) relied on paleontological studies for secondary data to explore how the ancestors of extant San communities of the Kuruman area of Northern Cape in South Africa (with traceable transitioning history stretching beyond 10,000 years) managed to overcome their own transitioning inertia through ongoing innovations to tools and methods of altering states of consciousness for both individuals and groups within a community. Springing from Maape's (2016) findings on historical inertia-mitigating tools and methods, Rukambe (ongoing) shifts the focus from the past to the future in order to substantiate possible inertia-mitigating tools for our own transitioning from the contemporary crises.

So far, the team's scholarship has identified the underlying circumstances and dynamics that underpin ongoing innovations as opposed to specific cases of one-off innovations. The team's core innovation is the substantiation of these mechanisms and dynamics, particularly adapting them for applications to a more specific innovation scenario. For example, in Maape (2016) the study team realized that past indigenous communities managed to transition and adapt through innately-understood (as opposed to consciously and rationally reasoned-out) methods and tools of mental reframing. However, what is truly innovative is the insight about the fundamental role of the body (especially when coupled with diverse cultural, mind-altering practices) in breaking existing schemas (which drive behavioural inertia) in order to bring about new ones, and thus the *re-meaning* of experiences to better engage with our rapidly changing world.

What the team's scholarship has managed to articulate is the contribution of ecological and social drivers and factors to what seems to be a primordial function of the human brain (as inevitably coupled to its body) in relation to paradigm shifting as a fundamental enabler of transitioning. This ability of the body–brain coupling, to make meaning and re-meaning of our experiences, is guided by cultural practices that have inevitably evolved across time, possibly since the emergence of early *Homo sapiens*. From this perspective of deep time and history, paradigm shifting emerges as a far more fundamental driver of innovation that underpins the commonly understood one-off version of technology solving short-term human problems (as important as this may be). Paradigm-shifting tools and practices are the crucial enablers that catalyze and guide the emergence of novelty in human adaptation. This relates directly to our species' capacity for changing our inner brain and body processes in order to overcome our status quo paradigm and behavioural inertia. Having prioritized the temporal dimension within the context of *constructivism*, what emerges from our narrated scholarship journey is a more empowering sense of the future as co-creatively emergent (rather than a prior condition existing independently of us as the actors and observers), with the resultant leveraging opportunities for transitioning towards diverse desirable futures for humankind where sustainable-city futures is one of the key ingredients.

The prototyping processes allowed the study team to engage in trans-disciplinary action research within an empirical context where research-derived principles could translate into practice innovations at a pilot level. The Climate Change Leadership prototyping consolidated insights on the relevance and contribution of a multi-disciplinary learning peer group, as well as the role of a prototype project for the engagement of the body as part of embodied knowing (rather than the common emphasis of classroom-based learning with the lecturer as an expert). Bringing together diverse disciplines can both enrich the learning process and create a networking platform for the participants during and after completing the programme. This is demonstrated by the confluence of diverse insights from the study team's various scholarship initiatives, (including human behaviour in relation to transitioning inertia) and the prototyping of the multi-disciplinary Master's programme, MArch (SEEC) at Wits University. Some of the students' research reports (mini-dissertations) also contributed insights, which were subsequently elaborated through in-depth studies by the study team, thereby creating opportunities for improved methods and findings on paradigm shifting and transitioning. One clear example is Paschini (2017), which is contributing significantly towards Rukambe (ongoing) as a PhD study (see Figure 9.1 for the envisaged link across the two studies).

The *botho/ubuntu* dialogue in Botswana is the only prototyping initiative that has not enjoyed follow-up iterations to improve on what was achieved in 2017. Yet it has already yielded its own unique insights, through neuroscience scholars in neuro-phenomenology directly engaging with *ubuntu* philosophers and indigenous knowledge practitioners such as traditional healers. Thus the event was a crucial demonstration of the trans-disciplinary collaboration that is the core feature of our scholarship. Finally, the newly launched prototyping towards a convergence of smart- and sustainable-city transitioning for Mombasa is expected to be the actual case where all the above insights will be applied, comprehensively tested and consolidated. In particular, we envisage strong synergy between Rukambe (ongoing) and the prototyping for Mombasa, with the added challenge of smart-city transitioning.

KEY INNOVATION RECOMMENDATIONS ARISING FROM INSIGHTS

Over the last ten years, the study team's journey has consolidated a significant amount of scholarship, as narrated in this chapter, building on prior scholarship:

- Almost 40 years of academic foundations by other scholars who inspired the study team's scholarship as narrated in this chapter: *genius loci*, *spirit of place* and *phenomenology in theory of architecture* (e.g. Norberg-Schulz 1979), *systems thinking* (e.g. von Bertalanffy 1968), *ecology of mind* (e.g. Bateson 1972) and *futures thinking* (e.g. Fuller 1970).

- Close to 30 years of incubation especially within sustainable-development paradigm, such as *our common future* (WCED 1987), *limits to growth* (Meadows et al. 1972) and *chaos* and *complexity theories*.

- Nearly 20 years of sustainable architecture and city transitioning (Kammeyer 2010; Gichia 2013; Maape 2016; and Rukambe ongoing).

Just as Kuhn (1962) highlighted the role of anomalous science findings in galvanizing scientific revolutions (and thus transiting to a new paradigm), the escalating crises facing humankind today demand a new model of reality, to guide the species in a manner that overcomes the prevailing individual and collective inertia. The team's transitioning journey, as narrated in this chapter, constitutes a specific attempt to consolidate a pathway for such a paradigm shift. Echoing Kuhn (1962) and Meadows (1999), the team's goal is to balance attention across *normal innovations* within a prevailing paradigm versus the more fundamental innovation (which we can now term as *revolutionary innovation*) in order to bring forth a new paradigm within which a *new-normal* innovation practice will emerge.

Even though the study team fully recognizes the critical need to prototype (and scale up) the specific innovations through action research as narrated in the chapter, the more critical challenge is how to scale up the pursuit of knowledge and understanding required in order to effect the paradigm shift. Some of the approaches towards the scaling-up are as follows:

- Embracing, promoting and intensifying multi- and trans-disciplinary collaboration opportunities, especially through emerging platforms such as City Labs, which are becoming common in cities globally. This would help to mitigate the perpetuation of the single-discipline expert, as the primary paradigm for our responses to the crises we now face.

- Curriculum innovations across all levels to align with the changing paradigm. In particular, insights from the team's own transitioning pathway emphasize the embedding of futures thinking and futures literacy (temporal cognition) as the foundational cognitive competence towards mitigating transitioning inertia at micro- (self) and macro- (collective) levels.

- A *constructivism* mindset is required for the above two recommendations to take effect, which ultimately highlights the growing need for multi-disciplinary, neuro-phenomenology research centres in Africa, where neuroanatomy, brain physiology and psychiatry (as pursued in medical sciences) collaborate with psychology, philosophy, anthropology and palaeontology among other disciplines. This is currently missing in our academic institutions. The team's commitment to pursuing the transitioning journey (especially in the last ten years) could not have been sustained without the confidence that we are building on systematically established scientific findings, especially from neuroscience

- Ultimately, systematizing the scale-up recommendations across communities, cities, economies, countries and globally would require expedited policy innovations at all these levels. However, the inertia is most pronounced at the political level, which is unlikely to be the first cog of the wheel to move. Instead, it most likely will be moving in a slower reaction pattern, in response to faster transitioning moves in other sectors and arenas.

ACKNOWLEDGEMENTS

Foremost, the team extends sincere gratitude to the various reviewers of this chapter, as well as editors of the book, for the intensive reviews and feedback provided to us in the course of developing the chapter right from the conceptual note. In addition, it is our great privilege to have been afforded this opportunity to share our scholarship journey in the form of this chapter in the second volume of the Africa Innovations book.

The authors also acknowledge the invaluable support and contribution by colleagues (both students and staff) at the School of Architecture & Planning at University of the Witwatersrand (Wits) in the process of incubating and growing the initiatives, studies and programmes reported in this chapter. Most of the studies highlighted in this chapter were supported by other supervisors and examined by reviewers, some within and others external to the School/Wits. We hereby extend our sincere appreciation for the invaluable contribution they have all made to the team's experience.

In addition, the team extends deep appreciation to all the participants, facilitators, and subject-matter-expert presenters as well as GIZ and the Global Change & Sustainability Research Institute (GCSRI) at Wits for the invaluable peer-to-peer learning opportunity through CLP and CL+ as presented in this chapter. The ongoing collaborations with the network of our CLP and CLP+ Alumni are also deeply appreciated.

We truly value the contribution of Ms Karen Fitzgerald who was one of our invited expert-dialogue anchors (CL+ 2014) on neuroscience and contemplative practices based on her ongoing PhD studies at University of Cape Town. Besides her invaluable sharing and dialogue-contribution during her session, Karen subsequently facilitated the team's link with the Mind & Life Institute (USA), especially through Prof Clifford Saron (contemplative neuroscience scholar at the University of California, Davis). It was this link that opened the door for the team's participation and contribution to the *botho/ubuntu* dialogue in Botswana in 2017.

Finally, the team warmly extends our thanks to the Mind & Life Institute (USA) for the invaluable and unique opportunity of having invited us to serve and contribute towards the programme planning for the *botho/ubuntu* dialogue (the 32nd Dialogue with the Dalai Lama) in Gaborone, Botswana.

For the conceptualization, development, launch and ongoing revisions to the Master's programme, the MArch(SEEC), as presented in this chapter, the team gratefully acknowledge initial EU-funding that supported the generative collaboration project among several African and European universities under the title of Promoting Renewable Energy Africa (PREA), from 2006 to 2009.

BIBLIOGRAPHY

Ariely, D. (2008) *Predictably Irrational: The hidden forces that shape our decisions,* London: HarperCollins Publishers.

Barrett, L.F. (2017) *How Emotions Are Made: The secret life of the brain,* New York: Houghton Mifflin Harcourt.

Bateson, G. (1972) *Steps to an Ecology of Mind.* New York: Ballantine Books.

Bello-Schünemann, J. (2018) Defining the future of Africa's brave new world. *Africa in fact: The Quarterly Journal of Good Governance Africa* (45): 13–18.

Carr, E.H. (1961) *What Is History? The George Macaulay Trevelyan Lectures delivered in the University of Cambridge January–March 1961,* United Kingdom: Penguin Books.

Damasio, A. (1994) *Descartes' error: Emotion, reason and the human brain.* New York: Avon Books.

Damasio, A. (2000) *The Feeling of What Happens: Body and emotion in the making of consciousness,* London: Vintage Books.

Damasio, A. (2003) *Looking for Spinoza: Joy, sorrow, and the feeling brain,* New York: Harvest Books.

Damasio, A. (2010) *Self Comes to Mind: Constructing the conscious brain,* London: Vintage Books.

Davies, J. (2016) *The Birth of the Anthropocene,* Los Angeles: University of California Press.

de Rivero, O. (2010) *The Myth of Development: Non-viable economies and the crisis of civilization.* London: Zed Books.

Eberhard, J. (2009) *Brain Landscape: The co-existence of neuroscience and architecture,* Oxford: Oxford University Press.

Eze, M.O. (2010) Ubuntu: Toward a new public discourse. In Eze MO (2010) *Intellectual History in Contemporary South Africa,* Springer Publishing.

Fleming, P. (2017) *The Death of homo economicus,* London: Pluto Press.

Freeman, W. (2001) *How Brains Make up Their Minds.* Columbia, USA: Columbia University Press.

Fuller, B. (1970) *The Buckminster Fuller Reader,* London: Jonathan Cape Ltd.

Gergen, K. (1997) *Realities and Relationships: Soundings in social construction,* Cambridge, MA: Harvard University Press.

Gergen, K. (1999) *An Invitation to Social Construction,* London: Sage Publications.

Gergen, K. (2000) *The Saturated Self: Dilemmas of identity in contemporary life,* New York: Basic Books.

Gergen, K. (2001) *Social Construction in Context,* London: Sage Publications.

Geszler, D. (2017) Mapping the transition pathway to low-carbon homes for South Africa. Unpublished Masters Dissertation, School of Architecture and Planning, University of the Witwatersrand, Johannesburg.

Gichia, S. (2013) Re-thinking cost-benefit evaluation for sustainability: A prospect theory perspective on choice and decision making for solar water heating in southern Africa. Unpublished PhD Dissertation, School of Construction Economics & Management, University of the Witwatersrand, Johannesburg.

Goldhagen, S.W. (2017) *Welcome to your world: How the built environment shapes our lives,* London: Harper Collins.

Guldi, J. & Armitage, D. (2014) *The History Manifesto,* Cambridge, UK: Cambridge University Press.

Irurah, D.K., Malbert, B., Karam, A., Castell, P., Keiner, M. & Cavric, B.I. (2004) Opportunities and strategies for sustainable urban development. In M. Keiner, C. Zegras, W.A. Schmid & D. Salmeron (eds.) *From Understanding to Action: Sustainable urban development in medium-sized cities in Africa and Latin America,* Berlin: Springer.

Kahneman, D. (2011) *Thinking Fast and Slow,* London: Penguin Books.

Kahneman, D. & Tversky, A. (1979) Prospect Theory: An analysis of decision under risk. *Econometrica* 47(2): 263–292.

Kammeyer, H. (2010) Reciprocity in the evolution of self through the making of homes-as-artefacts: A phenomenological study of the Basotho female in her vernacular architecture. Unpublished PhD Dissertation, University of Pretoria, Pretoria, South Africa.

Kierkegaard, S. (1843) *Jornalen JJ:167* (1843) (English translation of Soren Kiekegaard Skrifter), Soren Kierkgaard Research Centre, Copenhagen 1997. Volume 18: 306.

Kuhn, T (1962) *The Structure of Scientific Revolutions,* Chicago: University of Chicago Press.

Lewis, S.L. & Maslin, M.A. (2018) *The Human Planet: How we created the Anthropocene,* London: Pelican Books.

Lewis-Williams, D. (2002) *The Mind in the Cave,* London: Thames & Hudson.

Lowenthal, D. (2015) *The Past is a Foreign Country,* Cambridge: Cambridge University Press.

Maape, S. (2016) Architecture for resilience. Dialogues with place in indigenous communities of Kuruman during the Holocene period. Unpublished PhD Dissertation, School of Architecture and Planning, University of the Witwatersrand, Johannesburg, South Africa.

Maape, S. (2017) A phenomenological approach: Deep history for architectural students – An exploration into embodied learning as a method for teaching deep history and for creating more inclusive teaching styles. Proceedings – Architectural Education Forum, Symposium 2016, Architectural education at different scales, September 3 to 4, 2016. School of Architecture & Planning, University of the Witwatersrand, Johannesburg, pages 56–61.

Markard, J., Raven, R. & Bernhard, T. (2012) Sustainability transitions: An emerging field of research and its prospects. *Research Policy* 41: 955–967.

Mallgrave, H. (2011) *The Architect's Brain: Neuroscience, creativity, and architecture,* Oxford: Wiley-Blackwell.

Meadows, D. (1999) Leverage points: Places to intervene in a system. Hartland: The Sustainability Institute.

Meadows, D., Meadows, D., Randers, J. and Behrens III, W. (1972) *Limits to Growth: A report for the Club of Rome's Project on the predicament of mankind*, New York: Potomac Associates Book.

Mind & Life Institute (2017) Botho/Ubuntu: A dialogue on spirituality, science and humanity – Programme of the 2017 Mind & Life XXXII Dialogue with the Dalai Lama, 17–19 August, 2017. Botho University, Gaborone, Botswana (see additional content on proceedings on www.mindandlife.org/mind-and-life-dialogues/)

Neumeier, M. (2013) *Metaskills: Five talents for the robotic age*. New Riders, USA

Newen, A., de Bruin, L & Gallagher, S. (eds.) (2018) *The Oxford Handbook of 4E Cognition*, Oxford: Oxford University Press.

Norberg-Schulz, C. (1979) *Genius Loci: Towards a phenomenology of architecture*, New York: Rizzoli.

Orrell, D. (2012) *Economyths: How the science of complex systems is transforming economic thought*, London: Icon Books.

Pallasmaa, J. (2005) *The Eyes of the Skin: Architecture and the senses*, Chichester: John Wiley & Sons, UK.

Pallasmaa, J. (2009) The thinking hand: Existential and embodied wisdom in architecture. In *Architectural Design (AD) Primer*, Chichester: John Wiley & Sons.

Pallasmaa, J. (2011) The embodied image: Imagination and imagery in architecture. In *Architectural Design (AD) Primer*, Chichester: John Wiley & Sons, UK.

Paschini, M. (2017) The relevance of the creative process of design in leadership competencies for sustainable city transitions. Unpublished masters research report, School of Architecture and Planning, University of the Witwatersrand, Johannesburg.

Ramose, M.B. (1999) *African Philosophy Through Ubuntu*, Harare: Mond Books.

Robinson, S. & Pallasmaa, J. (2017) *Mind in Architecture: Neuroscience, embodiment, and the future of design*, Cambridge, Massachusetts: MIT Press.

Rovelli, C. (2015) *Seven Brief Lessons on Physics*, London: Penguin Books.

Rovelli, C. (2016) *Reality Is Not What It Seems: The journey to quantum gravity*, London: Penguin Books.

Rovelli, C. (2018) *The Order of Time*, London: Penguin Books.

Rukambe, V.I. (2016) A rite of passage: An exploration of cultural catalytic spaces in the urban context. Unpublished MArch(Prof) mini-dissertation, Faculty of Engineering , Built Environment and Information Technology, University of Pretoria, Pretoria.

Rukambe, V.I. (ongoing) Memories of futures-past and visions of future-futures: A temporal perspective on sustainable city transitions for African cities. Ongoing Doctoral study (now in fieldwork/data collection stage), School of Architecture & Planning, University of the Witwatersrand, Johannesburg.

Schiller, R. (2013) *Irrational Exuberance* (Revised and expanded third edition 2016), Princeton: Princeton University Press.

Sharmer, O. (2016) *Theory U: Leading from the future as it emerges* (Second Ed), San Francisco: Berret-Koehler Publishers.

Simon, H. (1979) Rational decision making in business organisations. *American Economic Review* 69(4): 493–513.

Tait, J. (2018) *The Architecture Concept Book: An inspirational guide to creative ideas, strategies and practices*, London: Thames & Hudson.

Thaler, R. & Sunstein, C. (2008) *Nudge: Improving decisions about health, wealth and happiness,* New Haven: Yale University Press.

UN-Habitat (2014) UN-Habitat-State of African cities 2014 report. Re-imagining sustainable urban transitions. [online] Available at: https://www.gwp.org/globalassets/global/toolbox/references/the-state-of-african-cities-2014_re-im-agining-sustainable-urban-transitions-un-habitat-2014.pdf 2. [Accessed April 5, 2019].

Varela, F. (1999) *Ethical Know-how: Action, wisdom, and cognition,* Stanford CA: Stanford University Press.

Varela, F., Thompson, E. & Rosch, E. (1991) *The Embodied Mind: Cognitive science and human experience,* Cambridge, Massachusetts: MIT Press.

von Bertalanffy, L. (1968) *General System Theory: Foundations, development, application,* New York: George Braziller.

World Commission on Environment and Development (WCED) (1987) Our common future. WCED.

Wuellner, C.F. (2011) Beyond economic and value wars: Mythic images of future cities. *Futures 43* (2011): 662–272.